Celebrate!®

OMNIBUS

EDITED BY EUGENE T. AND MARILYNN C. SULLIVAN

WILTON ENTERPRISES, INC., CHICAGO 60616

Library of Congress Catalog Card Number: 76-17859
International Standard Book Number: 0-912696-09-5

CELEBRATE! OMNIBUS is published by Wilton Enterprises, Inc.,
Chicago, Illinois 60643. NORMAN WILTON, Publisher;
EUGENE T. and MARILYNN C. SULLIVAN, Co-editors; SANDY
LARSON, Designer; CAROL ZALESKI, Layout; MARIE KASON,
VALERIE WOZNEY, BRUCE BURROUGHS, SCOTT LEESON, Decorators;
HELENE GALE, MARSHA ADDUCI, Copy editors; MELISSA RENCKLY,
VIRGINIA COLWELL, Editorial assistants; DIANE KISH,
Reader's editor; EDWARD HOIS, Photography.

CONTENTS

THIS BOOK is for our decorating friends—for those friends who subscribed to CELEBRATE! Magazine when it was being published in 1973 and 1974 . . . and for more recent friends who may never have seen any of its issues.

For many months we have had numerous requests from early subscribers for special issues of CELEBRATE! no longer available. From friends more recently attracted to the satisfying art of cake decorating, we get equally urgent requests for ideas they can translate into beautiful, colorful cakes for occasions all through the year.

To us nothing seemed more logical than to put the best of twelve sparkling issues of CELEBRATE! Magazine—each a proven collector's item—into a single handsome volume.

So here is CELEBRATE! Magazine again—two years' issues of an informative, full-color publication bound in a permanent, hard-cover book. It's designed for many years of ready reference and pure pleasure. We've omitted just the original advertisements the magazine carried, and articles we felt to be dated. All the exciting cakes, advice from decorating experts and tips for more successful decorating are here—just as fresh and stimulating as ever.

We hope you enjoy CELEBRATE! OMNIBUS— and we are confident it will be a continuing source of inspiration for many years of happy decorating.

Norman Wilton

PUBLISHER

VOLUME ONE

Celebrate!®

JANUARY / FEBRUARY

Decorating directions for
Tulip Wedding Cake on page 15

DUTCH DUO

That Dutch-doll-of-a-cake dressed in the garb of a Klompen dancer—an enchanting centerpiece! And individual Dutch windmills rest invitingly before each place. Use wonderful "wonder molds"—large and small sizes—for these double delights.
See "how-to" on page 13.

Capture the charm of Dutch Delftware

The famous blue and white pottery has been a collector's joy and many a housewife's pride since about 1600. CELEBRATE! was inspired to create this cake with the candy box look; topped it with our new-to-do frosting tulips in a glow of color.

Directions for decorating on page 13.

A Glorious
Springtime Wedding to do yourself

You can do this . . . and just as beautifully as it's pictured here. Starring our own
tulip-trim cake, first-time ever design and a charmingly set table
with both eye-and-taste appeal. This lovely reception will take time and planning, we know.
So Celebrate! helps you with both: lists a suggested menu,
gives you an organized plan-ahead schedule to simplify your work.

Turn to page 16 "Fancy Foods," for details of the reception.

how to make a perfect tulip

Here are the easy step-by-step directions for creating lovely icing tulips. A decorating "first" for the readers of CELEBRATE!

1. Trace Petal Patterns. With a nail, etch four large and four small tulip petal patterns on the reverse side of an Egg-Shaped Cupcake Pan. The large petals are traced on the fuller half of the egg and the small petals on the narrower half. See step 2 for position of petal on pan. Lightly cover petal area on the pan with shortening.

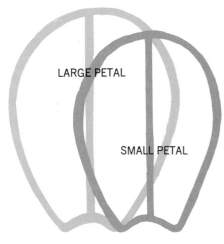

LARGE PETAL

SMALL PETAL

2. Outline Design. With stiffened Color Flow icing and tube #2 or #3, outline the petal design, keeping lines clean and smooth. Set aside to dry (about 20 minutes).

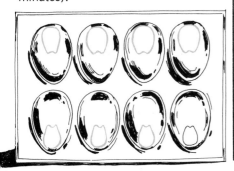

3. Fill in Petals. Fill in each petal with tube #104 and a stiffened, thin layer of Color Flow. (The petal will "belly" if the Color Flow is not firm.) With a moist brush, lightly smooth surface of petal. To vein, use tube #2 and put a thin line of icing down the center back of the petals. Place aside until dry (about 4 hours). (Prepare stamens at this time —see step 6.)

4. Release Petals. Once dry, place pan into a preheated oven (250°) for 30 seconds. (This will melt the shortening, thus loosening petals.) Take pan from oven and gently push bottom of tulip petal outward with thumb. Petal will release from pan.

5. Assemble Tulip. Place aluminum foil on the inside of a small tapered cup or glass. With tube #8, pipe a mound of stiffened Color Flow icing in the bottom of the foil cup. Place three large petals in the icing mound. With a small brush, smooth the icing upward onto the petals. Add another mound of icing in the center and place the three small petals inside the larger. Again, brush icing in center upward on to the inside of the petals.

6. Make Tulip Stamens and Pistil. Trim tips from artificial stamens. Using tube #65 and dark icing, insert about ½" of stamen into end of tube. Slowly squeeze bag and pull stamen from tube. Let stamens dry. With tube #9 and green icing, pipe center pistil in tulip. Fasten 6 stamens at the base of pistil with dots of wet icing. Let completed tulip dry overnight.

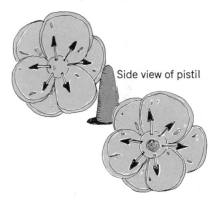

Side view of pistil

How to Make the Tulip Arrangements For Wedding Cake on Page 5

Make five icing tulips. With tube #112 and royal icing, press out 12 leaves from 1 to 2 inches on wax paper. Let dry. Place a ball of tissue paper in a Wilton Heart-Ringed Vase. The tissue should be level with the top of the vase. Cover the tissue with a layer of green royal icing. Pipe 4 mounds of icing inside vase and arrange tulips. Place fifth tulip in center using small mound of icing to secure. Attach leaves with icing.

Tulip

Clean as a lady,
cool as glass,
fresh without fragrance
the tulip was.

The craftsman,
     who carved her
of metal, prayed;
"Live, oh thou lovely!"
Half metal she stayed.

Humbert Wolfe

So much *Love*

FEBRUARY
14

Decorating directions on page 15

GOES INTO MAKING a Cake

10

DECORATE
A CAKE WITH
daisies

Marguerites, shastas, wild field-blossoms . . . what a wonderful variety and range of colors to mix and meld and trim a cake with. The flowers can be made in royal icing days or weeks ahead. Then you can decorate a one-mix cake in a simple but beautiful manner to set off your daisy clusters—and have a spectacular centerpiece cake ready in just a short time. Experiment with the contrast colors . . . see how beautifully they blend.

Bake a two-layer cake in oval pans and frost with pale yellow buttercream. Pipe top and bottom shell border and fleur de lis with tube #16 in white icing.

Make daisies ahead of time in royal icing with tube #102 and #104. For natural-looking curved petals, place daisies on Flower Formers to dry. Pipe stems with tube #3 and attach daisies with a dot of icing. Use tube #65 for green leaves.

Flowers with a Secret

Are they real? Look a bit more closely. The charming petite flower arrangements on the facing page are made of *icing!* A fun idea that's surprisingly easy to do. And what a party-brightener!

Can't you just see a bridal shower table with a little cherub, knee-deep in blossoms, marking each place? Or the wee watering cans filled with tiny roses and jonquils for take-home baby shower favors. And wouldn't the little swans bearing roses and apple blossoms be a sensation at a wedding or anniversary reception?

There's just no end of exciting possibilities for these enchanting mini-bouquets. Give them as hostess gifts. Display them on a knick-knack shelf. Cluster several together for an unusual centerpiece. Use them as never-before prizes. Or for pretty cake ornaments that will live on as treasured keepsakes.

A switch of flowers will adapt your designs to any season or reason. Use holly-and-berries or brilliant poinsettias for Christmas. Red rosebuds for Valentine's Day. Shamrocks for St. Pat's. Colorful mums and leaves for fall. Match them to the bride's bouquet — or use the birthday girl's flower of the month!

Putting them together is the easiest part. Make up lots and lots of little drop flowers, tiny roses, daisies or whatever you like best. And of course, pipe leaves in green. Use royal icing for all and they will hold up beautifully.

But do try to keep them quite small. (The tallest arrangement we've shown is only 10½ inches high, vase and all!) Then collect some pretty petite vases like the ones used here. All the same or all different—depending on just how you're planning to use them.

Attach leaves and blossoms to florist wire stems with a dot of icing. (Use stems in different lengths for variety and a natural look.) Put some sand or sugar at bottom of vase to make it tip-proof. Then fill with green icing almost level to top to provide anchorage—and start arranging things!

You can mix colors as wildly as you wish. It's almost impossible to make a mistake with flowers. If you like, use long leaves and ferns to define a basic shape first as florists do. Then fill in with blossoms.

To add color to your vases, brush with tinted icing as we did, or spray with regular paint ahead of time.

Easy? Indeed! And yet they turn out looking like little works of art. And, unlike your born-to-be-consumed cake, they'll still be around to pay tribute to your talents when the party's over! —HELENE GALE

How to Decorate the Klompen Dancer
shown on page 6

To make Klompen dancer, bake a cake in the big Wonder Mold Pan. Insert Doll Pick and ice entire cake in light blue. Make ruffles with tube #104. Using zigzag motion, pipe green trim on skirt with tube #14. With tube #16, outline apron and "fill-in" with pink stars as shown. Using tube #44, make white bow and red-and-yellow yoke on bodice. After piping each stripe on yoke, smooth with small damp paint brush. Add buttons and fringe with tube #1.

To make Dutch bonnet, cut two layers of net using pattern in CELEBRATE! Charter Pattern Book. Baste layers of net together. Prepare a sugar solution of ½ cup confectioners sugar and ½ cup water in sauce pan. Stir gently over medium flame until sugar is completely dissolved. Bring to boil and allow to simmer for 3 minutes. Make an aluminum foil ball the size of the doll's head, affix to dowel rod and secure rod with ball on top in an upward position. (A block of styrofoam is handy to push the dowel rod into.) Dip entire net in the warm sugar solution and fold end of net to make brim. Wrap net so rounded ends touch to give cone-like appearance. Then shape bonnet on aluminum ball. Secure by placing pin through rounded ends into ball. Let dry. Place bonnet on doll. Use circular motion and tube #1 to trim brim. Add dots of icing with same tube. The Klompen dancer is ready to entertain your guests.

How to Decorate the Windmills
shown on page 6

Bake 4 cone-shaped cakes in the Small Wonder Mold Pan and a small 1½" deep sheet cake. Cover blade pattern (CELEBRATE! Charter Pattern Book) with waxed paper. Follow design with tube #3, leaving small hole in center of blades. Outline doors and window frames with Color Flow and tube #3— fill-in with blue Color Flow. Allow to dry.

Cut four 3¾" diameter bases from sheet cake and ice in white. Ice towers in blue and place on bases. Secure doors and windows with icing. Make balcony fence and tiny stems and "flowers" with tube #3. Then, carefully push a toothpick through center hole of blades and into side of cake. Cover end of toothpick with a dot of icing. Let the gentle Dutch breezes blow!

How to Decorate the Delft Tulip Cake
shown on page 7

First make 7 icing tulips in the colors shown. See step-by-step instructions on page 9. With tube #112 and royal icing, press out 12 leaves from 1 to 2 inches long on wax paper. Dry thoroughly and set aside.

Next, make scalloped extended circle for cake top, 8 squares for sides and 8 scalloped bevels for cake base, using pattern in CELEBRATE! Charter Pattern Book and Color Flow icing.

When doing Color Flow panels, use tube #2 to outline flower and leaf designs. Do scrolls and center circles with tube #1 and light blue icing. Fill in petals and leaves with same tube and same color icing. Outline petals and overpipe center circles on side panels with dark blue. Fill in background with white icing. Allow Color Flow panels to dry for at least 48 hours before placing on cake.

When tulips and panels are ready, prepare cake. Bake a 12" square cake, chill, pin pattern to top and cut off corners for an 8-sided hexagonal shape. Frost all over in pale blue icing.

Attach side panels first, matching them up evenly with sides of cake, using dots of royal icing for "glue." Next, attach bevel panels at bottom of side panels, piping a mound of icing at base of each side panel first to lift bevels and angle them slightly outward. After side and bevel panels are attached, pipe beading all around square panels and between bevels with tube #4. Pipe the tiny beading between squares with tube #1.

Then attach top piece to cake with small mounds of royal icing (so it rises about ⅛" above surface) and pipe beaded edging on it and on the bevels at bottom with tube #2 and light blue icing. Do beading around center of top with dark blue icing and same tube.

To arrange tulip bouquet at top, pipe 6 small mounds of icing at center opening. Press 6 tulips into mounds to form a circle, then add another mound in middle and press in seventh tulip. Place a little icing on ends of leaves and attach them between tulips as shown. Your Delft Tulip Cake is ready to charm your circle!

DECORATE
A PATRIOTIC
PORTRAIT
directions on opposite page
★★★★★★★★★★★

Lincoln Cake
shown on page 14

Make portrait and color flow stars first. Tape Lincoln Pattern from CELEBRATE! Charter Pattern Book flat on board and tape clear plastic wrap on top. Fill in pattern with tube 14 stars, keeping stars very close together to prevent cracking. Start with flesh tone areas. Then deepen color to fill in facial shadows, beard and hair. Fill in whites of eyes to complete face; suit, collar and background to complete portrait. Dry thoroughly, at least 24 hours. Tape clear plastic wrap over star patterns from CELEBRATE! Charter Pattern Book, outline with tube 2 and fill in with color flow.

Make cakes. Ice sides of 14" and 10" two-layer rounds white, ice 10" cake top white, 14" cake top red. Carefully peel plastic wrap off portrait and attach 10" cake top with icing, framing with tube 16 shells. Pipe tube 46 stripes on 14" cake top and tube 3 triple drop string borders on both tier sides. Peel color flow stars off wrap and attach with icing. Border cakes with shells using tube 20 for 10" cake, tube 20 for 14" cake top, and tube 32 for 14" cake base.

Cupid Cake
shown on page 10

To make raised heart for cake top, cover Cupid pattern (Sugar Plum Pattern Book) with wax paper or clear plastic wrap, smoothing to remove all wrinkles. Use deep pink Color Flow icing and tube #2 to outline ruffle border, lovebird and cupid. Let outline dry at least an hour to prevent colors bleeding, then use pale pink Color Flow to fill in as shown. (Leave heart-shaped background around cupid blank to achieve a cut-out effect.) Let dry.

To do deep pink under-heart, draw a line just inside scallop edge of pattern, so it forms a simple heart shape. Use this for your pattern, outline and fill in with deep pink Color Flow icing. Let both hearts dry at least 48 hours before placing on cake.

To do cake itself, bake a two-layer cake using 9" heart shaped pans and one package of cake mix. Frost top and sides with pale pink buttercream icing and pipe big puff garlands at bottom with tube #17. Place tiny stand-up ruffles in between with leaf tube #66. Do top garland drape border with tube #16, add latticework and deep pink stringwork with tube #2. Use tube #14 to finish top edge with shell border.

To add hearts to cake top, attach plain heart first with dots of royal icing. Then attach raised heart on top, using small mounds of royal icing to raise it about ⅛" above plain heart. Finally, with tube #2 and deep pink icing, edge raised heart with small dots.

Tulip Wedding Cake
shown on page 5

A day or two before decorating cake, prepare two icing tulip arrangements in bowls. (See page 9.)

Then prepare cake tiers — bake two layers each, 18", 14" and 10" round, fill and frost with white buttercream icing. Assemble as shown with four 10¼" tall pillars and two 14" separator plates, placing bottom tier on a 22" diameter cake plate or board.

Next, decorate cake, starting at bottom and working your way up. For bottom tier, do reverse shell base border with tube #32. Then mark off space for drape garlands with stringwork, using tube #4 and leaving about ½ inch between for bells. Pipe zigzag garlands directly over the strings with tube #17, then drop three rows of string-work atop them with tube #4. Pipe reverse shell border all around top edge of tier with tube #17. For top surface, cut a paper pattern to mark off curves all around inside edge, matching them to the garlands. Then pipe a zigzag line over your markings with tube #14. Attach 2 x 1¼" filigree bells between curves and garlands all around, using royal icing for "glue". Outline scallops of separator plate with tube #14, use #4 to overpipe with short curves.

On center tier, do the framed angels first. Fold a piece of paper 3¾" square in half and draw half of the heart-shaped scallop pattern on it. Cut out, pin to cake and trace shape with a pin. Remove pattern and use tube #4 again to follow outline with tiny reverse shells. Attach angels with horn or violin inside with dots of royal icing. Then pipe borders—do large bulbs at base with tube #22, draped with #4 string-work, top shells with #17.

For top tier, do lily of valley vine first. Beginning exactly at center, pipe a horizontal curved line, first up, then down, all the way around. Next pipe branches at top and bottom of vine, striving for a natural look. Pipe long leaves with tube #66 and do the tiny lily of the valley blossoms with tube #81, turning your hand over on its back with curved opening of tube on surface. As you press out icing, turn your hand back around and pull outward.

Finally do top tier borders—using tube #16 to pipe full garland at top. Use tube #4 to drop one string under garlands and another straight across, and also to trace curves on top of tier with an "e" motion. Attach plastic doves between garlands and finish with reverse shells at base, using tube #16. When cake is in place at reception, put one tulip bowl arrangement in center of bottom tier, and one on top tier.

Easter Bunny Cake
shown on page 30

First make ears & eyes. Draw a bunny ear, 4½" long and 1½" wide at widest part and tape wax paper or clear plastic wrap over it. Outline with Color Flow icing right out of the batch, then do a second outline about ¾" in from first. Immediately, without waiting for outlines to dry, fill space between them with white Color Flow icing, just soft enough to flow out of bag, but still quite thick. Then, without waiting for the white area to dry, fill in pink center. At once, very carefully lift and lay on a curved surface. Repeat for second ear. Let dry 48 hours, then peel off paper, turn ears over. Place toothpick at base of each ear so half extends below it, then cover it and rest of ear with icing. Let dry another 48 hours. Ice a 5" styrofoam ball with white royal icing. (This is bunny's head.) Attach ears to head with toothpicks. For eyes, draw ½" diameter circles, outline and fill with Color Flow icing. Dry and attach, using dots of royal icing for "glue".

Trim body at top and bottom as shown

Next, make head, body, paws. Bake 2 cakes in egg-shaped pans. Bake 4 standard cupcakes. Swirl cupcake tops in pink icing.

Assemble Bunny, then ice. Put body and paws together as shown, using toothpicks to fasten. Ice all white first, filling in where paws meet body for a more natural look. Outline jacket freehand. Ice blue and pipe a green collar with giant rose tube #127, pressing out a broad band of icing all around neck. Do all zigzag edging with tube #15, & bow tie with tube #3. Attach head with toothpicks. Draw pink nose with #3.

Easter eggs
Mold Easter eggs of sugar and tempered chocolate (or summer coating) in egg-shaped molds. To add trims, use your imagination! We attached colorful icing drop flowers, made with tube #16. Piped tiny leaves with #6, stems, bows and stringwork with tube #2. Used #44 for lines, #103 for graceful ribbons and bows. Make up icing, tint different colors and "let it happen!"

HERE is the suggested menu for the lovely wedding reception shown on page 8. We have planned for 35 to 40 guests and any of the recipes below may be doubled or tripled. Of course you may want to substitute specialties of your own for some of the tidbits.

Read through the recipes and you will see that everything can be made ahead and refrigerated or frozen, or prepared ahead for last minute touches before serving time. (Starred items (*) may be refrigerated or frozen as indicated in the recipe. In either case, they should be placed in a wax paper-lined box, then covered with a plastic bag . . . tied or sealed. Allow at least two hours for thawing, before heating or serving time.)

You may need to borrow refrigerator and freezer space, and certainly you will need several pairs of willing hands to put everything together just before the reception— but we know your work will be well repaid by the pleasure of your guests.

RECEPTION MENU

Baby hamburgers with tiny buttered buns
Curry shells   Ham towers
Lovebird paté   Crackers
Smoked turkey pin wheels
Saucy shrimp   Bride's crowns
Miniature puffs stuffed with chicken salad
Tulip sandwiches   Salmon treats
Black and green olives   Tiny tomatoes
Salted almonds   Mints
Champagne   Tea   Coffee
Wedding Cake

*Baby Hamburgers

1 pound beef ground fine
2 slices very dry toasted bread soaked
   in water until they swell. Then
   squeezed dry.
2 tablespoons fine-chopped parsley
2 tablespoons grated onion
¼ teaspoon black pepper
1 teaspoon salt
¼ teaspoon garlic salt
2 large eggs

Combine ingredients and mix until thoroughly blended. Measure with tablespoon and shape into small balls. Saute in hot butter until brown. Remove from pan, pour off excess fat and make sauce. Put meat balls into sauce and simmer 5 minutes, or until done. Cool and refrigerate until ready to serve. Or freeze, a week or more ahead. Reheat, and serve in a chafing dish with tiny buttered hamburger rolls at the side. Makes 35.

SAUCE

1½ cups hot water
   1 package instant beef broth seasoning
   2 tablespoons cold water
   1 tablespoon cornstarch

Pour hot water into drippings from meat, scrape gently; add 1½ teaspoons cornstarch blended in 2 teaspoons cold water, and instant beef broth seasoning. Cook until it thickens, simmer 5 minutes longer.

Taste and season more if desired.

Miniature hamburger buns, approximately 2″ in diameter, should be ordered **well in advance** from your local bakery.

Fancy Foods

BY MARIE

*Curry Shells

FILLING

1½ tablespoons butter or margarine
   3 tablespoons chopped onion
   3 teaspoons curry powder
1½ teaspoons flour
   1 cup + 2 tablespoons light cream or
     milk
   ⅛ teaspoon pepper
   ¼ teaspoon garlic salt
   3 tablespoons drained chopped
     chutney
1½ tablespoons lemon juice
   3 6-ounce packages frozen crabmeat,
     lobster, or tuna, finely diced.

Melt butter in a large skillet. Add curry powder and flour and stir to blend. Gradually stir in cream. Cook until thickened, stirring constantly. Add garlic salt, pepper, chutney, lemon juice and seafood. Keep hot over simmering water. Spoon into shells.

PASTRY SHELLS

2 sticks butter or margarine
2 3-ounce packages cream cheese
2 cups sifted enriched flour

Let butter and cream cheese soften in mixing bowl at room temperature about 1 hour. Add flour ½ cup at a time; work with wooden spoon thoroughly after each addition. Refrigerate dough about 30 minutes. Pinch off small pieces and shape into 1″ balls. Put each in cup of small (1¾″) muffin pans. Press dough against bottom and sides, lining each cup evenly. Bake at 425° for 10 to 12 minutes or until pastry is golden. Let stand 5 minutes; lift out of pan. Cool on wire rack. Makes approximately 48 shells.

Shells may be baked and stored in a wax paper-lined box for a day or more at room temperature. Filling mixture may be made a day or two ahead and refrigerated. Before serving, fill shells with seafood mixture and heat for 8 to 10 minutes in 350° oven on cookie sheet. (Freezing is not recommended as shells may become soggy.)

*Ham Towers

HAM SALAD FILLING

1 cup finely chopped cooked ham
1 tablespoon piccalilli
2 teaspoons prepared mustard
¼ cup mayonnaise
2 tablespoons minced onion

Mix all together well, and refrigerate until ready to use.

PASTRY CASES

You will need 3 packages of refrigerated crescent roll dough. Unroll 1 package of the dough and place on lightly floured pastry cloth. Roll gently to eliminate perforations in dough. From ½ dough, cut 12 circles with 2″ cutter. Place on cookie sheet. This is important: Dip bottom of small glass in flour, and press firmly into these 2″ rounds to flatten center; then prick center edges with fork. Take other half of dough and cut 12 more circles with 1½″ cutter, taking center out, thus making "doughnut" circles. Place "doughnut" circles on top of full circles. Bake on cookie sheet at 350° for 10-13 minutes until brown. Repeat operation for each package to make 36 pastries. Mound one full tablespoon of ham salad on each, bringing to a slight point. Garnish with parsley sprig if desired. Store in refrigerator (overnight only), or freeze ahead. Makes 36-40.

To serve hot after freezing or refrigerating, thaw and place on cookie sheet in 350° oven for 8-10 minutes, until golden brown. Keep hot on a buffet warming tray.

To serve cold after freezing, follow procedure above and let cool for 10-15 minutes before serving. If not frozen, serve right from refrigerator.

*Lovebird Paté

3 pounds chicken livers
7 to 9 finely chopped green onions
   and tops (to taste)
¾ cup sweet butter
4½ teaspoons each sherry and brandy
3 teaspoons salt
¾ teaspoon each nutmeg, coarse
   ground pepper
Generous pinch each (to taste): thyme,
   basil, marjoram, fresh parsley

Use large frying pans or dutch oven. Saute livers and finely chopped green onions in ½ cup butter for 3 to 4 minutes to brown livers outside, stay pink inside. Place livers in a bowl. Add remaining butter to frying pan, melt, then stir in rest of ingredients. Pour mixture over sauted livers. Puree in blender, ⅓ of amount at a time. Spoon all into oiled lovebird mold. Chill overnight or longer.

*Smoked Turkey Pinwheels

2 3-ounce packages smoked turkey
1 pound loaf sliced sandwich bread
Small jar sweet pickles, midget size,
   one end cut off each and quartered,
   long way
2 3-ounce packages cream cheese

Remove all crust from bread. Overlap 2 slices at edges and press lightly with rolling pin just to seal. Spread bread with softened cream cheese tinted yellow. Cover with 4 slices smoked turkey (2 on each slice of bread). Put 2 sweet pickle quarters together to form one long quarter that fits the width of bread. Roll tightly around pickle to form a pinwheel on sheet of wax paper: then roll wax paper around pinwheel and twist ends tight. Slip into plastic bag and freeze. Remove 2 hours before serving time. (May be prepared days in advance.) When partially defrosted, cut crosswise in about ½-inch slices with a very sharp knife. Makes about 40 pinwheels.

*Saucy Shrimps

1½ pound sliced loaf of wheat or rye
   bread
Butter for spreading
1 small bottle cocktail sauce
½ pound frozen cooked shrimp,
   medium size
1 8-ounce package cream cheese for
   white borders
1 3-ounce package tinted cream
   cheese for rosettes and leaves
Food coloring as needed

Cut the bread into rounds with a 2″ cutter. Butter rounds. Spread about ½ teaspoon cocktail sauce to about ½-inch from edge.

Lay shrimp on top of sauce. (Sauce should show around shrimp.) With #16 tube, pipe zigzag white cream cheese border around edge of bread. With same tube, pipe pastel cream cheese rosette on top center of shrimp. Pipe green leaves with tube #65. (Tint cheese with food coloring.) These canapes can be frozen, or refrigerated a day ahead. Makes about 38.

*Bride's Crowns

1 loaf sliced sandwich bread
12 hard-cooked eggs
¼ cup soft butter
¼ cup mayonnaise
4 ounces cream cheese, softened
1 teaspoon salt
¼ teaspoon dry mustard
¼ teaspoon garlic salt
2 teaspoons vinegar

Cut 36 small (approximately 1¾″) rounds of bread, spread with butter, sprinkle with a little garlic salt. Using egg slicer, cut hard-cooked eggs into rings. Remove yolks carefully. Place white rings on bread rounds. Put yolks and ends of whites through a food mill. Combine them with rest of butter and ¼ cup mayonnaise, the softened cream cheese, vinegar, salt, and dry mustard. Add garlic salt. Blend all thoroughly. Add seasoning to taste.

If mixture seems too heavy, add a little vinegar or lemon juice. If too soft, add a little more cheese or additional hard-cooked egg. With #1-C star tube press mixture into the egg rings, about 1″ high. Use tube #16 to decorate tops with tiny pink-tinted cream cheese rosettes and tube #65 for the green leaves. Can be stored for a day or two in refrigerator. Makes about 36.

*Miniature Puffs Stuffed with Chicken Salad

CHICKEN SALAD

4 4½-ounce jars boned chicken
   or
1 pound chicken breasts, cooked
½ cup minced celery
2 teaspoons minced green pepper
1 teaspoon salt
½ teaspoon pepper
½ cup mayonnaise
2 teaspoons chopped pimiento

Mince the chicken and mix well with other ingredients. Refrigerate overnight until ready to use; or fill cream puffs and freeze several days ahead.

CREAM PUFFS

1 cup water
½ cup butter
1 cup sifted flour
¼ teaspoon salt
4 eggs

Put water and butter in saucepan and bring to boil. Lower heat, add flour and salt all at once; continue to cook stirring constantly, until mixture leaves sides of pan and forms a ball. Remove from heat and add eggs, one at a time. Make sure each egg is well-blended before adding the next. Drop by heaping teaspoonful on ungreased cookie sheet. Bake at 425° for 30-35 minutes until golden brown. Immediately remove from cookie sheet with spatula and place on wire rack to cool. This makes 36-40 tiny cream puffs. Cut small slice from tops of puffs and remove any soft dough inside them. Fill puffs with chicken mixture, mounding slightly, and replace tops.

Cream puffs can be made 2 or 3 days in advance, then filled with mixture, and frozen. If puffs are soft after defrosting, reheat in 400° oven for approximately 10 minutes.

*Tulip Sandwiches

2 1-pound loaves sliced white or wheat
   bread
2 8-ounce packages cream cheese
   flavored with 1-ounce roquefort or
   bleu cheese, or onion juice
1 3-ounce package cream cheese
Vegetable food coloring
2 green peppers cut in thin julienne
   strips approximately ¼″ x 1¾″

Cream the cheese and seasoning to fluffy consistency. Tint with food coloring 1 8-ounce package yellow, other one orange. Tint 3-ounce package green for stems and leaves. Cut bread into tulip shapes with tulip cutter. Pipe blossoms first with tube #30 and yellow or orange cheese. Pipe stems with #6 tube and leaves with tube #70, using green cheese. Place green pepper strips on stems. Will make 26 - 30 tulip sandwiches. Can be made a day ahead and refrigerated.

Salmon Treats

4 cucumbers, about 2″ round
1 box melba toast rounds
16-oz. of canned salmon, minced
¼ cup mayonnaise
Butter for spreading

Score unpeeled cucumbers down their whole length with a fork. Cut in ¼″ slices. Sprinkle cucumbers with salt. Refrigerate in bowl of cold water about 1 hour. Remove from refrigerator and dry slices thoroughly on paper towels before placing them on buttered rounds. Mix fish and mayonnaise and spread over cucumber to edge. Place on buttered toast rounds. (You may spread the cucumber slices with the fish mixture the day before, and refrigerate. Then, just before the reception, place on buttered toast rounds.) Decorate top with mayonnaise star, using #16 tube. Makes 40 to 45.

John McNamara pipes a jolly green leprechaun

Here is a cake to beguile all the Irish! John McNamara, Mr. Figure-piper himself, tells just how to do it.

Ice the cake in a soft green. A gold border, using up and down motion (#17 or #27 tube) is run around the bottom. Overpipe the hanging drapes.

Green piping jelly (#3 tube) shamrocks are used on the sides·

A small round cake or sponge cup is used for the tree stump. This gives extra height to the cake and also the brown color makes a "break" in the all-green color scheme. Ice top of stump in pale yellow. Streak a bag with brown color, then fill with brown icing. Using a #10 tube with upward and downward strokes, cover the sides of the cake creating a rough effect. Insert a plastic straw into the stump for the "backbone" of the figure.

For the leprechaun figure use a darker green. Starting on the stump run a heavy tapering line up the front of the straw with #7 tube. Repeat on the back. Smooth off the "joint" seams on the sides with the tip of the tube (for the body). Insert straw into the body at front bottom and pull out legs, bending at the knee. For arms, insert straw at top of body and pull out, keeping

arms close to the body for support. Pipe right arm upward from elbow.

Shoes are a circle with a pointed line pulled to the toe. Make the head in light pink with a #7 tube. Leave enough of the straw to support the head and clip the rest off. Start at the shoulders and go up the front of the straw, then the back. Insert tip of the tube in forehead and "blowout". Do the same for each cheek. Add small ball for chin.

Nose is a thin line piped from forehead downward. Ears are small pointed lines. Hands are added by making a small ball at the end of sleeves for palm and then pulling each finger out separately in position desired. For lines on nose, ears and fingers a #3 tube

may be used. Use piping jelly for eyes and mouth. White hair is added with a #3 tube and the figure is finished off with the green hat, using tube #7 Circle and pull to a point. Boiled icing is best for upright figures.

Remember to keep the end of the sleeves and legs blunt for strength in attaching hands and feet.

The mushrooms are made of a baked meringue mixture (like meringue shells). Stems and caps are made separately, then glued together with a little icing. Use a large round tube. Add "Erin go bragh" in gold icing.

John McNamara's Boiled Icing

6 ounces water
1 pound 4 ounces granulated sugar
½ teaspoon Cream of Tartar
8 ounces egg whites

Put water, sugar and cream of tartar in pan and cook to temperature of 232°. While syrup mixture is cooking, whip eggwhites until fluffy in mixer. After syrup has reached its temperature, add it slowly to whipping eggwhites. Then reduce mixer to medium speed and run until icing stiffens, 10 minutes. Makes 5 quarts.

JOHN McNAMARA is well known as the "decorator in the window" at the Farmer's Market in Los Angeles. He taught in the Los Angeles County schools for many years and has been for many years an instructor of Cake Decorating at the Los Angeles Trade Technical College. Mr. McNamara is known as a foremost authority on figure piping and has appeared on many TV shows.

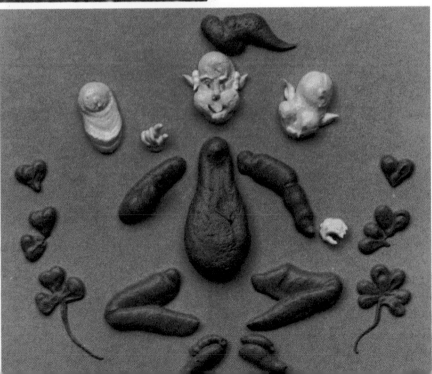

VOLUME ONE

Celebrate!®

MARCH / APRIL

Decorating directions for Cupid Cake on page 27

Let the cake blossom in the garden

"A garden is a lovesome spot" . . . and long a favored one for both wedding and reception.
Appropriately placed in your garden, this glorious 3-tiered cake will beckon as a happy
harbinger. Dancing cupid pillars and a heart-framed cupid at top are especially pretty
in the outdoor setting, and the lavish trim of flowers reflects the real blooms in the leafy
background. Here, indeed, is a wedding cake that adds so many romantic touches to its
storybook setting that it is certain to leave fond memories of this perfect day.
Decorating directions on page 27. Serves 250.

Flower Basket

*A petite cake . . . beguilingly decked with posies in their baskets. This is the
perfect cake for a bride who cherishes the quaint, lovely traditions of
marriage celebrations. The fragile lattice trim and baskets are made on
specially-shaped Australian nails . . . the warm color scheme is
accented by iridescent pillars. Serves 100. Decorating directions on page 27.*

QUEEN of HEARTS

Utterly exquisite, eye-thrilling, towering! A decorator's showpiece that *must* be a prize-winner. Six individual heart-shaped cakes beneath arched columns surround a sparkling fountain. This might be your masterpiece! Serves 300.

Directions on page 28.

CLASSIQUE. The formality of tradition, the symmetry of sculpture, here in the fresh loveliness of white. A cake of beautiful dignity to adorn a formal wedding table. A variety of simple borders, each executed to perfection, give this cake its timeless elegance. Serves 225. Directions on page 28.

Dear Ann,
    Please join us for tea, on Tuesday, April 3rd, at 4:30 p.m. We have some exciting news to announce. See you then?
    Mary.

TO TELL THEM LOVE'S IN BLOOM—*center your announcement party around this cake crowned with luscious buttercream flowers. Surprisingly quick and easy to prepare and delicious from outside in! Just make up lots of colorful buttercream flowers and leaves ahead of time and freeze. Use daisies, wild flowers and roses as we did or your own favorites. The day before the party, simply bake a cake in a bundt pan, brush it with shiny apricot glaze. Then mound icing in garland shape, arrange flowers and leaves on top, refrigerate until party-time. They'll say it's too pretty to eat!*

A CAKE FOR A SHOWER . . . *has parasols to foretell sunny skies, bells to ring out the happy news and dainty curving borders to complete the feminine effect. Tell your guests the party color scheme, and suggest that their package wrappings carry it out. Here the soft pink tones are complemented by the tones of the roses that bud nearby . . . and what a nice gesture to give one to each guest at the end of the party! Plan a simple menu that appeals to girlish tastes—hot bouillon, a fruit or sea-food salad with tiny hot rolls, or creamed chicken on toast points. Add some tangy relishes and serve coffee or tea to accompany the cake. Decorating directions on page 27.*

TO MAKE IT YOURS ALONE...
match your wedding cake ornament to your color
scheme, your flowers, your bridesmaid's gowns.
It's fun and so easy! Just make up tiny icing flowers or
use flowers of new soft-look plastic, pouffs of tulle,
mini-pearls or tiny birthstone gems. Attach with glue
or dots of royal icing!

LACE HEART COVER CAKE
shown on page 19

First, prepare flowers: a couple of days or weeks ahead, press out drop flowers with tube #225. Center each with dot of yellow icing and reserve.

Next, prepare cake. A day before serving, prepare two tiers, one 14 inches round and 4 inches deep (two 2-inch layers) and another in 9 inch heart shaped pans (two 1½ inch layers). Fill and frost white and divide round cake into 12ths. Assemble so point of heart cake is about 3 inches in from edge of round cake.

Then add heart designs. With Pattern Press, press 6 scalloped heart shapes into sides all around. Press another into top of heart cake, but enlarge by tracing ½" outline all around it.

Now decorate. Outline all heart shapes with green icing, using tube #14 and a circular motion. Fill in with cornelli lace, using white icing and tube #1. (Hold tube to the surface and run curly lines of icing all around to create a free-hand lace effect.) Repeat on side of heart cake. At each 12th point on top of round cake, press out a dot, about 1½" in from edge, and another about 1" in from edge. Drop two rows of stringwork scallops from dot to dot all the way around with tube #3 and fill with more cornelli lace. Then border with tiny dots, using tube #1. Repeat on heart cake top, but pipe 2 straight strings instead of scallops. About 1¾" up on sides of round cake, press out dots as guide, then drop stringwork all around with tube #3. Do green circular motion border on base of round cake with tube #21 and heart cake with tube #17. Use #17 again to do white shell border at top of heart cake and #19 at top of round cake.

Finally, attach flowers and pipe tiny leaves with tube #67.

GARDEN WEDDING CAKE
shown on page 20

First, prepare flowers: make many wild flowers ahead of time with tube #103 and royal icing. Attach artificial red stamen with a dot of icing. Dry thoroughly and reserve.

Next, prepare cake tiers: bake two 2-inch round layers in each of the following sizes — 18-inch, 12-inch and 8-inch. Fill and frost with white buttercream icing and assemble with 10-inch separator plate and pillars as shown.

Then decorate: Do each tier starting in with largest and working upward. **For 18-inch tier,** divide into sections 5 inches wide. At each division, pipe a large upright shell with tube #199 and pull up to top of tier for "post" effect. Do regular upright shells for rest of bottom border with same tube. Drop a stringwork guide for garlands between posts with tube #5 and overpipe with tube #7, using a zigzag motion. At each side of garland, pipe a butterfly string bow with tube #4 and attach flowers as shown. Finish 18-inch tier with a top border of shells piped with tube #21, then circle them with string, using tube #4 again. **For 12-inch tier,** do draped flower garlands, centering each over post on tier below. Pipe a mound of icing in shape of garlands and press flowers in as shown. Do more butterfly bows between garlands, again with tube #4. Finish with shell borders —tube #21 at top, #17 at base.

For 8-inch tier, pipe a curving vine all around sides by running tube #3 along surface, pressing out icing evenly. Pull off little stems at intervals and pipe leaves for these and main vine with tube #66. Attach flowers to vine as shown and finish tier with a reverse shell at base, using tube #18 and a plain shell at top, using tube #17. Use remaining flowers to trim top ornament and base of pillars.

FLOWER BASKET CAKE
shown on page 21

A clever Australian technique is used for the blooming flower baskets and lacy arches that brighten this charming tier cake.

Prepare baskets and arches first. To make these, you will need special Australian icing net nails—the arch border and the basket. Rub a little oil on nails first. Then, using royal icing and tube #1, pipe free-hand lace for arch borders, latticework for half and whole baskets. Overpipe vertical lines on baskets and do tiny zigzag overpiping on basket tops ,and edges and tops of arches to add strength. Dry thoroughly and lift off nails when ready to place on cake. Note: handle carefully as they are very fragile! In fact, it is wise to make some extras.

Then make flowers. Pipe tiny red roses and yellow jonquils with tube 101s on florist's wire wrapped with pale green florist's tape. Dry thoroughly on wires. Pipe leaves with tube #65 on wax paper squares, insert wire and dry on curved shape. Just before you are ready to add bouquets to cake, assemble flowers and leaves by winding together with more florist's tape. Assemble finished flowers into bouquets, again with tape. Bend bottom of stems into a small circle to use as anchor in baskets.

Prepare cakes. Fill and frost a 2-layer 8-inch tier and a 2 layer 12-inch tier. Place on foil-covered cardboard circles, 12 inches and 16 inches in diameter.

Make patterns for tier tops. Fold parchment cake circles the diameter of tiers into sixteenths. Unfold and use to mark off tiers into sixteenths. Refold and, measuring 2 inches up from wide end, cut a curve, pointed at folded side and curving up about an inch and a quarter to other side. Unfold into 8-petal design pattern. Pin to tier tops and trace onto cake with a toothpick. Place iridescent pillars on larger tier as shown.

Now decorate. Trim base of pillars and outline patterns on tier tops with beading, using tube #2. Do beading trim at inner points of petals with same tube. Attach arches and half baskets with dots of royal icing. (Handle carefully!) Then pipe bulbs of icing at stem end of bouquets and carefully attach them inside side baskets. (Anchor one leaf to side of cake with dot of icing to hold bouquets in place.) Attach bouquets in whole baskets same way, center on tier tops and pipe beading around bases. Last, do beading borders and trim at base of both tiers, working them around baskets. Use tube #3 for 8-inch tier and #4 for 12-inch tier. Add a thin line of scallops with tube #1 for a finishing touch on separator and base plates. Assemble tiers, using icing as "glue" on tops of pillars.

PARASOL SHOWER CAKE
shown on page 25

Prepare flowers first: pipe many small apple blossoms, using tube #101s and pink royal icing. Reserve.

Next, prepare cake: bake a 10-inch, 2 layer cake and frost white. Divide cake top into 16ths. With a toothpick, draw a curve from mark to mark about an inch in from edge.

Then decorate: trace top-of-cake curves with beading, using tube #2. Use same tube to drop stringwork loops all around edge. To do these, drop a string from one 1/16th mark to a point halfway to next 1/16th mark, and repeat all around. Working from center of loops, do another row, and another, and another (4 in all). Pipe small beading at top edge of cake with tube #4 and large bulbs at base with tube #10. Trim top edge beading with pink row of beads and bottom bulbs with mock fleur-de-lis and circles, using tube #5. Trim tiny plastic parasols with reserved drop flowers, attaching with icing. Add tube #1 stringwork and tube #65 leaf trims to parasols and push into cake. Top with a tulle-trimmed triple bell ornament.

QUEEN OF HEARTS
shown on page 22

First, prepare cakes: bake three round tiers, all 2 layers (each layer about 2" high), one 16", a second 12" and a third, 8". Bake 6 nine-inch, two-layer heart shaped cakes. Fill and frost.

Decorate heart cakes first, before assembling. Make a paper pattern in a scalloped heart shape, trace on cake tops with a toothpick. Then outline with tube #15 and a circular motion. Draw a second heart inside first and outline same way. Pipe reverse shell border at base of heart cakes with tube #74, do full garlands at top with tube #15 and drape stringwork over them with tube #4.

Assemble tier cake with 5" Roman pillars. Place atop arched Roman pillar tier set with Kolor-Flo Fountain inside. (When transporting finished cake, carry top tier and separator, also heart cakes separately and assemble all at reception.)

Decorate tier cake. For 16" tier, pipe bottom border of large curved shells with tube #32. Then drop a string guideline with tube #4 all around top for garlands, leaving about 1" space between. Then do zigzag garlands over guidelines with tube #17 and use tube #4 again to drape three rows of string over them. Attach artificial flowers and bells and do reverse shells around top edge with tube #75.

For 12" tier, pipe reverse shell border around bottom with tube #20 and do a garland at top just like the one on 16" tier. But this time, use #15 for the zigzag garlands and #4 for string and leave only ½" space between garlands. Finish with a top border of straight shells, piped with tube #17.

For 8" top tier, achieve the rich crown effect by piping vertical rows of shells with tube #14 up sides about 1½" apart. Pipe full garlands around bottom and top of tier with tube #14 and trace a curving vine between rows of shells with tube #3. Deck vine with lily of the valley buds, using tube #81.

CLASSIQUE WEDDING CAKE
shown on page 23

Prepare cake first: bake 3 tiers of two 2-inch layers each, 16", 12" and 8"

round. Fill and frost white.

Next, assemble with classic 5" tall Grecian pillars and 10" round separator plates.

Then decorate: for 16" tier, do base border of stars with tube #22 and circle each with string, using tube #3. For garland, drop a guideline first, making each drape 3" long with ⅓" space between. Pipe garland with tube #15 and a back-and-forth motion. Do lattice work with tube #2 and stringwork trim with tube #3 again. Finish top edge of tier with reverse shell using tube #15. And do zigzag curves on top of tier with tube #14. For 12" tier, do shell bottom border with tube #17 and pipe a tiny ruffle between each with tube #102. Pipe short, puffy upright shells for top border with tube #18 about 1" apart. Do zigzag trim with tube #14. Do stringwork trim and triple stringwork drape under shells with tube #2.

For 8" tier, do same star base border as on 16" tier. Do garland guideline with tube #3 and garland with tube #14. Drop strings over garland with tube #3 again. Do small shell top border and curves at top of tier with tube #14.

"IVY" GRADUATION CAKE
shown on page 32

First, make Color Flow ivy leaves. Make patterns, cover with wax paper or clear plastic wrap. Then, using Color Flow icing outline with tube #1 and fill in. Place at different angles over a curved shape.

Next, prepare cake. Bake two tiers, one 6 inches in diameter, the other 12 inches in petal-shaped pans. Make each tier of two 2-inch layers. Fill and frost in buttercream icing, the smaller tier in pale green, the base tier in white. Assemble as shown, being careful to place smaller tier on a cardboard circle, lined with wax paper first.

Then decorate. Following petal shape of cake, pipe "v"-shaped side scallops and puff base scallops using a zigzag motion. Do top edge-of-cake scallops with an upside-down "e" motion. Add a vertical overline at each scallop point. Use tube #16 for all borders on 6" tier and tube #18 for all borders on 12" tier. Pipe scrolls on top of base tier

with tube #14, vines on both tiers with tube #2. Attach ivy leaves with dots of royal icing. Place a spray of leaves at base and add a tiny ribbon-tied "diploma". Top with Proud Graduates.

CARNATION CAKE
shown on opposite page

A radiant cascade of carnations makes this Mother's Day cake unforgettable. Make all your pretty carnations ahead of time, the rest of the decorating is easy.

To make carnations. Add confectioner's sugar to royal icing until dry enough to achieve broken petal effect. Attach 2" square of wax paper to #7 flower nail with icing, and touch wide end of tube 104 to nail center. As you squeeze out icing, revolve nail counterclockwise and move tube to outer rim, lifting it slightly and jiggling your hand for a ruffled petal effect. Now ease off pressure as you return to center of nail; then repeat procedure until you have a full circle of petals. Add row upon row of petals to this first full circle, making each successive petal row shorter and more upright than the last, until flower is round and full. Slide wax paper and finished flower off nail to dry, and repeat entire procedure until you have a dozen carnations.

To make cake. Bake a two-layer 10" round cake and ice pink. Cut a paper circle the exact diameter of the cake top and fold in half three times. Cut off an inch of curve, unfold pattern and trace on top of cake with a toothpick. Cover pattern outline with tube 14 zigzag, adding tube 14 fleur-de-lis between curves. Next, using curves of cake top as a guide, divide cake base into 8ths and pipe tube 199 upright shells at each marked point. Add tube 14 zigzag to cake base, going around outer bottom edge of each upright shell. Frame cake base, above and below zigzag, and cake top with tube 14 shell borders. Pipe several tube 5 stems on cake top and attach carnations to stems with icing, draping some of the flowers onto the side of the cake. To complete the cascade of carnations, add green sepals to flower bases with tube 5, and trim with tube 65 leaves. When you see your carnation creation complete, you're sure to want to use these fabulous icing flowers to top off other party treats.

a special cake for mom

Directions on opposite page

Easter morning in the park...

. . . a walk in the fresh morning air . . . and here in the flowers, the Easter
Bunny dressed in a new spring suit! He's guarding a clutch of pretty Easter
eggs molded in sugar or chocolate. You can duplicate this storybook picture
with ease . . . and thrill every child you know. (And after Bunny has been
admired, he tastes delicious!) Decorating directions on page 15.

SHINING BEAUTY FOR YOUR EASTER TABLE

What a sweet surprise! Nearly all the exquisite things on this page are made of sugar. The basket, flowers, leaves, ribbon bow and dessert dishes are all transluscent pulled sugar. The nests that hold the molded ice cream "eggs" are sparkling spun sugar. And you can do them yourself! See page 58.

directions on page 28

TO CONGRATULATE THE GRADUATE!

You've something to be proud about—whether your graduate is moving up from grammar school, high school, college or even kindergarten! Express your joy in a cake decked with traditional ivy. Here two colorful designs show how to do it. At left, a tier cake salutes graduates celebrating together and is large enough to serve a gathering of 32 guests. To make "Ivy" cake *see step-by-step decorating directions on page 28.*

To make "Good Luck" cake, *first do Color Flow design for top, using pattern from*

Sugar Plum Pattern Book.

Cover with wax paper or clear plastic wrap; outline with Color Flow icing. Dry thoroughly, then fill in with softened Color Flow icing. Dry 48 hours more. Fill and frost a 10″, two-layer cake, 4 inches high. Attach Color Flow design to top and frame with small shells, using tube #14. Do second ring of shells with tube #20. Pipe #14 zigzag at cake base and drape #104 ribbon garlands over it. Do vine with #1, leaves with #67. Serves 14.

NORMAN WILTON DISCUSSES
commonsense
FOR THE CAKE DECORATOR

TIPS ON DECORATOR ICINGS

While every decorator has little special techniques and work habits of his own, there are some few "dos and don'ts" it pays anyone who picks up a decorating bag to remember. If some of the suggestions seem almost too obvious to talk about, remember it is the **obvious** that is most often overlooked.

First, to achieve really precise and consistent results in doing side borders it is absolutely essential to **keep your work at eye level.** This is particularly true in doing stringwork. Unless you are in a comfortable position to check on the distance each loop is dropped, the completed running series of loops is going to be conspicuously uneven and distracting. With proper pressure control and the use of a disciplined rhythmic motion, stringwork that's done in **full view** can be a mark of distinction on any cake. Try to do your stringwork in as relaxed a posture as possible: pull out, let the string drop, then tack in. Repeat the process in a steady, continuing motion—pull out, let drop, tack in. Though it is not essential that the cake be on a turntable when this work is being done, you will find that the use of a heavy, solid-sitting turntable does make the operation faster and easier. The position of the decorating hand can be maintained at the best working level and more precise control can be exercised.

When scrolls and garlands become major adornments in side borders these scrolls and garlands should also be worked out at eye level. Make a drop first as a guide. This can be lifted off if a mistake has been made. Since they often serve as the basis for stringwork, all three of the artistic devices should be as well-executed as possible. Other-

wise one poorly done decoration will be high-lighted by the others.

Shells need not be done at eye level, since—even when looking down at an angle—you ar able to see the shell in all stages of formation. Simply exercise the proper pressure control, move forward at an even pace and you are assured of a neat, even border. One point should be stressed in connection with forming shells. The icing **must** be of the right consistency. If it can be drawn to a peak and then holds, you are sure of success. If it does not peak in this manner, shells will not stand up.

Icing that can be pulled to a peak and hold is also of the right consistency for roses, ribbon borders and leaves. For lilies of the valley or scroll work you will need to thin down icing that meets the peak-and-hold test.

While the right consistency of icing is of top importance in achieving really distinguished results, the best rule is to **use what works** best. Use what you find easiest. The harder it is to squeeze through a tube, the more difficult it is to use. Generally you will find a light **boiled** icing the most manageable and easiest to control.

When colored icing is to be used you will find liquid colors more convenient for everything except striping a bag. In this case a paste color is clearly the best. The liquid colors are easier to blend to get exactly the shade wanted.

These are easy-to-follow, common sense tips. Put them to use and see for yourself how much more professional your decorative effects become!

USES OF BOILED ICING

Boiled icing can be adapted to a number of decorating techniques and, when handled properly, is easy to use. Be sure no grease or oil touches the icing. Keep all pans, stirring spoons and decorating tools clean and grease-free and you will find the icings we mention here all work well. (Note: Don't use plastic bowls or utensils when making boiled icings. It is impossible to get them absolutely grease-free.)

For producing flowers and borders the two most generally used boiled icings are both made with powdered suger, but one utilizes **meringue powder** while the other substitutes **egg whites.** Each has its advantages and, since each flows smoothly out of the tube, you can be the judge of which best suits your needs.

A decorator who wants to work with the same batch of boiled icing for a period of four or five days can rebeat the **meringue** boiled icing and it will rise to its original consistency. It will also not spoil, even when kept for a week. The

egg white icing will not return to its original consistency or volume when re-beaten. Further, this icing will spoil rather quickly. On the plus side, most people would agree the icing made with egg whites does have the edge in taste.

All boiled icings, whether made with meringue powder or egg whites, have a tendency to crust, particularly in dry weather. This can be prevented by adding a small amount of nulomoline before the batch is beaten for the last time. In cool weather add about four ounces to a 12-quart batch so the decorated cake can later be cut without having the icing shatter. Essentially the same results can be obtained with glycerine. As the temperature and humidity rise, decrease the amount of the softening liquid that is added.

A third variation of boiled icing—one particularly adapted to figure-piping—can also be used with great success. This is **John McNamara's Boiled Icing.** (See recipe on opposite page) It is very stable, unusually light and ideally suited to piping high figures that hold their true form.

Wilton Boiled Icing—Meringue

4 level tablespoons Wilton Meringue Powder
1 cup warm water
2 cups granulated sugar
¼ teaspoon cream of tartar
3½ cups sifted confectioners sugar

Boil granulated sugar, ½ cup water, cream of tartar to temperature of 240° F. Brush sides of pan with warm water to keep crystals from forming. Meanwhile, mix Wilton Meringue Powder with ½ cup water, beat 7 minutes at high speed. Turn to low speed, add confectioners sugar, beat 4 minutes at high speed. Slowly add boiled sugar mixture, beat 5 minutes at high speed.

Keeps a week in refrigerator, covered with damp cloth. Rebeat before using again. Makes 5 cups.

Wilton Boiled Icing—Egg White

2 cups granulated sugar
½ cup water
¼ teasp. cream of tartar
¾ cup (approximately 5) egg whites at room temperature
1½ cups confectioners sugar, sifted

Boil granulated sugar, water, cream of tartar to 245°. When boiling starts, brush sides of pan with warm water to prevent crystals forming. Brush again halfway through, but do not stir. Meanwhile, whip egg whites 7 minutes at high speed. Add boiled sugar mixture slowly and beat at high speed until icing stands in soft peaks. Turn to second speed, gradually add confectioners sugar and beat all at high speed for about 7 minutes more or until icing stands in stiff peaks. Cover with damp cloth while using. Rebeat before using again. Not recommended for flowers; fine for borders and stringwork.

We are reprinting John McNamara's recipe for boiled icing here, for your convenience.

John McNamara's Boiled Icing

6 ounces water
1 pound, 4 ounces granulated sugar
½ teaspoon Cream of Tartar
8 ounces egg whites

Put water, sugar and cream of tartar in pan and cook to temperature of 232°. While syrup mixture is cooking, whip egg whites until fluffy in mixer. After syrup has reached its temperature, add it slowly to whipping egg whites. Then reduce mixer to medium speed and run until icing stiffens, about 10 minutes. Makes 5 quarts.

Once you have done a little experimenting with all three of these boiled icings your decorating skills will be broadened tremendously. Then you can be the judge of which boiled icing best suits the project of the moment. It's the perfectionist approach that produces the real decorating triumphs!

USES OF BUTTERCREAM AND ROYAL ICINGS

Much Used Icings

It is important for every serious decorator to know the characteristics of both royal and buttercream icings, since each has qualities the other lacks. Accordingly, you should first make some decisions on the cake or other food you intend to decorate and then choose the icing that best suits the need. You may end up using only royal or only buttercream. Or you also may—particularly if you're a perfectionist—use buttercream for some areas and royal for others, depending on the overall effect you want to achieve. The common sense rule is simply this: decide what you wish to accomplish and then use the icing that does each decorating technique best.

Versatile Buttercream

Buttercream—essentially a mixture of butter, powdered sugar and shortening—is very versatile and widely used. Various consistencies of buttercream (ranging from medium soft to rather hard) can be made by increasing the amount of sugar in the batch of icing. The more powdered sugar that is added, the stiffer the icing.

To streamline your work, particularly if you believe that different consistencies of buttercream will serve your need from start to finish, you should remove a portion of the original batch to **ice** the newly-baked cake to a smooth finish. This covering need only be a thin one, just enough to seal in the crumbs on the surface of the cake and keep them from working through the smooth surface of the final, or second coat icing. When you remove this small portion for the initial icing, put the remainder in the refrigerator to keep it cool. (It's important to keep buttercream as cool as possible at all times! If this portion of the initial batch still seems a bit stiff, thin it for easy spreading with the addition of a little milk. This "seal-in" first coating will usually dry in 20 to 30 minutes when the humidity is not excessive. At any time when the humidity is excessive the most practical approach is to work with boiled icing, rather than the more perishable buttercream. Both, of course, are very edible.

When the initial "seal-in" coat of buttercream is dry, ice the cake finally to a smooth finish and let this coating dry before starting your borders. These require a medium stiff icing, so you may wish to add a small amount of powdered sugar to get the workable texture that feels right for border work.

When you do the borders in buttercream you may follow up by adding flowers and leaves. Or merely pipe on the stems of the flowers, then add the leaves and provide for room to add the flowers once the borders and leaves are sufficiently set to allow the flowers to be added.

If you are using **only** buttercream icing, you do have a measure of flexibility when it comes to adding the flowers. First, you can make some kinds of flowers directly on the cake merely by using icing that has been somewhat stiffened with additional powdered sugar. Once finished with your borders, you may add slightly more powdered sugar to thicken the icing sufficiently **to be sure** the piped-on-the-cake flowers hold their shape. Or, if you wish to work up the flowers in advance, you may make an ALL FLOWER batch of buttercream icing, appropriately thickened with powdered sugar to be of just the right consistency for flowers, and then indulge yourself in a session of making **only flowers** which can be placed in the freezer for whatever time you need before applying them to the carefully iced and already bordered cake. They will thaw quickly.

Note that many flowers such as the rose, aster and daisy must be made on a nail and so must be made ahead with the freezer method.

It should be well understood that any piece **should not** be iced with buttercream, if it is intended as a display piece. Buttercream is a **workable** and **edible** icing that provides for a large degree of flexibility in its use, but it is not long-lasting.

Royal Icing Adds New Dimension

Royal is the icing to use when you wish to make **near permanent** flowers or other decorations in advance. It can be made either by using powdered sugar and egg white or by using powdered sugar, water and meringue powder. The egg white version seems to make the tougher of the two versions, though both become very hard.

Either the meringue or egg white variations of royal icing can be beat to different consistencies to meet specific needs. Should you be doing latticework, for example, it is necessary to have strong icing. To accomplish this, merely avoid overbeating the mixture. The reason for this is easy to understand: the more this icing is whipped, the more air cells are formed. The air cells tend to weaken the structure and make the dried icing more brittle. It is possible to whip either of the royal icings by adding either water or egg white. Whipped sufficiently, either will become practically as light as boiled icing. Once hardened, however, either will practically disintegrate under the lightest touch.

Once you have experimented a bit with the effects of beating royal icing to various consistencies, you can judge the strength you need in the icing and control the beating to produce this strength. Where the cost of making a sizeable quantity of large flowers may be a factor, you can make them of more aerated material, still strong enough to be **carefully** placed on the cake after they are dried. On the other hand, when making flowers with thin narrow petals, beat the icing much less to give it the body to hold the more delicately-formed shape.

As is the case with boiled icings, any grease will break down your royal icing. Therefore be sure to keep all pans and utensils grease-free.

Depending upon the need that any particular decorating project dictates, you can also use both buttercream and royal icings on the same cake. The fact that both icings can be varied to consistencies to suit definite needs provides a great deal of flexibility for you. Merely remember that buttercream, while it lacks the long-lasting quality of royal icing, is much more palatable. Therefore, it's best to use buttercream to make any decoration that is to be eaten and to use royal for such trims as the flowers which can easily be removed and held as keepsakes or mementoes indefinitely. Stated most simply, decorations from buttercream are made for consumption; decorations from royal are made more for display. Or, use royal icing only for dummy and display cakes. You be the judge as to which best meets each decorating need!

More icing recipes on page 65

commonsense
FOR THE CAKE DECORATOR

Decorating tubes and their uses

We all know that even when equally-skilled decorators make the same flowers and borders, differences in the completed decorations are always apparent. Both can use identical tubes and work with the same batch of icing in an effort to produce identical-twin decorating results. But this seldom, if ever, happens. The differences are most frequently the result of variations in the control of pressure used on the decorating bags.

This emphasizes one very important point: the more you **perfect your pressure control** on the icing being forced through a decorating tube, the more varied are the artistic results you can achieve with a single tube. It's comparable to a virtuoso violinist getting everything to be had from his instrument!

Which are the four most versatile tubes?

As an interesting experiment, imagine you were forced to make a choice of **just four tubes** from the over 150 now available. Which ones would you pick in order to get the widest range of effects?

While every decorator need not agree with my selection of the four that rank highest in terms of the versatile decorating effects they make possible, here's my choice:

Number 104—basically a flower tube, but adaptable to many other uses;

Number 19—a star tube that's a "star performer" in many areas when you know its full capabilities;

Number 3—a writing tube that, with a bit of imagination and dexterity, can be put to many different jobs; and, finally,

Number 67—a "middle of the road" leaf tube that is capable of creating many bits of decor you may never have thought to ask it to perform!

The many uses of tube 104

As a flower tube, 104 is ideal for making a perfect rose, the bloom that is still the favorite on wedding and other major celebration cakes. For cakes of some-

what smaller proportion, 104 can be used equally effectively for the rosebud or the half carnation. With equal ease it can turn out the most natural-looking sweet peas or, if you prefer, half carnations.

The pansy, poppy and the jonquil are also easily achievable with 104 and—by relaxing pressure slightly—the dahlia, daisy and wild rose may be added to your flower repetoire. These are normally made with 103, but by gently easing pressure through 104 you can watch perfect specimens "bloom" before your eyes.

Ribbons, swags and classic ruffled borders are simple to produce with 104, too. These borders are attractive used alone or serve as good basic elements for intricate trims.

With 104—as with numbers 19, 3 and 67 in our trimmed-down selection—it is important 1) to keep the icing at the right consistency (stiff icing must be thinned, if it is to be brought to a point, but should be stiff for petals); 2) observe to be certain tube opening is at all times as it was designed, not unduly pinched or opened; and 3) tube is in proper position to permit it to produce the formation you want.

By using fewer tubes as suggested in this "grand experiment" you will learn the little subtleties of pressure control faster for the very understandable reason that through the carefully-measured pressure you apply, you will be "compensating" for larger or smaller openings in tubes for which you are now substituting 104. Through this process, though, you will be sharpening your control techniques and will find this will improve your decorating. Particularly when you are making flowers with 104, try to relax and

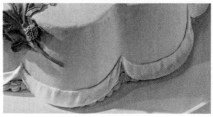

avoid tension. The flowers that you form will more closely resemble those that nature provides as elegant models.

Here's one last suggestion. Both metal and plastic tubes can do a good job, but I much prefer metal when you are striving for perfection. With an inexpensive "tube saver" tool you can keep tube openings precisely as they should be to secure perfect icing formations. In your search for perfection, you deserve to use the best tools!

Decorating Tubes and Their Uses
Tube 19: A star performer

Now that you have seen that tube 104—normally thought of as essentially a flower tube—can be used in many other ways, we are sure that you will see the value of "experimenting" a bit with every decorating tube. Next we will explore just a few of the additional ways tube 19 can be used. Tube 19 is a middle of the road star tube that can produce an amazing variety of effects by skillful pressure control and by employing just the right techniques.

1. Start by using light pressure and pressing out a row of little stars. Increase the pressure and make larger stars. Join the stars for a pretty border.

2. Start with light pressure then heavy, then light again—using a zigzag motion—to make a sculptured garland border.

3. Pipe a horizontal straight line with tube 19. Line up shells below it, then above it. Pipe a final row of shells in the middle, right on top of the line. Result: a heavy sculptured border, important enough for the largest cake.

4. Make a dainty reverse shell border by combining comma-shaped shells in reverse directions. Very pretty for a top border. By varying the pressure you can make this border large or small.

5. Pipe fleur-de-lis, combining three shells—the first one straight, then a curved one above and an opposing curve below. This adds a classic touch to cake top or sides. Join the fleur-de-lis if you wish.

6. Now make a rope-like border with curved shells, keeping them uniform.

7. Evenly spaced shells make this traditional border. You can embellish it, or leave it plain. Even pressure makes it perfect.

8. The border demonstration ends with a line-up of stars.

Tube 19 can make a flower basket

Versatile 19 is not a basket weaving or a flower tube, but it can produce a very pretty, stylized basket of flowers!

1. Start by describing the shape of the basket.

2. Then fill in with a broad horizontal zigzag to give dimension. Cover this with a similar zigzag in a vertical direction. Now your basket has a rounded form.

3. Pipe five curving vertical "ribs"—then with contrasting color, pipe three horizontal strokes over alternate ribs.

4. Continue the horizontal strokes over alternate ribs, producing a woven effect.

5. Pipe a "handle" on the basket using an "e" motion. Finish the top of the basket with the same technique, and the bottom with a rope-like border. Add a flowing "ribbon" around the handle—then pipe stems and

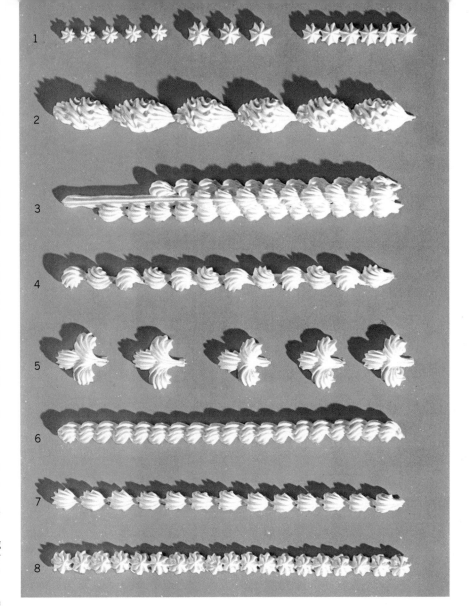

leaves. Make rosette "flowers," using a tight circular motion.

With the icing ready, this flower basket can ornament the top of a cake in less than 15 minutes.

Know the joy of discovery—take a little time to experiment with tube 19. You'll create many more effects with just this one tube and expand your decorating skills.

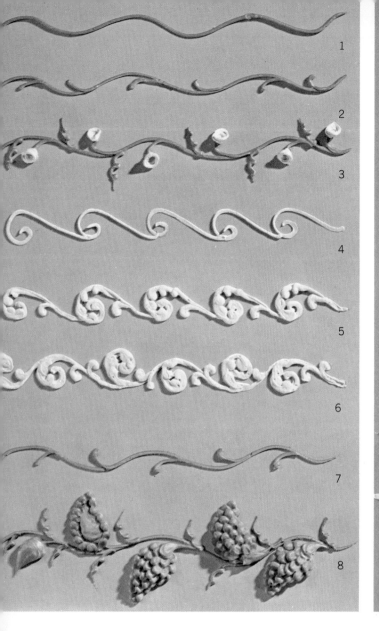

1
2
3
4
5
6
7
8

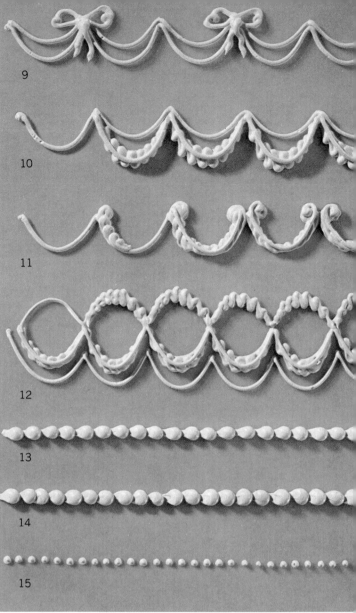

9
10
11
12
13
14
15

A further discussion of versatile decorating tubes

Most people think of tube 3 as primarily a writing tube for script and small block letters. Indeed it is well adapted to that purpose, but it has many other uses.

Tube 3 can pipe many graceful borders for side, top or base of cake, lavish stringwork, and, by increasing your pressure, can even do figure piping.

The fifteen borders shown above are merely representative of the decorating possibilities of this very frequently used tube. Put your skill and imagination to work and you will discover many more. Before seeking still more decorative devices, however, here are exercises to try:

1. Keeping the tube nearly horizontal and using a rhythmic motion, press out a long curving line.

2. Add short stems to the line by working them well into the main curve and joining them smoothly.

3. Pipe little spiral "flowers" at the end of the stems, and corkscrew "tendrils" between them. A dainty, graceful border for top or side of a cake.

4. Tube 3 pipes a series of upside-down "C's." Finish each "C" with a long tail, join the next to it smoothly.

5. Ornament the border by going over it with a feathery "e" motion. Add short curves to the long "tails."

6. Make a different border by alternating upside-down and right-side-up "C's," joining them smoothly. Ornament as before. These traditional borders look lavish on the side or top of a cake. Practice to achieve graceful, uniform curves.

7. Make another smooth curving line and add short stems.

8. Using heavy pressure, press out a tapered oval of icing at the end of the stems. Border it with quick bulbs of icing. Working from the tip of the oval to the stem, cover the oval with

bulbs. Finish the grape cluster by going over the stem in a small shell. Add spiral tendrils. This makes a very rich looking grapevine border that is quick to do.

9. Now try stringwork with tube 3. Touch the tube to the surface, draw straight away, touch again. Never bring the tube down in an arc. Draw it straight out, pause slightly, move back and touch. Rhythm and timing will make the curves perfect. Drop another line of stringwork below the first. Finish by piping a little icing bow at alternate points of the stringwork.

10. Pipe a line of curved stringwork. Pipe another just below it in a deeper curve as a guideline. Cover the guideline with an "i" motion of the tube, making the "i's" deeper at the center of the curves. Pipe curves of stringwork on top.

11. Drop a guideline of curved stringwork. Cover with a series of tiny "e" motion curves. Finish by covering with curves of string for a decorative plume effect.

12. Pipe a row of curved stringwork. Swing practice board around and join with another row of string. (You can turn a buttercream-

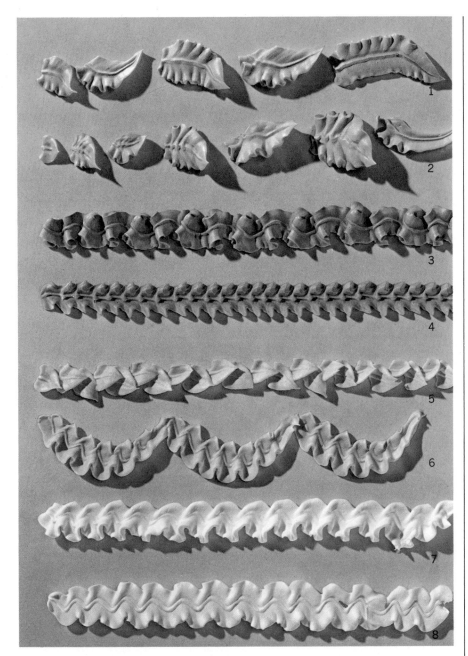

extending the decorative effects that tube 3 can produce. Just as tube 3 is normally thought of only as a "writing tube", tube 67 is generally considered only a "leaf tube". It is a leaf tube—and more.

Using tube 67, many variations from the conventional leaf form can be made. Boiled icing, thinned down to the consistency in which it might be used for figure piping, works especially well for both leaves and unique borders.

1. & 2. To produce the different leaf shapes shown, thin boiled icing as suggested and start by applying moderate pressure, then less. Finally stop completely and pull icing out **gently** to a point where it will then break off. To get ripples in the leaf, squeeze with greater pressure without moving. The slower you move and the more pressure you apply, the more ripples you produce. Move faster and decrease pressure to make leaf more smooth and ripple free. The 67 tube, with substantial variations in pressure, can be used to make many sizes of leaves, and with practice your control of the size and shape of each leaf will greatly improve. While this work with a single tube provides good practice in developing fine pressure control, greater refinement can be achieved by using four or five different tubes. It is also easier when more tubes are used.

3. This unusual looking border is made by holding the 67 tube at a 45° angle (with one edge in the air) and then following the procedure for making a reverse shell. Squeeze to the left, squeeze to the right and follow this shift back and forth in a rhythmic pattern. The result: a border that's unusual and highly decorative.

4. Accomplish this symmetrical border by maintaining steady pressure while moving along at an even pace. Pause at regular intervals and start again with a slight nudge forward.

5. Shift from left to right repeatedly to make this all-leaf border. Start **under** each leaf. The border is particularly impressive on the side of a cake.

6. The 67 tube is easily adapted to this fluted garland. Start with light pressure, jiggling and increasing pressure as you go down and around. Then decrease pressure on the upward movement.

7. Here the 67 tube is used with one edge in the air, and tipped both up and to the side at 45° angles.

8. With the tube flat to the surface and held at a 45° angle, track along under steady pressure, using a zigzag motion. This border can be used for top, side or edge of a cake.

Here, just as with writing tube 3, you've seen some of the many borders and decorations tube 67 can produce, in addition to its variety of leaf-making effects. Practice all the decorations you see on these two pages and you'll soon be creating your own eye-appealing effects with tubes 3 and 67.

iced cake upside down by covering the top with wax paper.) Cover the curves with "i" motion movement. Overpipe the lower curves with string, then add curves of stringwork below. An intricate-looking border that is easy to put on the side of a cake if you practice control and rhythm.

13. Press out a line of shells using rather heavy pressure, relaxing, stopping pressure and pulling away. Join for a border.

14. Press out a reverse shell border.

15. Using light pressure, make a row of tiny dots. Hold the tube perpendicular to the decorating surface and try for similarity of size and spacing.

These are just a few of the decorative trims tube 3 can produce. As you practice and gain control of pressure, you will think of many more ways to use tube 3. It certainly is one of the most versatile tubes.

A Leaf Tube—and so very much more

It's a source of surprise to many decorators that a tube normally used to produce a particular decorating motif can actually be used to achieve quite a different design. That, of course, is part of the pleasure of cake decorating. The more you use a particular tube (and experiment with icings of different consistencies), the more you learn how really creative you can be.

In the 15 borders shown on page 38, we ventured out a little farther than usual in

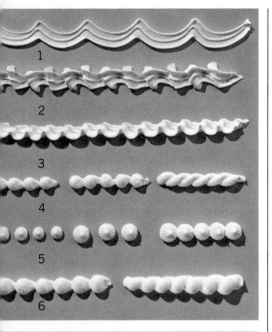

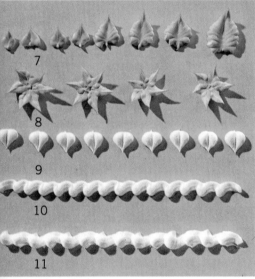

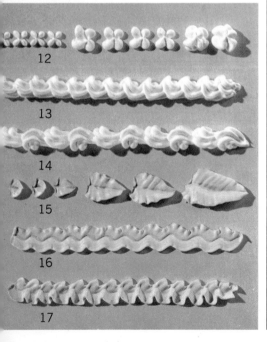

commonsense

18 special-effect tubes

At some time or other every imaginative decorator enjoys producing borders and trims that are different from those normally used, but are highly artistic.

Now we want to introduce you to a number of tubes which can vastly broaden your decorating horizon and add a whole new dimension to your decorating pleasure.

The Essex group is a newly-added line of deep-cut tubes of the type used principally by English decorators. The 5-tube Stellar Series is a new group of deep cut star tubes that every decorator can put to use in creating a whole galaxy of stunning effects.

Essex Tubes Create Entirely New Decor

With all of this group, boiled icing, stiffened a bit with royal icing to keep border patterns sharp and precise, may be used.

1. To produce this plain but graceful border hold tube 355 flat to the surface at a 45° angle and—maintaining even pressure—move the tube along with a slight looping motion to create a ribbed ribbon effect.

2. Here tube 355 is held at a 45° angle. Merely make a series of reverse shells, maintaining a consistently steady pressure.

3. Tube 355 is made to produce this graceful border with the tube held flat against the surface. Turn the tube slightly on its side at a 45° angle. Then, holding steady pressure and proceeding with a looping motion, form the fluted border.

4. 5. & 6. Tubes 362, 363 and 364 resemble 199, but all have finer cuts and more precise grooving. In 4, tube 362 produces unusually neat shell, reverse shell and rope borders. In 5, tube 363, held vertical produces precise stars. And in 6, tube 364 produces finely cut shell and modified shell borders.

position of tubes 352 and 353 in making borders 7, 8, 9, 10 and 11.

7. & 8. Tube 352, using careful pressure control makes a variety of heart-shaped leaves. Tube is held on end (as it would be to make a sweet pea) and at a 45° angle. With a slightly thinned down icing, squeeze, move out, stop pressure and continue moving till leaf breaks off to a point. Larger leaves are made with continued heavy pressure.

9. Make this simple heart by positioning tube 353 on end, in the same position tube 104 is used when making sweet peas. Apply pressure at 45° angle. Relax pressure as you move to a perpendicular position; move away from top of heart to form point.

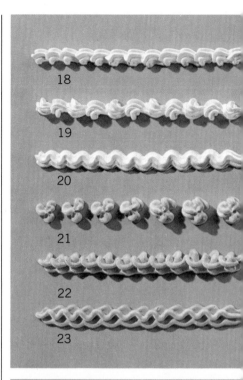

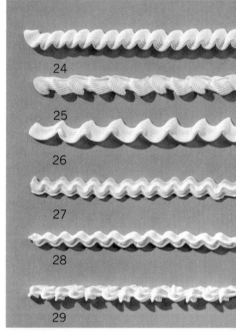

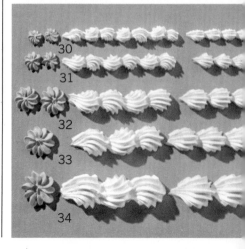

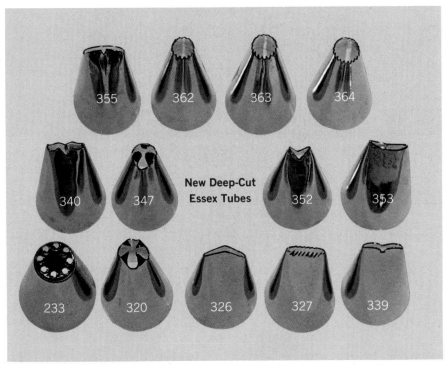

New Deep-Cut Essex Tubes

(tubes pictured: 355, 362, 363, 364, 340, 347, 352, 353, 233, 320, 326, 327, 339)

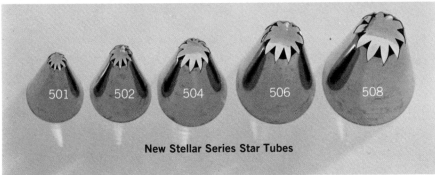

New Stellar Series Star Tubes

(tubes pictured: 501, 502, 504, 506, 508)

steady pressure, complete border.

23. Again using 347, hold tube at 45° angle to the surface and, with even pressure, move tube from side to side to complete border.

24. Hold tube 327 at a 45° angle to the surface and, tilted to the side at a 45° angle, apply steady pressure while completing the border with a series of "i" motions.

25. With tube 327 again held at a 45° angle to the surface and tilted to the side at a 45° angle, complete the border with reverse shell motions made under even pressure.

26. Still using tube 327, with tube point touching surface and short end slightly up, complete border with a number of evenly-spaced arcs formed under steady pressure.

27. Lay broad side of tip of tube 339 flat at a 45° angle and, with steady pressure, complete border with a slight side to side motion.

28. Hold tube 339 on side (the same 45° angle used for making a sweet pea) and use a side-to-side motion to complete border.

29. Again using tube 339, hold tube at a 45° angle—and tilted slightly to the side. Then follow through the reverse shell motions to complete the border.

Novelty tube

No photo of work that can be done with tube 233 is shown, but it's versatile . . . makes icing "fur", a superb chrysanthemum. Even "grass" or a "shag rug"!

**Stellar Series
Ideal for Multi-Tier Cakes**

30.-34. Tubes 501, 502, 504, 506 and 508 are all deep-cut star tubes capable of producing highly-defined borders that achieve very clear sculptured effects. Using these five deep-cut tubes, it is now possible to start with the base borders of large wedding cakes using tube 508—the largest of the group—and proceed upward to smaller tiers, using a smaller tube in the series for each tier. Each of the tubes also makes a very fine simulated daisy. Used individually or in combination, the tubes in the Stellar Series produce dramatic decorating results.

10. Stand tube 353 on end (in the same position 104 is used for making a sweet pea) and, holding it at a 45° angle, make a series of arcs while using a steady, even pressure.

11. As in border #10, hold tube 353 on end at a 45° angle, standing on narrow edge. Make border in same way you would do a reverse shell, using steady pressure.

12. To make these 4-petal floral designs hold tube 320 perpendicular to the surface. For small design squeeze lightly and lift up. For middle design squeeze with slightly more pressure, turn with tube held in same position and draw up. Use this same position to make the largest design, only applying slightly more pressure.

13. Hold tube 320 at a 45° angle and make a series of semi-circular loops, holding pressure steady and continuing an "i" motion.

14. Here hold tube 320 at a 45° angle again and proceed to make a continuing series of reverse shell motions.

15. To make small, medium and large leaves with tube 326, hold tube at 45° angle, apply pressure, ease off to no pressure and draw to a fine point. For large leaves, use more pressure at start.

16. Hold tube 326 at a 45° angle and, applying steady pressure, turn and move tube in a slight side to side motion while squeezing.

17. Again hold tube 326 at a 45° angle, tilting it slightly to one side. With a side to side motion—again applying even pressure —complete this fluted border.

18. Hold tube 340 flat to the surface at a 45° angle. Then, keeping pressure steady, make continuing arcs to complete.

19. Maintaining tube 340 in the same flat-to-the-surface position and 45° angle used in border number 18, follow the reverse shell technique to make this border.

20. Again using tube 340, hold the tube flat to the surface at a 45° angle and use a side-to-side, wavy motion to complete this border.

21. Hold tube 347 perpendicular, apply even pressure while making a small arc, stop squeezing as you pull away. For the larger design, follow the same motion as you would for a bulb border: squeeze, build up with a slight arc motion and stop squeezing as you pull away.

22. Hold tube 347 at a 45° angle and, continuing a slight up-and-down "i" motion at a

41

HOW THE EXPERTS DO IT

Make an English wedding cake with Betty Newman May

Decorating with precision is the English way. Whether it's row-upon-row of stringwork or raised panels of Color Flow used on the cake featured here, the English achieve a dimensional decorating effect with precise geometric patterns and designs. It takes lots of practice and patience to master these techniques, but the results are breathtaking and well worth the effort.

This English wedding cake is a beautiful example of the use of Color Flow panels to give a dimensional look to decorating. To make this cake, you'll need the Color Flow patterns from the CELEBRATE! Charter Pattern Book. Then just follow these step-by-step directions to achieve this stunning English-decor cake. This handsome example of the art was created by decorating expert, Mrs. Betty May.

The English customarily choose fruitcake for weddings, so use your favorite recipe to bake one (in two layers if you wish), 10 inches round and 4 inches high. Cover with rolled Marzipan and reserve until Color Flow pieces are ready to be attached. Then ice it very smoothly with royal icing. To get the proper glossy smoothness, it's a good idea to ice cake on a turntable.

To do Color Flow pieces. (The English call this technique "flow-in", but it is the same as our Color Flow.) Begin at least a week before wedding. Tape patterns A, B, C and D shown below on a piece of glass or hard plastic to keep them absolutely flat and cover with wax paper or clear plastic wrap, smoothing so not a single wrinkle remains. Use Color Flow icing straight from the batch for outlining, thinned for filling in. (Be sure to thin icing according to directions on Color Flow package!)

For patterns A & C, outline all pattern lines with tube #2, except outer circles. Use tube #1 for these. Then use tube #2 to overpipe the first outline whenever the patterns show a dotted line. (These are the "riser" lines that will support the upper filigree—patterns B & D.) Flow in softened icing to the level of the first #2 line on A & C as shown in photos below. (When filling in areas, be sure to use decorating bag with cut tip only—a tube might break outline!)

For patterns B & D, outline entirely with tube #1 and fill in with softened icing. Let patterns A, B, C & D dry for at least 48 to 72 hours.

Meanwhile, outline pattern E for sides of cake with tube #1, first attaching the pattern on the curve of a propped-up 10-inch cake pan (or styrofoam cut to exactly the same shape) and covering it very smoothly with wax paper or clear plastic wrap. After completing outline, let dry on curved shape. Repeat for 6 identical pattern E pieces.

When patterns A & C are thoroughly dry, overpipe all riser lines 4 more times (so you have a total of six #2 lines, one on top of the other). Let dry again and pipe on small free-hand flowers, leaves & vines, also beaded borders of royal icing with tube #1, as shown.

Now assemble. Place iced cake on foil-covered circle or plate. Slip Collar A (pattern A) over top. Put dots of moist icing on riser points and slip Collar B (pattern B) over, adjusting so lines fit. Pipe flowers & leaves on cake side at this point—do freehand with tube #1 —lining up with points of Collar B. Then pipe a double line of royal icing with tube #2 on back of pattern E pieces and place over flowers. Attach pattern C on cake top, piping moist icing at points of riser lines. Then add pattern D on top of it.

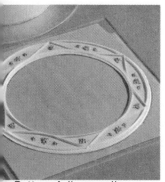

Pattern A (base collar for bottom of cake)

Pattern B (filigree collar for bottom of cake)

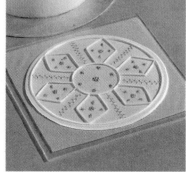

Pattern C (base cover for top of cake)

Pattern D (filigree cover for top of cake)

Celebrate!

MAY / JUNE

Directions for making this Fabulous
French Dinner on pages 56-57

F DESSERTS FOR THE 4TH

It's the newest idea in partying and a perfect way to celebrate Independence Day. Even "bombs bursting in air, and the rockets' red glare" could hardly be more American (and certainly not nearly so delicious) than these three tried-and-true desserts. Certainly the men in your party will give them the proper rousing salute. Set the table on the patio and invite friends and neighbors to an unforgettable dessert buffet. Or serve all three as the bang-up finale to a back-yard barbecue. Happy feasting on a memorable Fourth!

STRAWBERRY SHORTCAKE**

Outstanding because of the delicious contrasts of color, texture, flavor and temperature. An American classic!

> 2 quart strawberries, hulled, cleaned and
>   slightly crushed, sweetened to taste
> 3½ cups sifted flour
> 6 teaspoons baking powder
> 1 teaspoon salt
> 6 tablespoons sugar
> 8 tablespoons chilled butter
> 1½ cups rich milk
> 2 cups heavy cream, whipped
>   whole berries for garnish

Chill the crushed berries. Combine the dry ingredients and sift into a bowl, cut in butter with a pastry blender until mixture is the texture of coarse cornmeal. Make a well in the center, pour in the milk, and stir lightly until just blended. Put into a 10″ round pan and bake at 375° for about 25 minutes, or until done.
Split the cake while still warm, butter the bottom half generously and top with about half of the chilled berries. Cover with the top half and the rest of the berries.
Top with whipped cream and whole berries. Serves eight.

CHOCOLATE PEPPERMINT CAKE*

A pretty, well-flavored cake topped with a "web of chocolate."

> 1¾ cups sifted flour
> 1 teaspoon baking soda
> ¼ teaspoon salt
> ¾ cup butter
> 1¼ cups light brown sugar
> 3 eggs
> 1 teaspoon vanilla
> 4 ounces unsweetened chocolate, melted
>   and cooled
> ¾ cup water
> 1 recipe Seven Minute Icing
> 2 ounces unsweetened chocolate, melted
>   and cooled

Continued on page 51

CAKES FOR
men

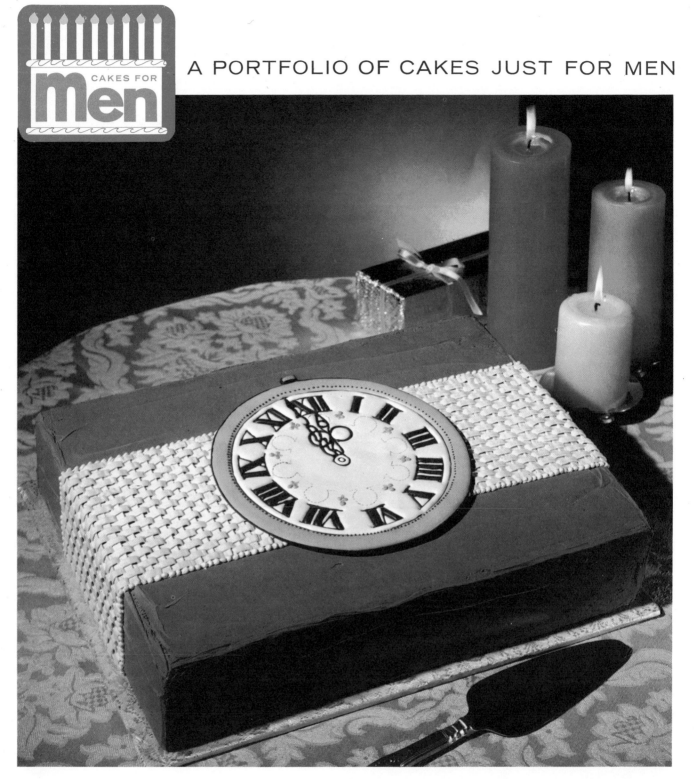

At last—cakes a man can identify with. Gone are all the ribbons, ruffles and roses. Here instead are clean, masculine lines, bold colors, designs with a man's interests in mind. All have a party look, but are definitely "his," not "hers."

TELL HIM HE'S THE ALL-TIME GREAT with this striking wrist-watch cake. Set the hands to his age (if he's 35, set hour hand to 3, minute hand to 5). A Color Flow design so it won't take much time to do!

First make Color Flow "face." Use Color Flow watch pattern from Sugar Plum Pattern Book. Outline details with tube #2 and chocolate icing, pipe gold fleur-de-lis and tiny dots with tube #1. Paint in dashes around fleur-de-lis with a tiny bit of chocolate icing on a fine pointed brush. **Prepare cake.** Bake a two-layer sheet cake, 11″ wide, 15″ long and 4″ high (two 2″ high layers). Fill and frost with chocolate icing. Attach watch face to cake top with dots of royal icing. Pipe on a yellow basketweave band, using tube #44. Edge with tiny shell-shaped beads, using tube #4.

SPELL OUT WHAT HE MEANS TO YOU
Give him the word in the sweetest way possible whether he's "Dad" or "Hubby," "Uncle" or "Gramp." Write it on the cake or with cake letters.

IN ANY LANGUAGE, HE'S GREAT! That's the message on this happy centerpiece. And it couldn't be easier to do. **First prepare cake.** Bake a two-layer sheet cake, 13"x9"x3". Fill and frost with buttercream icing. **Then add borders.** For scalloped frame on top, start with a piece of greaseproof paper, 8"x3½" and cut a scallop pattern. Center pattern on cake top and outline with a toothpick. Remove pattern and trace design with tube #14 and a wide "e" motion. Pipe top shell border

with tube #19, bottom one with tube #199. Edge bottom border with tiny red "U's" and tube #1. **Add writing.** Begin with message in scallop frame, then in script or print, write Dad's name. In English of course, "Pop," "Daddy," "Dad" and "Father." In Spanish, "Padre" or "Papa." In German, "Vater" or "Pater." In Polish, "Tatus" or "Ojciec." In Portuguese, "Avos." In Swedish, "Fader." In Hungarian, "Atya." Or your own pet names.

A "TWEED" CAKE FOR PAPA! Topped with a cheerful Color Flow greeting. **First, make letters.** Use Color Flow "Happy Birthday Papa" pattern from CELEBRATE! Charter Pattern Book and outline letters with tube 2 and chocolate icing. Fill in with Color Flow and dry.

Then prepare cake. Bake a two-layer cake, two 10 inch layers 2 inches high. Fill and frost with light chocolate. **Next pipe tweed design.** We suggest a bit of practice first on the side of an angel food cake pan. Raise cake to eye level—and press out vertical lines all around, about ½ inch apart, using dark chocolate icing and tube #3. To keep lines straight, hold decorating bag with hand turned to left, so back of hand faces upward. Start at top of cake and draw icing down or start at bottom of cake and pull up (whichever gives you the best control and straightest lines.) Keep tube just at surface either way to avoid digging into icing. When lines are drawn all around, add chevron stripes. Starting at top of a line, draw a slanted line downward to next line over, pausing at a point about ½ inch from top. Then slant upward again to top of the

line to make a "V." Continue this way all around cake and repeat until entire cake is patterned. Then pipe shell borders. Use tube #21 for top border, #199 for base border. Then attach Color Flow message to top of cake with dots of royal icing. Let the party begin!

A CAKE THAT'S LETTER-PERFECT—a great tribute for him on his birthday, Father's Day or any day you want to make happy for him. Actually the easiest of all to do. **First, prepare cake.** Bake a 9"x13" sheet cake and chill. Attach "DAD" pattern from CELEBRATE! Charter Pattern Book to cake top with toothpicks and cut out letters with a sharp knife. Use another toothpick to trace lines where letters join. *Ice cake* in three colors, keeping colors separated by placing wax paper over ones not being iced. **Then pipe white borders.** Do shell border around bottom of cake with tube #21. Pipe top rope border with tube #16. Do rope borders outlining insides of letters with #14.

Does he dream of days gone by?

Make him a cake that takes him back to gentler days, simpler ways. Happy way to hail a bicycle buff, also. And not time-consuming either, as it's an easy Color Flow creation. Here's how to do it. **First, make bicycle scene.** Use Color Flow Bicycle pattern from CELEBRATE! Charter Pattern Book. Outline bicycle scene with tube 2, fill in with Color Flow and set aside to dry thoroughly. **Then prepare cake.** Bake a cake 10″ square, 3″ high (two 1½″ layers). Fill and frost in pale blue-green butter-cream icing. **Now decorate cake.** Attach Color Flow bicycle scene and bird with dots of royal icing. Pipe top bulb border with tube #10, bottom one with #12. Flatten bottom bulbs with a damp fingertip and pipe on "spokes" with tube #1 to give a wheel effect.

WHAT'S THE NAME OF HIS GAME?

Every man has his favorite pastime. His game may be one he enjoys taking an active part in—or simply watching. Or he may like to play the waiting game at the end of a fishing pole. Whichever is his, he'll get a kick out of the cake that salutes it!

DEAL HIM A WINNING HAND with a cake that Color Flow magic makes easy to do. **First, prepare cards** for cake top and hearts, clubs, spades and diamonds for cake sides, using patterns from CELEBRATE! Charter Pattern Book. Tape wax paper over patterns, outline with tube 2 and fill in with Color Flow. Let dry thoroughly and reserve. **Then make cake.** Bake an 11"x15" sheet cake at least 3 inches high and frost in yellow buttercream icing. Attach cards and decorate. Use dots of royal icing to attach cards to cake top, other designs to cake sides. Do top shell border and bottom full garland border with tube #18. Pipe ruffles between garlands with tube #102.

GIVE YOUR FISHERMAN A CREEL that looks real! You can do it with an ordinary cake pan and a couple of plain round tubes. The "catch" is molded of marzipan. **First mold the marzipan fish** using your favorite recipe for marzipan. Shape in sugar mold and define scales and paint fins and tail with a small brush and food coloring. Set aside to dry. **Then make cake.** Bake two 9" round cakes, chill and cut in half. Lightly ice between layers and stack the four halves, one on top of the other. With a serrated knife, cut top diagonally down. Place on square cake board and spread green icing around for "grass"— rough with a spatula for natural effect. To do basketweave use tube #9 and dark icing down, #7 and

CAKES FOR **men**

light icing across. Outline basket lid and border side and bottom with large shells, using tube #199. Do small opening at top of lid with dark icing, framed with bulbs, done with tube #7. Attach fish head with more icing.

MAKE THE RIGHT MOVE with a chess cake, complete with all the chess "men." Arrange them in a challenging pattern and he'll want to finish the game before he starts on the cake! The board is Color Flow, the chessmen a "painted" set. So easy even the children can help! **First make 36 red squares.** (You'll need 32 for the board, plus a few extra in case some break in handling.) Draw a 1¼″ square pattern, outline with tube #2 and fill in with Color Flow icing. Dry and reserve. **Then make cake.** Bake a cake 12 inches square and about 2 inches deep. Frost cooled cake with buttercream icing. **Attach squares to top** and decorate. Draw a checkerboard pattern on top first with a toothpick, then attach red squares with dots of royal icing as shown. Pipe borders with a shell motion, doing bottom one with tube #10, top with #7. **To complete chess setting,** buy an inexpensive set of chess men and "paint" with royal icing. Place these on cake.

TELL HIM WHAT HE MEANS TO YOU It isn't always easy to come right out and say it. But his birthday or special day gives you a chance to let your cake speak for you. He'll love it!

SAY HE'S THE KING of his own Castle with this cake of whimsical charm. It's a breeze to do with our easy Star Method. **Do Star Method king first,** using pattern from CELEBRATE! Charter Pattern Book. Tape

pattern flat on table and tape smooth, clear plastic wrap over it. Then fill in pattern with royal icing tinted as shown, using star tube #14. Do lighter areas first, then darker ones. Do white part of eye last. Be sure to pipe stars very close together, so picture will not crack or fall apart after drying. Dry at least 24 hours and carefully peel plastic wrap away before attaching. **Prepare cake and decorate.** Bake two layers in an 8″ square pan. Fill and frost with white buttercream. Attach picture to top with dots of royal icing. Then pipe rope borders, using tube #17 for bottom, #15 for top. Pipe the fleur de lis with #15 also.

SAY HE'S A HONEY with a beehive cake that'll start everyone buzzing. Much easier than it looks and he'll say you're sweet for doing it. **Make flowers ahead.** Pipe small roses for top of hive with tube #101 and tiny drop flowers for hedge with tube #13. **Then bake cake** in a Wonder Mold pan, using a single cake mix. **To decorate,** start at bottom of cake and with light brown icing and tube #32, pipe a continuous circle until you reach the top. Ice semi-circle at front for door a dark brown. Ice cake board green and rough with spatula for a grass effect. Ice path pink and pipe a dark brown fence with tube #32 and a hedge next to it with tube #65. Use #13 again to pipe a window and press out a doorknob on "door." Then pipe a vine with tube #5 over top of hive, add leaves to it with tube #65 and attach tiny roses as shown. Finish with drop flowers attached to hedge and artificial bees here and there. Add sentiments on a tiny sign (2″ square of paper on a toothpick).

Beehive and Fishing Creel cakes by Florene Ramboldt

HOW TO DECORATE THE FONDANT CONFECTIONS ON PAGE 53.

The "Pink Rose" wedding cake is given a richly festive air by the satiny gleam of the fine fondant icing. So decorations are kept quite simple for a look that is both elegant and sweetly innocent.

Prepare roses first. Make them a day ahead if of buttercream, or a week or more ahead, if of royal icing. (You can make buttercream roses a week ahead also, but be sure to freeze them.) Use tubes #101, #102 and #104 to make three sizes. Make enough—at least 75.

Next prepare cake. Bake three round layers— 6" (two 1½" high layers), 10" (a 1½" and a 2" high layer), 14" (two 2" high layers). Cool and fill with buttercream. Then ice all layers with a thin coat of white buttercream. Coat tiers with fondant as directed on page 52. Assemble with 3" high Grecian pillar separator set with 8" round plates.

Then decorate. Pipe shell borders at base of all tiers, using tube #13 for top tier, #14 for center tier and #16 for base tier. Edge separator plate on center tier top with tiny reverse shells, using tube #14. Pipe mounds of icing at points where rose clusters will be placed, then press in reserved roses, using all sizes. Do larger clusters for top tier and top of center tier. Pipe leaves with tube #65. (Note: if you attach buttercream roses while still frozen, they will soften perfectly by serving time and stay much fresher.)

The petits fours and mints are decorated much alike. To make petits fours, bake sheet cake in size most appropriate for number of guests to be served, but keep it about an inch high. Chill and cut into a variety of shapes, using cookie cutters or a paper pattern and a very sharp knife. Keep them fairly small—our round ones are 1¾" in diameter, our diamonds 2½" long and our squares and heart shapes about 2". Seal with a thin coat of buttercream icing, then coat with fondant as directed on page 52. To make mints, see directions on same page.

To decorate: make up lots of tiny drop flowers with tube #225 and roses with tubes #101s (piped on toothpicks). Use tubes #101s and #1 for string designs and #65 for leaves. Then follow ideas on page 53 or do your own thing! Pipe borders of tiny scrolls, zigzags or dots, or hearts made with two tear drops. Pipe fleur-de-lis or spirals, even tiny birds (Wilton Encyclopedia tells how)!

PARADE OF DESSERTS
continued from page 45

Cream the butter, add sugar gradually and cream again until fluffy. Add the eggs, one at a time, beating well after each ad-

dition. Add the vanilla and 4 ounces of chocolate, mix well.

Mix the flour with the baking soda and salt and sift together. Add to the batter, alternately with the water, stirring just enough to blend thoroughly. Pour into two 8" layer pans that have been buttered and dusted with flour. Bake at 350° for 25 to 30 minutes. Cool.

Fill and ice the top and sides of the cake with pink Seven Minute Icing. When the icing has set, decorate with a web of chocolate. Fit a pastry bag with tube #1 and fill it with the 2 ounces of melted chocolate. Then drop a spiral line beginning at center of cake top and ending at edge. Draw a knife lightly from center out to edge for a spider web effect.

SEVEN MINUTE ICING*
A very fluffy white icing that never fails.

- 2 egg whites
- 1½ cups sugar
- 5 tablespoons cold water
- ¼ teaspoon cream of tartar
  few drops peppermint flavoring
  red food coloring

Place all the ingredients except flavoring and food color in the top of a double boiler and beat with a whisk or electric beater until well-blended. Then place over rapidly boiling water and continue to beat for 7 minutes.

Remove from heat, add the peppermint flavoring and a bit of red food coloring. Continue to beat until the icing reaches spreading consistency.

PERFECT LEMON PIE*
An old-fashioned pie that surpasses any of its modern variations.

- ½ recipe pie pastry (see below)
- 1 cup sugar
- 6 tablespoons corn starch
- ⅛ teaspoon salt
- 2 cups water
- 3 beaten egg yolks
- 3 tablespoons butter
- ⅓ cup fresh lemon juice
- 2 teaspoons coarsely-grated lemon rind

Bake a one-crust pie shell with fluted edge. Cool. Mix the sugar, corn starch and salt in a heavy saucepan and pour in the water. Cook over low heat, stirring constantly until mixture thickens and becomes clear. Pour a little of the mixture into the egg yolks, blend quickly and pour back into the mixture in the saucepan. Cook and stir over the lowest heat for 3 minutes. Remove from heat and beat in the butter, lemon juice and rind. Cool and pour into the pie shell. Cover with meringue, sealing edges well and bake at 350° for about 18 minutes, or until delicately browned. Cool several hours before serving.

MERINGUE*
- 3 egg whites
- 6 tablespoons sugar
- ⅛ teaspoon salt

Beat the egg whites with salt until stiff. Fold in the sugar gradually.

PIE PASTRY*
A perfect tender pie crust can be achieved by keeping in mind 3 prohibitions: don't use too much flour, or the crust will be tough; don't use too much shortening or it will be crumbly; and don't use too much water, or it will be heavy. On the positive side, have all the ingredients as cold as possible. This will make a 9" one-crust pie.

- 1 cup sifted flour
- ½ teaspoon salt
- ⅛ cup ice water
- ½ cup vegetable shortening

Mix the flour with the salt and sift into a large bowl. Cut two-thirds of the shortening into the flour with a pastry blender until it is the consistency of corn meal. Cut the remaining third of the shortening until the particles are the size of large peas. Sprinkle with water and blend lightly with a fork until it just holds together in a ball. Wrap in wax paper and chill for a half an hour or more. (It will keep for days in the refrigerator.)

Roll the chilled dough between sheets of waxed paper, lifting the rolling pin at the end of each stroke. Trim it in a circle one inch larger than the pan. Fold in half and lay the fold across the center of the pan. Then unfold. Fit it loosely into the pan and make a crimped edge with your thumb and forefinger. Prick all over with a fork. Bake at 450° for about 15 minutes.

*From the American Heritage Chapter of the Wilton Book of Classic Desserts
**We doubled this recipe

BALLET OF LOVE CAKE
shown on page 54

Its time-saving secret—the roses have the look and feel of buttercream, but are actually a new kind of plastic!

First, prepare cake. Bake two each of 14", 10" and 6" round layers. Fill and frost with pink buttercream icing, assemble with Dancing Cupid separator set (12" plates).

Next, pipe borders. For 14" tier, do large shells at base with tube #22, then drop a string guide for side garlands with tube #4. Drape garland over string guide with a circular motion and tube #71. Drape stringwork above garland with tube #3. For 10" center tier, do reverse shell base border with tube #22. Then repeat garland done for 14" tier, this time doing just a single stringwork drape over it and adding fleur-de-lis between garlands with tube #15. For 6" tier, do shell border at base with tube #16, do same garland as tiers below, but this time, use tube #72, and drape one string above and one below. Do reverse shell borders at top of **all** tiers with tube #72.

Add flowers, using attached pick to push into cake, using artificial roses described above.

the fine art of

fondant

BY NORMAN WILTON

Fondant is the elegant coating for cakes and petits fours with the fine, shiny finish. It is the only ingredient in mints and the rich, creamy center for chocolates and bon-bons. Fondant takes a bit of doing, but is well worth the effort. Because it has so many uses, and because, tightly covered, it will keep at room temperature for weeks, I've given a recipe that yields about 10 pounds. Cut it in half if you have only a small table on which to work.

FONDANT RECIPE

7 pounds of granulated sugar
4 cups water
1 pound glucose

Combine all ingredients in a large, heavy saucepan. Heat until all the sugar is dissolved. When syrup looks clear, wash down sides of pan with a brush dipped in warm water to remove any clinging sugar crystals. Repeat this procedure several times. Increase heat and boil until it reaches 240° F. on a candy thermometer.

1. At once, pour mixture onto a marble slab or mar-proof plastic table top and let it cool to lukewarm. (You can make a "frame" with dowel rods to contain it on a small table.) When mixture begins to set and you can touch it comfortably at edge, start to "work it" with a candy scraper.

2. With your hand holding the scraper palm up and blade of scraper lying almost flat, push under edge of mass and move toward center. Lift as much as possible and fold over onto rest with a circular motion. Repeat the under, up and over movement again and again. Approach mixture from all sides, keeping it in motion.

3. Soon fondant will begin to thicken and whiten as you work. Keep pushing, lifting and folding over. When it becomes so stiff and thick you can stand the scraper straight up in it (this takes about 4 minutes), pile in a mound, cover with a damp cloth, let rest a few minutes.

4. Then knead the stiff, chalky mound of fondant like bread dough and very quickly it will soften and become smooth and creamy. This formula does not have to be ripened, but can be used immediately. (Keep covered with a damp cloth while using to prevent drying out.) Or store at room temperature in air-tight container.

HOW TO ICE WITH FONDANT

Seal cake first, preferably with a thin coat of buttercream icing. This gives the fondant a white undercoat to help mask the cake and provide a crumb-free surface. Under "Versatile Buttercream" on page 35, read how to use this "seal in" technique. Put two cups of fondant into a double boiler and add desired flavoring and food color. Warm over heat, stirring constantly until fondant is of a pourable consistency. (Do not overheat or it will become too thin and may lose its shine.) Fondant should be thick enough to cover cake, soft enough to pour and spread by itself. Set cake or petits fours on a wire rack and pour fondant over, touching up bare spots with a spatula. Place plate under rack to catch fondant that drains off to use again.

HOW TO MAKE A "BOB"

This is the easy way to double your batch of finished fondant without having to start from scratch again. You simply combine it with a second recipe of ingredients cooked to 240°. Put finished fondant into mixture at that point and stir for about 3 minutes. Magically, you will have double the amount of fondant, ready for pouring over a cake or into mints. For candy centers, just let it cool and thicken, then knead until creamy. For just a couple of extra pounds, mix part of finished fondant into an equal amount of recipe ingredients.

HOW TO POUR MINTS

Heat some fondant to 160° F. in top of double boiler, stirring occasionally. Add food color and flavoring while heating. Place wax paper on table—or a length of fine-ribbed rubber matting (to make stick-proof edges in bottom of mints). Close bottom opening of mint patty funnel with point of wooden stick, then add fondant.

Lift stick to let just enough fondant run out on paper or mat to form patty, then push stick down again to stop flow. Go along, moving stick up and down in a regular rhythm.

Page 51 gives decorating directions for the fondant confections on the facing page.

What could be more romantic than happy little cupids dancing around a wedding cake? A delightfully fresh and young approach to a spring or summer nuptial day. The cake is lavish as any bride could wish, yet borders are simple to do and flowers need no doing at all. Serves 155. Decorating directions on page 51. Or choose a lovely, lace-bedecked look from a land far away, shown at right. The graceful flowers are modeled of gum paste, the cake is covered with plastic icing. The effect on your guests, sensational! Serves 70. Decorating directions for Australian Rose Cake on page 58.

Ballet of Love

Cake by Hazel Riseborough, Victoria, Australia

French Cuisine to Delight American Men

ARE YOU looking for a dinner menu to honor Dad on his day? A special meal to fete his birthday, or just to tell him how much he means to you?

CELEBRATE! asked master chef John Snowden for his suggestions. He responded by preparing the delectable meal on page 43. The recipes are all French, but the appeal is universal.

A hearty steak, cooked and sauced to perfection is the star attraction. Supporting it, green beans prepared to charm even a confirmed vegetable-hater, a salad of spring's first tender asparagus, and a garnish of crisp bacon chunks, fresh mushrooms and flavorful potatoes.

We asked Sid Langstadter, our wine consultant, for the right wine to complement this lavish dinner. He suggested a 1966 Chateau Moulin Rouge (Haut Medoc), a robust glowing red wine. If you prefer a California wine, choose Cabernet Sauvignon, or Pinot Noir. Serve it with the rich paté that begins the meal, and right through the main course.

End with fresh strawberries in a heavenly raspberry sauce. Accept the applause of replete and contented male diners.

MENU

PATÉ MOULÉ
(Molded Paté)

ENTRECOTE a'la FORESTIÉRE
(Steak Forestiére)

POMMES DE TERRE CHATEAU
(Chateau Potatoes)

PAN AU BUERRE
(French Rolls with Butter)

HARICOTS VERTS LYONNAISE
(Green Beans Lyonnaise)

ASPERGES VINAIGRETTE
(Asparagus Vinaigrette)

FRAISES a'la CARDINAL
(Strawberries Cardinal)

PATÉ MOULÉ

ASSEMBLE INGREDIENTS:

18 oz. pig's liver	3½ ounces butter
1 medium onion	6 ounces flour
1 lb. bacon fat	2 cups milk
½ teaspoon salt	2 jumbo eggs,
½ teaspoon pepper	separated
½ teaspoon ginger	1 sm. can truffles

TOOLS AND EQUIPMENT

3¾ quart saucepan
2 quart mold or bowl
Food chopper
10″ whisk
Cutting board

METHOD:

Put liver and onion through food chopper Out of 1 lb. of bacon fat cut enough strips with which to line the mold; the rest also goes through the food chopper with the salt, pepper and ginger.
Stir butter, flour and milk over a slow fire until they become a thick porridge, add the minced fat and let boil for a moment. Then add the minced liver and give it all a quick parboiling. Add 2 egg yolks and the can of truffles with the juice; finally add two whipped whites of eggs. Pour in a mold and bake 1¼ to 1½ hours in a 350° F. pre-heated oven.

ENTRECOTE a'la FORESTIERE

ASSEMBLE INGREDIENTS:

Boneless sirloin steak, about 3½ pounds
1 pound mushrooms
1 pound lean fresh unsmoked bacon
1 ounce chopped fresh parsley
4 ounces dry white wine
4 ounces concentrated beef stock
   (substitute 8 oz. beef broth boiled down to 4 oz.)
8 ounces butter
2 ounces vegetable oil
8 large whole mushrooms for garnish

TOOLS AND EQUIPMENT:

12″ sautépan (or frying pan)
Cutting board
Cook's knife
Large platter
10″ sautépan

METHOD:

1. Cut the fresh bacon into ½ inch dice. Cover with water in the 10″ sautépan and bring to the boil for two minutes. Drain and return to sautépan.

2. Pour two oz. oil over the bacon and fry until crisp on all surfaces. Drain, reserve, and keep warm.

3. Slice mushrooms thickly. Saute in the 10″ sautépan in 4 oz. butter until lightly browned. Flute the tops of the whole mushrooms and brown. Drain, reserve, and keep warm.

4. Season the steak with salt and pepper. Sauté it in the 12″ sautépan in 4 oz. butter over a hot fire. When bloody juice begins to seep through the top uncooked surface, turn the steak. Continue cooking until juice again appears on the top cooked surface. At this point steak is medium rare to medium, depending on thickness.

5. Remove steak to a platter and keep warm. Pour off the remaining butter.

6. Pour wine and beef stock into pan and boil down to ½ its volume. Stir in 1 teaspoon whole butter.

7. Pour sauce over steak.

8. Surround the steak on the platter with alternate heaps of diced bacon and sliced mushrooms. Put the potatoes on one side and garnish with whole mushrooms.

POMMES DE TERRE CHATEAU

ASSEMBLE INGREDIENTS:

6 Idaho potatoes
8 ounces butter

TOOLS AND EQUIPMENT:

5 quart saucepan with lid
12″ cook's knife
Cutting board

METHOD:

1. Peel the potatoes. Rinse well. Cut in large dice.

2. Cook in butter, in a covered saucepan. Shake pan frequently and cook until potatoes are tender, impregnated with butter and golden in color.

HARICOTS VERTS LYONNAISE

ASSEMBLE INGREDIENTS:

    2 pounds green beans
    ½ pound onions
    12 strips bacon
    ½ teaspoon leaf thyme
    Salt and pepper
    3 tablespoons butter

TOOLS AND EQUIPMENT:

    Large saucepan
    Large sautépan with cover
    Cutting board
    Chef's knife
    Colander
    Paper towels

METHOD:

1. Prepare beans for cooking by washing and cutting them into 2" lengths.

2. Cook beans in boiling salted water until they are tender but not soft. When beans are cooked drain them in the colander.

3. Cut onions in half from stem to root. Place them flat side down on a cutting board and slice them thinly. They will fall in half rings.

4. While beans are cooking fry the bacon until crisp. Remove from pan and drain on paper towel. When cool, crumble bacon.

5. Fry onions slowly in a small amount of butter in a covered frypan until golden.

6. Drain onions on paper towel.

7. Combine bacon and onions.

8. Ten minutes before serving put butter in the sautépan and allow it to melt. Add beans and toss to coat them with butter.

9. Add onions and bacon and season them with thyme, salt and pepper to taste. Mix and cook over gentle heat, tossing frequently for ten minutes. Check seasonings.

ASPERGES VINAIGRETTE
(Not shown on our cover)

ASSEMBLE INGREDIENTS:

    3 cans white asparagus or 2 pounds
      cooked fresh asparagus
    1 bunch romaine lettuce
    4 ounces white wine vinegar
    12 ounces olive oil
    ¼ teaspoon each: dry mustard,
      basil, oregano, and sage
    1 tablespoon capers
    Pimento
    Chopped parsley
    Salt
    Pepper

TOOLS AND EQUIPMENT:

    3 qt. bowl
    Wire Whisk
    Salad bowl

METHOD:

1. Wash, dry and chill the leaves of romaine.

2. In a 3 qt. bowl, mix oil and vinegar. Add herbs, salt, and pepper.

3. Drain asparagus. Marinate in the vinaigrette (oil and vinegar mixture) for 1 hour.

TO SERVE:

Arrange asparagus spears on torn leaves of romaine in a salad bowl. Top with strips of pimento, sprinkle with capers and chopped parsley. With a whisk, beat marinade briskly and sprinkle over all.

FRAISES A'LA CARDINAL

ASSEMBLE INGREDIENTS:

    1½ pounds fresh strawberries
    1 pound fresh raspberries
    2 teaspoons fresh lemon juice
    10 ounces powdered sugar
    4 ounces slivered, blanched almonds

TOOLS AND EQUIPMENT:

    Kitchen blender
    3 quart stainless bowl
    Fine wire strainer

METHOD:

1. Wash, drain and dry the strawberries.

2. Chill for several hours.

3. Wash raspberries. Drain. Pureé in blender, adding sugar gradually as the berries are pureéd.

4. Finish pureé with lemon juice. Chill.

TO SERVE:

Heap strawberries in a well chilled bowl. Cover with raspberry pureé. Sprinkle with slivered almonds.

JOHN SNOWDEN, Chicago's leading authority on "La Cuisine Francaise", teaches the culinary art in the classic tradition. He was born in Guadalajara, Mexico, and began his apprenticeship in Europe at the age of 15. He studied in France and Switzerland for nine years.

He is a fellow of the American Academy of Chefs and was a gold medal winner of the 1966 American Culinary Olympic Team.

For 25 years he operated gourmet restaurants, but in 1965 he left the business to devote himself full-time to teaching, lecturing, and writing. He then established his school of French cooking, Dumas Père, now located in Glenview, Illinois. Here is a kitchen accommodating 15 students, and a large conference/dining room.

His talent goes beyond his artistry in the kitchen. He is also a fine artist, having received his B.A. degree from the Art Institute of Chicago.

RECIPES TO PLEASE A CROWD

Many of you have asked for large-scale recipes to serve at banquets or other large gatherings. Here are two from Chef Snowden's files, guaranteed crowd-pleasers. Both can be prepared well ahead. Just add hot rolls, a casserole of fluffy rice and dessert (perhaps a specially designed cake) to round out a memorable meal.

Both of these recipes may be doubled, halved, or even quartered to suit the size of your group. Both can be easily and quickly served.

MEAT ROLLS

Portions: 100, 7 oz. ea. Temp. 350°F.
INGREDIENTS:

100 thin slices of round steak	24 lbs.
100 thin slices cooked ham	9 lbs.
1 quart vegetable oil	
4 cups chopped pork	32 oz.
4 dozen chopped, hard cooked eggs	6 lbs.
4 tablespoons salt	2 oz.
4 teaspoons pepper	⅔ oz.
8 quarts tomato sauce*	16 lbs.

METHOD:

Dip steaks in oil. Lay slices of ham over steaks and sprinkle with pork, salt and pepper and eggs. Roll tightly and fasten with skewers. Place in a baking pan with sauce and bake twenty minutes.

*TOMATO SAUCE

Quantity: 8 quarts
INGREDIENTS:

4 cups butter	32 oz.
8 cups minced onions	48 oz.
28 cups tomato pureé	14 lbs.
16 teaspoons salt	2⅔ oz.
8 teaspoons pepper	1⅓ oz.
16 tablespoons cornstarch	4 oz.
4 teaspoons paprika	

METHOD:

Simmer onions in butter until tender. Add pureé and seasonings, and cook five minutes. Add cornstarch that has been dissolved in a little water. Bring to a boil. Strain and pour over meat rolls.

SPRING SALAD TOSS

Portions: 100, 2½ oz. each
INGREDIENTS:

4 quarts shredded lettuce	3 lbs.
4 cups grated carrots	24 oz.
8 cups cut cooked string beans	32 oz.
8 cups cooked green lima beans	4 lbs.
4 cups minced water cress	1 lb.
4 cups grated onions	2 lbs.
4 cups diced radishes	24 oz.
4 tablespoons salt	2 oz.
4 teaspoons pepper	
6 cups bottled French dressing	3 lbs.

METHOD:

Combine all ingredients. Sprinkle with dressing. Toss and mix well. Serve in lettuce cups. If you wish to make the salad ahead of time, chill the vegetables in separate containers and combine them with the dressing just before serving.

AUSTRALIAN ROSE CAKE
shown on page 55

First model flowers. Use gum paste recipe given on this page. Roll out to about ½″ thickness. Trace petal shapes on it, cut out and curve carefully with finger and thumb—turning in petal tips as shown. Lay in small shallow bowl to dry overnight. (Mold petals for large center rose in small bowl about 3″ in diameter and a little less than an inch deep—a shallow wine glass might do.) Make large roses with 5 large petals, 1½″ long, 4 small petals, 1″ long, smaller roses with 5 petals, ¾″ long. To assemble, attach wax paper square in bowl, pipe dot of royal icing in center. Attach petals in circle, overlapping slightly. Push in pearltipped stamens about ½″ long.

Prepare cake. Make two square fruitcakes, one 6″, the other 10″, both 4″ high. Cover with plastic icing, using recipe below. Dust a pastry board lightly with cornstarch and roll out about ½ inch to ⅜ inch thick to size and shape of cakes. Roll back onto rolling pin, transfer to cakes. Dust hands with cornstarch, shape to cakes, stretching gently to get all ripples out. Polish with heel of hand until surface is smooth. Trim surplus with a sharp knife. Tuck net ruffle under base.

Make patterns for sides of cakes, top of base cake. Cut of greaseproof paper, trace on cake with toothpick.

Then decorate. Fill traced shapes with cornelli lace, using tube #1 to do little curly lines that do not cross. Edge with tiny dots, using same tube. At base of top tier only, pipe border of shells with tube #18. Press out small mounds of royal icing, attach flowers and artificial lily of valley. Add net to top flower for "ornament" effect. Pipe leaves with tube #65. Assemble cake with 3″ tall Grecian pillars and a single square separator plate.

PLASTIC ICING RECIPE

Easy to prepare if you don't mind using your hands—most home electric mixers aren't powerful enough.

    1 lb. confectioners sugar
    6 oz. glucose syrup
    4 oz. water
    ⅔ oz. unflavored gelatin
    Flavoring

Sift confectioners sugar directly onto pastry board. Put water and gelatin in a pan, stand it in boiling water. When gelatin has dissolved stir in glucose and flavoring, until they are completely blended. Mixture should be warm but not too hot. Pour onto confectioners sugar, combine into a clear, firm dough. (Adjust with a tiny bit more sugar or water if needed.) Dust with cornstarch, place in plastic bag. It will keep for some time. When ready to use, knead a bit until it is soft and pliable before rolling out.

GUM PASTE RECIPE

    ¼ oz. gelatin (one envelope)
    ½ cup water
    1 level teaspoon cream of tartar
    4 cups confectioners sugar
    1 cup cornstarch

Place first three ingredients on a low heat and stir. When dissolved, add confectioners sugar and cornstarch. Knead like pie dough until smooth. Cover with a damp cloth.

HOW TO MAKE
SPUN SUGAR NESTS
shown on page 31

How impressed and charmed everyone will be with these sparkling little nests filled with ice cream "eggs"! They're mostly plain sugar and great fun to make. The lavish scalloped plates upon which they lie and the shining flowers that embellish them (as well as the basket and flowers shown with them) are of fabulous pulled sugar, which you can also do yourself. Space does not permit our giving you directions for pulled sugar in this issue of CELEBRATE!, however, you will find full illustrated directions for this lovely art in the Wilton Encyclopedia of Cake Decorating and in CELEBRATE! II.

To make spun sugar, you must first find or fashion a "shaker". This very important piece of equipment is quite easy to make. Just cut a 4-inch square of wood, one-inch thick. Then drive about 50 three-inch nails through the

Spun sugar shaker

wood ½-inch apart. Arrange in rows as shown in sketch. Screw an easy-to-grip handle to top. You will also need two long narrow sticks—balloon sticks are fine—about 6 feet long.

Spun Sugar Recipe

    2 lbs. granulated sugar
    1 lb. corn syrup
    1 pint water

Combine all ingredients in a large, heavy saucepan. Cook until syrup reaches 290° on a candy thermometer. Wash down the sides of the pan at least twice with a brush dipped in hot water, to eliminate any clinging sugar crystals. Remove from heat and tint with food coloring.

To spin sugar, place the two sticks on a table about 1½ feet apart and let them extend about three feet beyond the table edge. (Place a weight on the opposite ends, so sticks won't roll or fall as you work.)

Next, stand on a chair to be at the proper height, with pan of syrup in your left hand. Dip shaker down into the syrup, lift it up and let it drain off slightly. Then hold it high in the air directly above the sticks and shake vigorously. Make long, sweeping back and forth movements so that sugar falls in fine strands over the sticks. Repeat

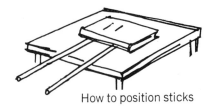
How to position sticks

until you have as much spun sugar as sticks will hold, then lift off and place on table. Continue making spun sugar until all the syrup is used up. (If remaining syrup has hardened, you may reheat it.)

To store spun sugar, place in a large air-tight can, cover with paper and seal tightly with a lid. It will last indefinitely in cool, dry weather, or in an air-conditioned room. (Do not refrigerate.)

To make nests, simply shape a small amount of spun sugar into a round bowl with your hands, working directly on table and using a delicate touch. Don't put ice cream in until just before serving, because the melting ice cream will melt the spun sugar. And just top ice cream with whipped cream & a cherry, because sauce will also melt the spun sugar. For a delightful centerpiece, shape a large spun sugar nest and fill with mint patties or chocolates. Sparkling spun sugar also adds a magic touch to a wedding cake, swirled around the base.

VOLUME ONE

Celebrate!

JULY / AUGUST

Decorating directions for Noah's Ark Cake on page 65

JACK

climbs the beanstalk on a cake that brings the favorite fairytale to life! He'll set the scene for a party featuring fun games like "Take a giant step," how many beans in the jar, how many beans can you carry on a table knife—and whatever climbing or chasing games you can invent. Serve a hot dog-and-baked bean casserole with corn chips and green dilly beans. Add cups of frosty punch or pop and finish up with Beanstalk cake and ice cream.

BEANSTALK CAKE. **First, do Color Flow designs.** (Do these at least 2 days before the party.) Use Jack-in-the-Beanstalk pattern from Sugar Plum Pattern Book. Tape plastic wrap over patterns, outline with tube 2 and fill in outlines with Color Flow. Important- do leaves, beans and Jack separately. Do not do whole pattern in one piece, as it would be impossible to transfer to cake top. Use pattern as a guide for putting all together later on. Dry leaves and beans in curved form, placing some over curve, some inside it. Dry Jack flat. See Color Flow tips page 92.

Then prepare cake. Bake a two-layer cake in a pair of oval pans, using just one cake mix. Cool thoroughly, then fill and frost with yellow buttercream icing. Do bottom shell border with tube #16.

Put design together. Using pattern for guide, find the point on cake top where Jack's lower boot will be. Then, starting at bottom border, pull a vine of icing up side and across top to boot point with tube #10. Repeat twice more, piping so last two vines are on top of first one. Turn cake around and continue vines across cake and down opposite side to a point about 1½" above border. Pipe a branch of the vine as pattern shows. Pipe small mounds of icing next to vine in places where leaves and beans are to go. Place them on top to elevate them slightly and push to touch vine. Some leaves go over beans, some under, all adding to the fascinating three dimensional effect—and to the "real" look. At this point, pipe tiny corkscrew tendrils here and there, as indicated, with tube #1. Finally, place Jack on another mound of icing. Then let the party begin!

JOLLY CLOWNS

dance a jig to start a circus party off just right. And make it a "real" circus! Send tickets of admission with invitations and ask everybody to come in circus costume —clown, acrobat, tightrope walker or wild animal! The more home-made the better! Get bags of peanuts-in-the-shell, popcorn, candy and potato chips, wrap hot dogs and hamburgers in napkins. Put all in shallow cartons (cut down from supermarket cartons), each with a carry-sling made of soft pajama cord. Put pink lemonade in a big picnic jug and the jug in a child's wagon. Give everybody play money when they arrive, so they can "buy" and appoint two or three guests to walk around "selling" the treats. Be sure to have a "balloon man" with one for each child. Mark off a circus ring in the backyard and let the kids who sing or dance or do tumbling, juggling or magic tricks be "entertainers." Give prizes for all performances. Serve Clown cake, ice cream bars.

JOLLY CLOWN CAKE. **First, make Color Flow Clowns** and balloons (do them at least 2 days before party). Use Jolly Clown pattern from Sugar Plum Pattern Book. Tape plastic wrap over patterns, outline with tube 2 and fill in with Color Flow. Make small round icing balloons for top of cake by pressing Color Flow icing straight from the batch through a #10 tube. Do flat balloons for sides of cake by outlining and filling in small circles the Color Flow way.

Then make cake. Bake a two-layer cake, 10" or 12" round and 4" high (two layers). Fill and frost with white buttercream icing.

And decorate. Pipe ribbon ruffle border at bottom with tube #104 and rosette border at top with tube #18. Pipe a small mound of icing at center top and pile up small icing balloons in a pyramid. Press a little icing on feet of clown figures and press into position in a circle as shown. Place small wads of foil between clowns to keep them upright until icing dries. Pipe strings on side of cake with tube #1 and attach flat balloons with dots of icing.

Who's zoo at your house? If zoo animals are favorites, bring them to the party! Here we show three charming—and easy—ways to do this. The cakes have simple shapes and borders—and the animal designs can be done almost entirely with a single star tube, using our easy Star Method. Put big bowls of peanuts-in-the-shell on the table and have lots of bright balloons everywhere. Hide stuffed toys and play "Animal Hunt." And give some cuddly animals as prizes!

TO DO ANIMAL DESIGNS use patterns from the Sugar Plum Pattern Book. Tape clear plastic wrap over pattern, outline with tube #6 making sure to include all features. Pipe small dots for eyes at this time. Then fill in with stars using tube #16. Be sure to pipe stars very close together or picture may crack or fall apart after it dries. Do whites of eyes last on owls. Re-pipe all features, making sure to reinforce eyes, mouth and whiskers. Dry thoroughly, at least 24 hours. Then peel off backing very carefully and attach to iced cake (see below), using royal icing.

TO MAKE AND DECORATE CAKES
Prepare a one or two-layer cake, depending on how many are to be served. Fill and frost with buttercream icing. **For elephant cake,** bake a 9x13" sheet cake and use tube #3 to drop strings across top and down sides for "cage" effect. Do bottom bulb borders with tube #12. **For bear cake,** bake a 10x10" square cake and pipe bulb borders, using tube #16 for top, #18 for base. **For owl cake,** bake a 9x13" sheet cake and pipe rosette borders, using tube #16 for top and #18 for base.

ANIMAL KINGDOM CAKES

VERY YOUNG

The littler children are, the more a pretty party cake enchants them. Especially if a colorful toy or dolly is part of it. And parties for wee ones are so easy to give. Cake, ice cream and lollypops will serve very nicely for refreshments. And games can be the simple, traditional ones children have played for generations. Give each child a rocking horse as a favor or have extra dolls at every plate. And don't forget the balloons!

MERRY-GO-ROUND of rocking horses—guaranteed to light up little eyes! Horses really rock and they carry candy and candles on their backs, too. Busy mothers of the sand-box set will be happy to see how easy this enchanting cake is to do.

Prepare cake first. Bake a two-layer cake, 10" or 12" round. Fill and frost with white buttercream icing. **Then decorate.** Cut a circle of greaseproof paper the size of cake top and fold into sixths. Place it on top of cake and mark off cake in sixths. Do small rosette at top center with tube #32, then use tube #46 to pipe 6 spokes from center to edge of cake and down sides to base. Do rosette borders, using tube #4B for base of cake, #32 for top. Position candle and candy-carrying rocking horses on cake top and decorate with tiny drop flowers (piped ahead of time with tube #225). Light the candles and sing "Happy Birthday"!

BASSINET BABY. Something for the girls of 2 and 3 and 4—a cake that's a bassinet with a dolly inside! (Makes a perfect baby shower cake, too.) Go-with favors could be miniature bassinets or tiny baby dolls in blankets. The cake is lots easier to do than it may look —and it's tops for toddlers!

First make sugar hood. Knead two cups yellow-tinted granulated sugar and four teaspoons water by hand, pack mixture into half of Egg Pan and scrape off excess with a spatula. Unmold immediately and cut into two pieces at a point less than half diameter of mold. Let dry one hour at room temperature before separating halves. Then take shorter piece (which you'll use for bassinet hood) and gently scoop out sugar from center with a spoon, leaving a ¼" shell. Let dry at least 4 hours more, then ice outside of hood white. Attach drop flowers (made ahead with tube #225) to inside of hood and add leaves with tube #65. Then pipe ruffles on outside of hood with tube #104 and zigzag at edge with tube #47 and set aside. **Next prepare doll head.** Use tube #2 to pipe squiggly yellow curls on small plastic doll head and figure-pipe a small pair of hands with tube #2. **Then make cake.** Bake a 2-layer cake in an oval pan set, using one cake mix. Cool thoroughly, fill and frost with white buttercream icing. **Decorate cake.** Do basketweave sides, using tube #47 for horizontal lines and #5 for vertical lines. Over this, pipe ruffle drape with tube #104 and fill with zigzag garland, using tube #47. Then drop a ridged line around top edge of bassinet with tube #16. Add a ribbon bow, using #104 again and attach little drop flowers all around.

At a point just beyond where hood will be attached, begin cornelli lace design for quilt, piping little wriggly lines with tube #2. Press out mound of icing for pillow and smooth it over with a wet spatula. Then pipe ruffles around it and across top of quilt with tube #102. While icing is still wet, push doll head gently into position and place hands atop quilt. **Finally, attach hood.** Pipe a line of icing around back of bassinet, then lift hood carefully on upturned fingers (touching only the sugar inside) and place on wet icing line— it's not necessary to press down.

sweet
stories

The 3
little
PiGs

Pinocchio

Little Jack
Horner
sat in the
corner...

directions on opposite page

HOW TO MAKE STORYBOOK CAKES
Shown on opposite page

First, do story patterns. You'll need a set of Book Cake Pans and Storybook patterns from CELEBRATE! Charter Pattern Book. Tape pattern to pan in position shown, making sure pattern follows curves smoothly. Tape wax paper or clear plastic wrap just as smoothly over pattern. Then outline with tube 2 and fill in with Color Flow. Let dry in position on pan, and when you remove, release very carefully, sliding wax paper off pan, up or down—**never** to the side. Design must dry on pan, so it will lie properly on curves of cake. **Then prepare cake.** Bake a cake in the two halves of Book cake pan, using a single cake mix for both. (Grease and flour before pouring in batter.) Bake according to mix directions, then place upside down on rack to cool for 5 minutes. Remove pans carefully. Place thoroughly cooled cakes together on a cardboard base and frost in buttercream icing. Pipe a line for binding around bottom of book with tube #57. Use table fork or decorating comb to draw "pages" on sides. Carefully peel wax paper off designs and attach to cakes with lines of royal icing, being careful to place with curve of cake. **For Pinocchio cake**—pipe in puppet strings with tube #2. **For 3 Little Pigs cake**—attach pig design in position first, then pipe leaves with tube #65 and attach drop flowers piped ahead with #225 for a garden path effect. **For Little Jack Horner cake**—Jack's shadow is done separately, so attach that Color Flow piece to cake first and then position Jack on top for a 3-dimensional effect. Pipe in "corner" with stringwork, using tube #2. Place cake on foil-covered board.

HOW TO MAKE NOAH'S ARK CAKE
Shown on cover page 59

First prepare cooky animals. Use cutters from Zoo Set, Gingerbread Family, Animal Pets and big Animal Set to cut designs from your favorite cooky dough. Cool and paint with softened Color Flow icing. Outline and pipe circles, collars, bows and hearts, with tube #1 or #2 and contrast icing. **Next make cabin.** Use House Sugar Mold to make house parts of sugar and water, using method described for Circus Train Animals on page 80. When thoroughly dry, assemble with royal icing. Pipe shingles for roof with tube #103.

Then prepare cake. Bake two 11x15" sheet cakes and chill thoroughly. Place one cake atop the other, and with a sharp knife and gentle sawing motion, cut into a boat shape, tapering slightly toward bottom. Fill and frost with pink buttercream icing. While icing is still wet, pull a spatula straight across sides to give the "wooden slat" effect shown. With tube #7, pipe a thick line of icing around top for railing, then do zigzag border over it with tube #16. **Put it all together.** Place cabin in position on "deck" of boat, securing with a few lines of icing. Position animals on deck, hull and cabin and secure with dots of icing. Let it rain!

SUMMER WEDDING CAKE TRIMMED WITH "OPEN STAR" TUBES
Shown on page 66

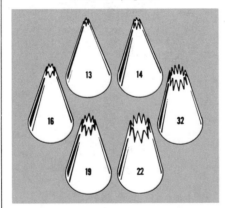

Here is ample evidence, indeed, of the marvelous versatility of the "open" star tube. You need just the 6 star tubes shown above to do this richly embellished "Baroque" wedding design.

All the star tubes used for this cake are of the "open" variety (with opening shaped like a star, but points left open). Icing presses through in a pretty ribbed design which lends itself to an almost endless number of beautiful shapes and borders—stars, shells, ripple garlands, rosettes and ropes.

Star tubes help you do a beautiful decorating job with very modest skills because they are so easy to handle. Even for beginners! Try this cake, see for yourself.

TO DECORATE "BAROQUE"
First prepare cake. Bake two 2-layer wedding tiers—one 10" round and another 6" round. Fill and frost white and assemble with 8" separator plates and 3" tall Grecian pillars. **Then decorate.** Do big shell borders for base of both tiers, using tube #32 for larger tier, #22 for smaller one and frame both with green zigzag, using tube #14. Do small shell borders with tube #19 for top edge of both tiers and add stars between shells with tube #14. Do green colonial scroll on side of top cake with tube #13 and zigzag on separator plate with tube #16. Use #16 again to do zigzag white garlands at sides of bottom cake and #14 for garlands of green upside down "e's" piped over them. Use #14 again to do circles, and fleur-de-lis between.

ICING RECIPES
Continued from page 35

Wilton Buttercream Icing
⅔ cup butter or margarine,
    cold and firm
4 cups sifted confectioners sugar
1 teaspoon vanilla
2 or 3 tablespoons cool milk or cream

Beat butter several minutes with electric mixer until creamy. Add sugar, about ½ cup at a time, beating well each time. Add vanilla, then milk or cream and beat well again. Store in air-tight container in refrigerator and whip up before using again. This recipe will produce approximately one quart of icing. To make it whiter, use vegetable shortening instead of butter or margarine and add butter flavoring.

Wilton Royal Icing—Meringue
3 level tablespoons meringue powder
1 lb. confectioners powdered sugar
3½ oz. warm water (slightly less
    than ½ cup)
½ teaspoon cream of tartar

Combine ingredients, beat at high speed for 7 to 10 minutes. Keep covered at all times with damp cloth. To restore texture later, simply rebeat. For lighter icing, add tablespoon water, continue beating. (This makes a more brittle flower.)

Wilton Royal Icing—Egg White
3 egg whites (room temperature)
1 lb. confectioners sugar
½ teaspoon cream of tartar

Combine ingredients, beat at high speed for 7 to 10 minutes. Very quick-drying, so keep covered with damp cloth. Yields less volume than meringue; beating won't restore.

Baroque

A cake for a small-but-elegant summer wedding . . . with swirls and scrolls as lavish as baroque art designs! Yet all done with simple star tubes. Serves 64. Directions on page 65.

*S*UMMER STAR. *For any shining hour the summer season might bring. Lavish enough for a family-only wedding or small anniversary celebration. Feminine enough for a sunny bridal shower; dainty enough for a welcome-baby shower. And simple to do! Serves 12.*

To do "Summer Star" cake. Bake a two-layer cake 8″ square. Fill and frost with white buttercream icing. Mark each side into thirds (make a mark every 2⅔ inch). With toothpick, draw guideline for scrolls from mark-to-mark on top and between center marks on sides as shown. Then with tube #2, drop slanted lines of green icing, first to left, then to right on top for latticework. Overpipe guidelines with scrolls, using tube #17. Do side scrolls with same tube, then overpipe second scroll right on top. Drop green lattice from top edge of cake to scroll, then do a final scroll on top to conceal lattice edges. Use tube #17 again to do "C" scrolls at each corner of cake side and to pipe shell border for top edge of cake. Also to pipe rosette with four shells around it for star effect on cake top. Finish with bottom shell border, using tube #20. Let the celebration begin!

Fancy Foods

BY MARIE

SPRING some creative summer touches next time you entertain. Use the vivid colors and sparkling freshness of abundant summer vegetables—and the pale golden coolness of rich creamery butter—to make beautiful bouquets you can eat. It's a quick, clever way to turn even the simplest warm weather fare into something that looks very special indeed. And you'll be amazed at how easy this handsome kitchen sculpture is to do.

VEGETABLE BOUQUET

Assemble the following. Firm, fresh radishes, cucumbers, carrots, turnips, cherry tomatoes, celery, baby beets (partly cooked), green onions, cauliflower, and brussel sprouts. Also, some fresh parsley for "leaves" and a large head of cabbage for a base, as well as a basket to put it in. You'll need a very sharp paring knife, a bowl of water with ice cubes in it, and a small amount of lemon juice.

First make base. Crumple some foil and place in bottom of basket to give bouquet height and to hold base firmly in place. Then set cabbage on top of foil.

Next make flowers. Do individual designs as directed below. As you finish each, drop it into the bowl of ice water to open "petals" and keep fresh until ready to assemble. If you are carving turnips or potatoes, have a separate bowl for them and add a little lemon juice to the water to keep them from darkening. Put beets in a separate bowl also as they turn water red.

Then assemble bouquet. Press a toothpick through each flower (or put flowers together with a toothpick) and push into cabbage in arrangement shown.

HOW TO CARVE "FLOWERS"

Daisy. Use turnips or potatoes dipped in lemon juice. Cut into thin slices and cut out with a daisy cookie cutter. Use a round piece of carrot for center and push a toothpick through to secure.

Daffodil. Cut a slice of turnip into 6 petals. From another piece of turnip, cut a cone shape and scoop out center of wide end. Put petals and cone together on a toothpick and dip top of cone into paprika.

Roses. Begin at base of radish, oval-shaped piece of turnip or carrot, or small peeled beet. Cut thin, half moon slices or "petals" all around at a 45° angle, leaving attached. Then cut a narrow wedge behind petals and remove. Do another row of petals, starting between petals in row below, and so on, until all that remains is a pointed center at top. Drop into ice water and petals will gradually open. For traditional radish roses, just cut petals straight down, do not cut wedge.

Tulips. Peel turnip or cucumber. Cut into oval (use rounded end of cucumber). Cut two long petals almost to base at opposite sides of oval. Hold back gently with fingers and cut two more in between them. Scoop out center, place black olive sections on toothpicks and push in for stamens.

Fantasy flowers. For radish, cut thin slices in accordion style from one end to the other. Or cut single deep petals from top to base and scoop out, carving center into a point. **For carrot,** cut into petals as just described for radish—or cut into daisy shape with small cookie cutter. **For green onion,** cut tiny vertical strips down from top of white head and frill out a bit with your finger, then drop in ice water to open even more. **For celery,** use a piece 2" long and cut one end into vertical strips. Put in ice water and strips will fan out prettily. **For cucumber,** cut into slices and notch deeply all around, then center with a tiny circle of carrot. **For cherry tomato,** cut 3 broad petals from top to base. Carefully scoop out pulp, and add center—a frill of green onion or a sprig of parsley. Use cauliflower "flowerets" and brussel sprouts whole.

Calla Lily. Cut a very thin slice of turnip. Curve into cornucopia shape, tucking a strip of carrot inside for stamen. Secure with toothpick.

VOLUME ONE

Celebrate!

SEPTEMBER / OCTOBER

Decorating directions for Autumn Wedding Cake on page 74

THE scarier, the better, that's the rule for Halloween parties! It's best to have them at night, unless your guests are very young. Then at least have them in the late afternoon. By all means, insist on costumes—and definitely home-made ones. (You'll be amazed how creative everyone turns out to be.)

For a really hilarious time, try an all-ghost, all-witch or all-monster party. With awards, of course, for the best version. Tell ghost stories with plenty of witches and monsters in them. One great idea is to have one guest make up a story, stop at a scary point and let the person next to him continue the tale. And so on around the room. The story that results will be incredible, unpredictable and great fun. Or play trick or treat, but don't actually play any tricks. Just sit around and dream them up. The one who thinks of the craziest stunt, wins the treat or prize. (A safe-and-sane version of the old custom.) Be old fashioned—bob for apples. Be new fashioned—play rock records and dance.

Be sure to include all the traditional favorites on the party table—popcorn, apples, doughnuts, peanuts, pumpkins (to do some in ice cream, see below) and of course, a punch bowl of cider. Center the table with a cake that's absolutely terrifying—and perfectly delicious.

BAKE A MONSTER
Make him ghastly. Green and knobbly, with a fiendish grin. He'll set the scene for a very scary evening and no one will know until serving time that he's just a softy inside.

Start with a 2-pc. stand-up tree pan and bake a single cake mix. Ice all over with soft buttercream tinted yellowish green. Follow the curves of the cake and add a few extra bumps and lumps here and there of icing. Do ears and nose ahead— ice standard-size marshmallows to match face and attach with toothpicks. Do eyes and teeth in advance, also. Draw 6 or 7 small rectangles for teeth and two circles for eyes, outline with tube 2 and fill in with Color Flow. Attach teeth as shown, pipe sides of mouth with tube #44 and lips with #3. Use #3 again for scar. Pipe close, wide zigzag lines for eyebrows, using tube

#5 and "pull out" short strings of icing at sides and around back of head for hair with tube #9.

WHIP UP A WITCH
Give her a sly and crafty air. Stringy hair. Eyes that hypnotize. A nose like a hose. And a mouth just made for mumbling incantations. As frightening as she looks, everyone will discover she's a regular cut-up at refreshment time.

To create witch, stir up a single cake mix and bake it in a Wonder Mold pan. Ice all over with flesh-tinted buttercream and pipe long straggly strings of yellow icing hair with tube #43, bangs with #4. Do eyes, and tooth in advance. Draw patterns, then outline with tube 2 and fill in with Color Flow. Do nose ahead also. Draw a hook shape. Cover with wax paper and figure pipe two half noses with tube #12. Let them dry, then place a toothpick on base of one half with part of it extending. Ice flat side of other half and press to first. Let dry and push into face. Pipe a round wart on nose with tube #10, and pipe pink dots for cheeks with tube #12 (flatten both with damp finger). Attach eyes with icing. Draw a jagged mouth with toothpick and trace with red icing and tube #5, then attach tooth. Roll a cone of colored construction paper for hat. Your witch is ready to cast a spell over all!

ICE CREAM PUMPKINS
For delicious individual servings! Easy to make with gourmet pumpkin molds. Simply soften orange-tinted ice cream and press into each half of the two-sided hinged molds, rounding one side slightly. Then close molds tightly, pressing until excess ice cream oozes out edges. Wipe clean, put into freezer until solid (about 5 hours). To unmold, pat with warm damp cloth for a couple of seconds. Then open and mold will release ice cream shapes easily. Return to freezer until serving time. Then pipe a stem of green icing with tube #10. Pumpkins will be about 2¼" in diameter.

O RNAMENTS
that are truly "you," because you make them yourself—with your own original ideas and designs! And with the quick, simple techniques shown here, you won't have to be an artist to create ornaments as beautiful as any you'll see in a store. (Another delightful getting-ready-for-Christmas project for the whole family!) To make them for your own tree or gifts, just . . .

PAINT WITH ACRYLICS. (Top left.) You'll need some clear plastic balls (come in 2 snap-together halves) and a range of colors in acrylic paints. An artist's paintbrush. A bowl of water for cleaning brushes or changing your design. Some gold cord for hanging. And any idea that pops in your head! Work with one half ball at a time and paint on the **inside**. Do your basic design first and let it dry thoroughly. This only takes about ½ hour, but be sure design is **completely** dry, before continuing. (If basic design seems too transparent, go over it one or two times more, letting dry between each coat.) Then paint background color right over it. Tie gold cord into a loop and place knotted end inside one half ball. Then snap other half on and cord will be attached. (Just be sure every bit of paint is dry inside before you put ball together.) That's all there is to it and see how beautiful! Other ideas . . . your monogram, newlyweds' first names, holiday greetings, favorite designs, and, most charming of all, the children's own drawings!

DECORATE SPARKLY MOLDED SUGAR. (Bottom left.) You'll need sugar molds from the Holiday, Christmas and Christmas Ornament Mold Sets, and some more clear plastic snap-together balls. Knead by hand 2 cups regular or tinted granulated sugar with 4 teaspoons water, pack into molds, scrape off excess and unmold immediately. To cut window in panorama ball, cut straight across top curve of half ball with a piece of string using a slow sawing motion (like slicing cheese). Let dry for two hours, then scoop out soft inside of half balls, and smooth window. (Hold half ball in palm of hand and gently clear sugar from window area, smoothing with fingertips.) **Decorate all** with royal icing using your imagination and tube #3 for string and ball trims, #16 for small shell borders, #67 for leaves. Pipe tiny figures with tube #4, use Tree Former as base for tiny tree. (Note: put objects inside half ball **first,** then attach window half with royal icing.) Add color to sugar before molding, or paint with tinted and softened Color Flow icing after molds are dry. Petal ornament is a styrofoam ball, iced and covered with petals made with tube #74. (Hold on skewer while working.)

MISTLETOE! FROM ANCIENT TIMES HONORED EVERYWHERE AS A MYSTIC BOUGH THAT MAGICALLY BROUGHT HEALTH AND GOOD LUCK. ENEMIES WHO MET BENEATH IT WERE SAID TO LAY DOWN THEIR ARMS IN PEACE. SO CAME THE CUSTOM OF GREETING EVERY-ONE UNDER IT WITH A KISS OF FRIENDSHIP AND LOVE. NOW CELEBRATE! SHOWS HOW TO MAKE MISTLETOE FOR THE FIRST TIME IN ICING. SEE PAGE 74.

HOW TO MAKE MISTLETOE "KISSING BALL"
Shown on page 73

Do this year's mistletoe ball in icing and hang over the entrance to your dining room! It's completely new and certain to enchant everyone.

To do: Coat a styrofoam ball with green icing, insert florist's wire all the way through it and make a loop at both top and bottom. Make mistletoe leaves ahead (see page 78 for step by step directions), some with wire stems and some without. Attach leaves all over ball with more icing, letting leaves without wire lie flat, pushing leaves with wire into ball so they turn out slightly. Pipe in white berries as shown with tube #7. Add festive green and gold ribbon at top and bottom.

HOW TO MAKE MISTLETOE ORNAMENT
Shown on page 73

Place this sweet touch of Christmas on mantel or table . . . or use it to crown a holiday wedding cake.

Make mistletoe in advance (see page 78 for step-by-step directions) and assemble several clusters. Use arched canopy trellis and weave a ¼" green ribbon through it as shown. Glue arch to Heart Base. Glue bench with Loving Couple to base. Put two clusters of mistletoe together and hang from top of trellis. Attach two clusters of mistletoe to top of trellis and center with ribbon bow. Pipe some icing on sides of bench and press in more bow topped clusters. Finish with single spray on front of heart base.

HOW TO DECORATE AUTUMN COVER CAKE
Shown on page 69

For the first time ever—a wedding cake decked with the vibrant colors of autumn leaves! And you can turn it out with ease, because you use just four simple borders and Autumn Leaf Patterns on page 78.

First, prepare leaves. Step-by-step directions are given on page 78.

Next, prepare cake. Bake 3 round tiers, 2 layers each—16" x 4", 10" x 4" and 6" x 3". Place base cake on a 22" board covered in gold color foil, and fill and frost all tiers with light golden yellow buttercream. Assemble with 5" tall Roman pillars and 12" separator plates.

Then decorate. For 16" tier—use tube #17 for top and bottom shell border and fleur-de-lis and #19 for garland. For 10" tier—use tube #17 for top and bottom zigzag border, fleur-de-lis and garland. For 6" tier, use tube #16 for top and bottom shell borders and fleur-de-lis. Arrange fall leaves around base of cake.

Between pillars. Glue a Petite Bridal Couple to a Heart Base, 4½" diameter. Add a few maple leaves as shown.

At top of cake. Place a small mound of icing in bottom of Heart Ringed Bowl. Press in a small styrofoam ball iced green. Push leaves on wires into ball.

Don't stop here. Carry the autumn leaf theme in other decorations for your wedding and reception. Frame tall candles with leaves for table centerpieces. Choose mums and fall leaves for wedding flowers!

HOW TO DECORATE MARZIPAN WEDDING CAKE
Shown on opposite page

A most unusual cake for a fall wedding, heaped with the happy fruits of a rich fall harvest. Most intriguing of all, the fruits are marzipan—the elegant almond paste candies in fruit shapes that once were made only by European trained pastry chefs. Now **you** can make marzipan and this gorgeous cake. (Amazingly, just two tubes are used for the cake's borders!)

Marzipan Recipe
1 cup almond paste (8 ounce can)
2 egg whites, unbeaten
3 cups powdered sugar
½ tsp. vanilla or rum flavor

Knead almond paste by hand in bowl. Add egg whites, mix well. Continue kneading as you add sugar, 1 cup at a time, and flavoring until marzipan feels like heavy pie dough. Divide batch for coloring, kneading in one drop of color at a time until natural shade is achieved.

To prepare fruit. Dust work surface with confectioner's sugar and roll marzipan into tube-like shapes ¾" in diameter. Cut tubes into 1½" pieces and model by hand. Roll ball shapes for apples, tiny oval shapes for grapes. To make grape bunches, roll marzipan into tear-shaped base and brush with glucose. Air dry until tacky, then attach grapes. Trim apples and grape bunches with florist wire stems and ready-made marzipan leaves. Brush fruits with corn syrup glaze, let dry and they're ready for the cake.

Next, prepare cake. Bake three round two layer tiers, 8" x 3", 12" x 4" and 16" x 4". Fill and ice all tiers with yellow buttercream. Place base tier on crystal-like plate and assemble with other tiers, using crystal separator legs and pairs of 14" and 10" separator plates. (Ice plates on tier tops to match tiers.)

Then decorate. Use tube #30 for the small pouffs on bottom of all three tiers. Do zigzag frame around pouffs and shell border under them with tube #16. Use #16 again for the triple shell borders at the top of all three tiers, and for the zigzag around crystal pillars. That's it!

Add marzipan fruits as shown. Arrange clusters between pillars and place some fruit on crystal-like tray. Mound some icing on top of 8" tier and press in a large fruit cluster.

MARZIPAN
WEDDING CAKE

Directions on opposite page

Fancy Foods

BY MARIE

HOME-MADE Christmas candy is one of the most welcome and traditional gifts of all. So appreciated because you make it fresh with good, rich things from your own kitchen. If you've hesitated to attempt candy-making, let this be your year to try it. It's really an easy task and everyone you favor with it will be **so** impressed! Incidentally, in this day of high prices, you'll find it is a good deal less expensive than "store-bought" candy of far inferior quality.

One thing that will keep your candy-making easy is to have a plan. Don't try to make too great a variety—about 4 different kinds should be enough. Try to choose candies that contrast in flavor, texture, color and appearance. And be sure to get yourself a good candy thermometer—accurate temperature is the secret of producing perfect candy every time. And do have some pretty fluted bon-bon cups on hand. Everything looks more tempting when presented attractively.

Set up a mini "assembly line" in your kitchen, enlisting some of the family to help. (You won't have to beg them.) Your only problem will probably be to keep them from taking too many samples! Prepare bon-bon and chocolate mint fillings ahead and let some helpers cut them into squares and roll them into balls. Let others do the dipping.

Search for pretty containers to "box" the candies for gifts. They'll look even more appealing.

Here we present four colorful candies to make for Christmas—pink and yellow bon-bons with creamy centers, the beloved melting chocolate mint squares, frothy light, white divinity brightened with red and green candied fruit, and crisp, crunchy, nut-topped English toffee.

CHRISTMAS DIVINITY

    3 cups granulated sugar
    ¾ cup light corn syrup
    ¾ cup water
    3 fresh egg whites (room temp.)
    ¼ teaspoon salt
    1 teaspoon vanilla
    ¼ cup pecans
    ¼ cup candied red and green fruit mix
        (cherries, pineapple, citron)

In a 2-quart saucepan, combine sugar, syrup and water. Cook to 262° F. While syrup is cooking, pour egg whites with salt added, into a mixing bowl. As soon as syrup reaches 262° F., remove from heat and let stand a minute or so while beating whites. Beat whites until they cling to bowl, then, **very slowly,** pour hot syrup over whites, beating constantly. (If you add the syrup too quickly it will cook the whites into lumps.) Continue to beat about 10 minutes, or until candy no longer flows from beater in a continuous ribbon, but in broken pieces. At this point mixture will start to appear dull and retain its shape when dropped from a buttered spoon. Quickly fold in nuts, fruit and flavoring. Pour into wax paper lined pan to form a sheet ¾" thick. When cold and firm, cut in squares. Keeps 3 to 4 weeks, wrapped in plastic wrap and stored in a tightly-closed container. Makes 2½ pounds.

ENGLISH NUT TOFFEE

    1 lb. butter
    2 cups sifted granulated sugar
    1 cup medium chopped nuts
    ¼ teaspoon oil
    ⅔ lb. milk chocolate

In 2-quart heavy saucepan combine butter and sugar. Cook over medium flame, stirring constantly until mixture comes to a full boil, or reaches about 242° F. After boiling begins, do not stir or beat until browning too rapidly on side or it curdles or separates. If mixture does curdle or separate at any time, beat it until smooth, using heavy wooden spoon. Cook the boiling toffee until it reaches 306° F., lowering flame during last few minutes of cooking. Remove from stove and pour into a 12x18" sheet pan that is very lightly greased (use about ¼ teaspoon oil). Spread with spatula to uniform thickness while still hot. Cut top into squares and brush with melted milk chocolate to cover, then sprinkle nuts over all immediately. Lay a piece of wax paper over top, place a cardboard square over that and carefully invert. Tap pan to loosen, then lift off. Quickly wipe candy with paper towel to remove any excess oil and brush with more melted milk chocolate to cover.

Sprinkle again with nuts. Let cool, then break squares apart. Makes about 2 pounds.

PASTEL BONBONS

Prepare a recipe of fondant as given on page 52. Spread in a pan, cover with foil and chill, then cut into squares. Or make squares into balls by pinching corners and rolling between palms. Use a fork or bon-bon dipper to dip into pastel coating (see below) or fondant softened for dipping.

To prepare pastel coating (a chocolate substitute that comes in pastels and does not have to be tempered). Just melt in double boiler. Bring water to rolling boil, turn heat off, let stand ½ hour. Then stir to blend—never beat. When it has a liquid look it is ready to use for dipping or pouring into mold.

Dipping tips: drop squares or balls into softened fondant or pastel coating. Lift on fork and swirl to cover completely. Lift out of pot, shake off excess, scraping bottom of spoon on pot edge to reduce dripping, drop on a wax paper-covered cookie sheet. Twirl last string of fondant or coating that flows off fork into a "C" on top.

MELTING CHOCOLATE MINTS

    1 lb. milk chocolate
    ⅔ cup whipping cream
    1 tablespoon warm melted coconut
        butter or plain white shortening
    ¼ tsp. oil of peppermint

Melt milk chocolate over hot water (about 175° F.). Beat after first 10 minutes and remove from heat as soon as it is fully melted. Temperature of chocolate when melted should be about 120° F. Bring whipping cream to a boil, then let cool to about 150° F. Pour warm, melted chocolate into mixing bowl. Add warm, melted fat and blend well. Add flavoring to hot cream, and add hot cream **all at one time** to chocolate. With electric mixer at low speed, beat until evenly blended and smooth. Now increase speed to high and beat about one minute more, until thick and smooth. Cover bowl and refrigerate for about 1 or 2 hours, stirring frequently to keep it uniform in temperature, but do not beat. After this much refrigeration and stirring, mixture will still be lukewarm. Beat at high speed for 1 or 2 minutes until lighter in color. Do not overbeat. Pour at once into 7-inch wax paper lined pan, cover with foil and put back in refrigerator until firm to touch. Cut into squares or roll between palms into balls. Dip in green pastel coating as for bon-bons.

Pastel Bon-Bons in a little copper kettle, a variety of candies in a basket, English Nut toffee in a miniature brass coal scuttle, Divinity in a red Chinese bowl and Melting Chocolate Mints on a blue ironstone platter.

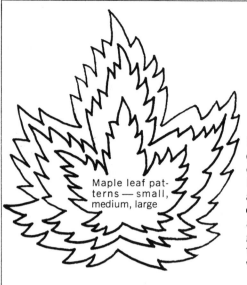

Maple leaf patterns — small, medium, large

HOW TO MAKE A MAPLE LEAF

Now the flame and gold and russet of glorious autumn leaves for your cake! (We used them for your Salute to Canada cake, facing page, and the beautiful fall wedding cake on our cover.) A CELEBRATE! first and easy to do! **First trace pattern,** given in 3 sizes at left. Cover with transparent paper, trace size you want.

Outline in Color Flow. Tape plastic wrap smoothly over pattern. Mix Color Flow icing, divide and tint in 4 autumn hues and soften as directed on page 92. Then fill a decorating parchment bag half full, cut a small opening in tip and roughly outline leaf patterns.

Fill in immediately with same icing and pull out points quickly with a damp #2 artist's brush.

Dry on curved form (Flower Former shown at left). Mix copper brown paste color with a drop of water, paint in veins (see below). Tint water copper, dip cloth-covered florist's wire for stems. Dry and attach with dab of unsoftened Color Flow icing, tinted to match leaves.

HOW TO MAKE MISTLETOE

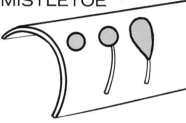

These pretty boughs have for centuries been a magical symbol of luck and peace, and an invitation to a kiss. Now, do them in icing! **Pipe leaves.** Attach wax paper to Flower Former with icing. Pipe small green dot on top, push in short length of fine florist's wire. Pipe elongated leaf over dot. Brush to taper at wire. Make 2 sizes with tubes 7 and 9.

Cover stems. When leaves are dry, peel off paper and cover stems with green florist's tape. To avoid breaking leaves, begin taping slightly below base, rolling between fingers. Cover wire left exposed with white icing berry.

For single spray. Tape stems of 3 or 4 leaves together, centering one, alternating others below. Pipe white dots for berries.

For multiple spray, shown below. Start with single spray, tape more sprays below it—to left, right, at center and so on. White berries are piped on last.

Salute
to
CANADA

A beautiful cake to hail our big-shouldered neighbor to the north! It's a land where all things—mountains, lakes and trees, even animals and fish—seem to come larger-than-life size. Where scenes of spectacular beauty are commonplace. And where the crisp elegance of England, the quaint charm of France and the quiet dignity of the Indian nations make a sparkling mix of cultures. From Montreal and Quebec in the east to central Toronto to breathtaking Victoria in the west, the landscape stretches like the stride of the legendary Paul Bunyan. Much of the vigor of Canada is expressed in its official coat-of-arms, around which we have designed our salutory cake. And its beauty is symbolized by its national emblem, the maple leaf—that adds glory to its golden autumns.

Prepare coat-of-arms. Use CELEBRATE! Charter Pattern. Outline with tube 2, then fill in with Color Flow. When dry, retrace outlines and do lettering with tube 1.

Next, make maple leaves in 4 autumn hues, 3 sizes. How-to on facing page.

Prepare cake. Bake and fill a two-layer tier, 9x13″ in size and 4″ high. And a two-layer tier, 4″ high baked in an oval pan set. Ice with white buttercream.

Then decorate. Pipe border of large shells around bottom of base cake with tube #199. Use tube #17 to do full garlands around top edge of base cake and for "e" motion scrolls on top of it. Do arch between garlands with tube #74 and drop stringwork with tube #3. Do full garlands at top edge of oval cake with tube #16, use #76 for arches between garlands and #3 again for stringwork. Set coat-of-arms on top of oval cake, attaching with dots of icing. Arrange leaves on cake as shown.

time for a fun cake!

TELEPHONE CAKE

Telephone Cake, crowned with flowers and wearing a Happy Birthday message on its dial. A great conversation piece with young people and it's easy to see why. To make, bake two cakes in 9 x 13 x 2" pans. Cut one cake into two halves, each 6½" x 9" and fill and stack as a layer cake. Chill and slice off front of top layer as shown in diagram below for a "desk phone" shape.

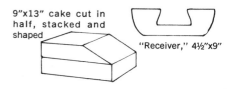

9"x13" cake cut in half, stacked and shaped

"Receiver," 4½"x9"

Position on serving tray and ice all over in buttercream tinted the shade you prefer. Pipe 3 circles in white with tube #7 for dial and do message with tube #4 in color to match flowers you are going to add. Edge all around top and lower edges with shells, using tube #19. Cut the other 9" x 13" cake into halves the long way, each 4½" x 13". Use one to cut out the "receiver," use the other for another purpose. Place next to phone and ice to match phone and add same shell border. Pipe more #19 shells right on tray for "cord." Attach buttercream daisies (made ahead with tube #102 and frozen)—any variety and color you wish—and position on phone and receiver. Pipe leaves with #67. Place Telephone Cuties among the flowers.

CIRCUS TRAIN

Four gay little cakes trimmed like circus wagons bring their favorite pets to the party! Making the "train" is nearly as much fun as serving it to 12 small circus fans.

First, shape the sugar animals. Knead together 2 cups granulated sugar, 4 teaspoons water, substituting the same amount of liquid food coloring for water to tint sugar. Then press into Merry Monkey and Panda chocolate molds and Elephant and Hound Dog candle molds, doing two half figures for each. Unmold immediately and let dry 5 hours, or 5 minutes in a 200 degree oven. When thoroughly dry, put halves together with icing and use softened tinted Color Flow icing to paint trims on elephant, monkey and dog, and to flow-in panda's eyes, nose and feet. Top monkey's head with plastic hat favor. The animals ready, make cakes, using a Daisy Cart cake kit. Bake the four 5" square cakes with a single mix. Cool, ice and add trims. Pipe all ball borders with tube 4, stripes with tube 47, zigzags with tube 16, scrolls with tube 3, ribbon garlands with tube 102.

Place on daisy-wheeled cake trays, bring animals aboard and let the good times roll! Serves 12.

Celebrate!®
NOVEMBER / DECEMBER

Decorating directions for color flow Christmas Village on page 92

Christmas Sweets from

around the World

Bring traditions from all over the world into your home this holiday season with Christmas treats from other countries! In the first row, from left to right, Germany's "Stollen" or Christmas Cake, France's yule log cake "Bûche de Nöel" and England's Plum Pudding. The second row of delicacies include "Thorner Lebkuchen" from Poland, "Basler Lekerli" from Switzerland and "Panettone" from Italy.

Recipes start on page 90

PUT ON A HAPPY FACE...

when the younger set gathers 'round your holiday table, with a cake like Santa himself. Bake in a Wonder Mold pan with a single mix, frost in icing tinted a skin tone (two parts brown, one part copper food color). Put features on first—round eyes and cone-shaped tongue done ahead with Color Flow icing, nose made of a miniature marshmallow dipped in pink icing, attached with a toothpick. Figure-pipe cheeks with tube #12. Do icing beard, eyebrows with tube #19 and a "C" motion. Twirl red construction paper into a hat, add a tassel of icing frills, piped on a styrofoam ball with tube #76. (Attach with toothpick.) Serve with greeting-topped ice cream.

LET SANTA DANCE...

'round a tree crowned holiday cake to add a frolicsome note to any Christmas party! Make the dancing Santas far ahead in Color Flow icing, using patterns from Sugar Plum Pattern Book. Do 6 in all and reserve. Make tree ahead, too—using tree-former and tube #74. On day or day before serving, bake a two-layer, 10″ round cake and frost snowy white. With tube #21, pipe top border of zigzag garlands, do draped garlands all around sides, and green shell border at cake base. Use tube #3 to pipe red string scallops on cake top between garlands. Attach Santas on side garlands with dots of icing so they stand out a bit. Place tree on top, attach candle with dot of icing.

Santa's coming...
let's bake him a cake!

HAVE YOU MET HIS ELVES?

Four little faces brighten four little cakes—Santa, Mrs. Santa and two mischievous elves, straight from Santa's own workshop! You'll do them all so easily, you'll almost think elves are helping **you.** Just bake a quartet of cakes in a set of 5" square pans, using one cake mix for all. Ice lightly in white buttercream and let crust slightly. Trace patterns from Sugar Plum Pattern Book onto greaseproof paper, then place on cakes. Punch through with a toothpick to transfer designs onto cakes. Outline with tube #2 and fill in with colors shown, using tube #16 for both stars and shell borders, tube #5 for holly berries on Mr. and Mrs. Santa cakes. A holiday hit!

HE'S A JOLLY ELF HIMSELF!

Sweet marshmallow santas—ready to perch atop a frosted cupcake, or any cake, to thrill each pint-size party goer. Make each of 3 standard and 9 miniature marshmallows. Thin tinted icing, making small containers of colors to be used. Push toothpick into one standard marshmallow and paint red for "body", cut another in half and paint red for "hat". Paint a third flesh-color for "face" (see santa face formula on opposite page). Stick into foam block to dry. Next, paint 4 mini marshmallows red, 4 green for "arms" and "legs", let dry. Assemble on toothpicks as shown, using white mini marshmallow for hat tassel. Pipe eyes, mouth, buttons with tube #2, beard and hair with tube #14 and "C" motion.

CONVERSATION-PIECE
CAKES FOR
CHRISTMAS PARTIES!

These will start the conversation going—
holiday cakes turned into angels, or
candles you can eat! Best of all, they're
a breeze to do.

Angels sing at the center of your holiday table—to symbolize the joy and harmony of the season. They're really bell cakes to turn out quickly and top with star method angels you were clever enough to do far ahead of time. You can be sure these cakes will capture the attention and admiration of everyone who sees them! To do them, you need just a pair of angel patterns from CELEBRATE! Charter Pattern Book and a set of bell shaped pans that take a single cake mix. And you can get along quite well with just average decorating skills. **Do angels ahead.** Tape wax paper over patterns, pipe in royal icing. Use tube #2 to outline details and draw out strings for hair. Pipe dots for eyes with tube #5, stars for mouth with tube #13 at this time. Fill in outline with stars, using #16 for orchid, #14 for everything else. Be sure to pipe stars very close together, so pattern will not crack or fall apart after drying. After doing stars, repipe eyes and mouth. Dry all at least 48 hours. Peel off backing carefully before placing. **Bake cakes** and ice with pale aqua buttercream. Press out white petals with tube #104 for wings, doing short ones at top, then drawing them longer and longer as shown. Pipe one or two rows of wings to lie under angels. Attach angels with dots of icing. Pipe shell motion border with tube #9.

Joyeux Noel is the wish expressed by this very unusual cake! Most surprising thing about it—the candles are actually small cakes themselves! And the "flame" atop each, as well as the real looking holly leaves are made of icing. It's a cake that will be remembered by all for holidays to come . . . yet not at all difficult to do. Here's how. **First do holly leaves and letters.** Outline patterns from CELEBRATE! Charter Pattern Book with tube 2 and fill in with Color Flow pulling out points with a paintbrush before icing dries. Dry finished leaves on a Flower Former for natural look. For letters, outline and fill in with stars, using tube #16 and royal icing. (Keep stars very close together.) Dry thoroughly and reserve. **Prepare cakes.** Do one 9x13" sheet cake and frost in aqua. Do four cakes in Little Loafer pans and ice in white. **Assemble cake.** Push 4 dowel rods into sheet cake and push little loafer cakes carefully onto them in upright position. **Then decorate.** Pipe mounds of icing on candle tops, smearing around to resemble melted wax. For flames, press out teardrop shapes on wax paper with tube #4-B. Insert toothpicks in wide ends and let dry. Peel off paper, hold upright, pipe second teardrop on back of first. Dry and carefully insert in candle cakes. Attach letters with dots of icing. Arrange holly leaves as shown, pipe berries with tube #8. Add shell motion borders with tube #10.

NEW WAX ORNAMENTS

TO MAKE YOURSELF

Jewel-like ornaments—with creamy surfaces that catch the light softly for a rich, elegant glow. They look a bit like ivory or porcelain, but they're actually wax, and you can make them yourself with very little fuss or muss. Hand-made ornaments are very much "in" and you couldn't choose a prettier kind to do. They are so attractive you might want to box several sets to give as distinctive gifts. And they'll turn your own Christmas tree into a holiday conversation piece!

To make them, simply use Christmas Ornament Molds and wax plus colors to tint it from your local craft shop. Melt and tint wax in a double boiler, pour carefully into oiled molds (deeply etched molds come 6 to a sheet of heavy plastic), let set overnight, unmold. Wash lightly to remove oil with a soapy cloth, then a damp one and dry. Paint with acrylic gilt color—or whatever color you prefer—and when dry, cover with a protective coat of clear gloss polymer medium (available at art supply shops). Attach hanging wire by laying a loop of wire on back of ornament and dripping wax from a candle onto it until sufficient to hold securely.

The molds can also be used to shape sugar ornaments or candy and even more easily. Another do ahead project for your holiday! Gather the family 'round the kitchen table —and get started right away. You'll find the more you do yourself for Christmas, the more enjoyable it seems!

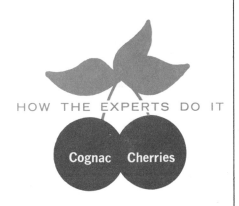

HOW THE EXPERTS DO IT

Cognac   Cherries

FABULOUS HOLIDAY TREAT

Lutz Olkiewicz, skilled Pastry Chef of Chicago's prestigious Drake Hotel and U.S. Gold Medal winner at the 1972 International Culinary Olympics, shares his famous recipe for Cognac Cherries with CELEBRATE! These delicious cordials, as much of a treat to look at as they are to eat, are sure to impress your family and friends. So to royally welcome the gay Christmas holidays, or to add an elegant touch to any occasion, just follow Mr. Olkiewicz's step-by-step recipe.

First, you will need to prepare the cherries for your candies at least 4 weeks in advance. Use only stoneless sour cherries—fresh, frozen or canned (well drained). The cherries should all be about medium-sized to allow room for the liqueured fond-

ant that will surround them.

Depending upon the number of candies you wish to make, fill a pint or a quart jar to the rim with cherries. Then pour in enough French Cognac or domestic brandy to cover. (Figure a pint jar to make about 50 to 60 candies, and a quart jar about twice that much.) Then seal the jar tightly and store in the refrigerator.

After the cherries have been refrigerated for 4 weeks, the next step is to prepare the foil bon-bon cups. Melt about 4 to 5 squares of semi-sweet or European dark chocolate in a double boiler until soft, but not warm. Remove the top of the double boiler and

cool the chocolate until it almost stiffens. Then replace the top of the boiler and reheat the chocolate till it's between 85° to 89° on a candy thermometer. This temperature gives the chocolate the proper consistency for a nice crack and sheen. If you find you need more chocolate later, merely repeat this same melting procedure until you obtain the necessary amount.

When the chocolate has reached the right temperature, pour some of it into a parchment decorating bag and fill each foil bon-bon cup to the top. After the chocolate sets in the foil cups for a few minutes, turn all the cups upside down on a screen. This allows the excess chocolate to run off, leaving a candy shell all ready to be filled.

Now, fill the chocolate-lined foil cups. Drain off the brandy marinated cherries and place one cherry in the center of each cup. Next, heat some fondant to about 60° (or until consistency is thick, not runny) and, using a decorating bag, pour the fondant over the cherries filling each bon-bon cup almost, but not quite to the top. After the fondant has settled for a few minutes, seal the top of the candies using more of the melted chocolate. Finally, place any fancy decoration you desire on the candies (designs in milk or dark chocolate, chips of fruit or nuts, etc.).

The picture to the left illustrates the steps we've just explained above. From left to right: the first row shows the empty foil bon-bon cups; the second row the cherry-filled, chocolate-coated cups; the third row the fondant-filled cups; the fourth row the chocolate-sealed cups and the fifth row, the final product—Cognac Cherries!

Before the candies are ready to be eaten however, they must go through a process of fermentation which takes about three weeks. After this time, the brandied cherries will have diluted the creamy fondant into a liqueur-flavored syrup, and at last the cordials are ready to delight the taste of any candy lover!

ENGLISH PLUM PUDDING

In England, it wouldn't be Christmas without plum pudding; the treat that's filled with all sorts of good things just like the holidays themselves. Spices, nuts, candied fruit peel and many more tempting ingredients are put into this delightful dessert. In this happiest season of the year, what could be a more festive finish to an enjoyable dinner than English Plum Pudding!

INGREDIENTS:

    ¾ cup dried currants
    1 cup seedless raisins
    1 cup white raisins
    ⅜ cup finely chopped mixed candied
        fruit peel
    ⅜ cup finely chopped candied cherries
    ½ cup blanched, slivered almonds
    1 small tart apple, cored and coarsely
        chopped
    ½ carrot, scraped and coarsely
        chopped
    1 tablespoon finely chopped orange
        peel
    1 teaspoon finely grated lemon peel
    ¼ pound beef suet, finely chopped
    1 cup flour
    2 cups fine, fresh white bread crumbs
    ½ cup dark brown sugar
    ½ teaspoon ground allspice
    ½ teaspoon salt
    3 eggs
    ½ cup brandy
    ¼ cup fresh orange juice
    2 tablespoons fresh lemon juice

PROCEDURE:

Place the first eleven ingredients in a large bowl and stir them with your hands until well mixed. Sift the flour with the allspice and salt and add to the fruit mixture. Mix well. Then add the bread crumbs and brown sugar and mix again.

In a separate bowl, beat the eggs until fluffy. Add the brandy, orange juice and lemon juice. Stir well. Pour this mixture over the fruit mixture and knead with your hands until blended well. Cover with a damp towel and refrigerate for at least 12 hours.

Next, butter two 1-quart pudding molds, or several small individual molds, and spoon in the pudding. Adjust the covers so they fit tightly. Then butter the seams where the covers meet the sides of the molds. (The English use a bowl-shaped mold without a cover and tie a floured cloth cover over the rim with a string.)

Put the covered molds on trivets placed in a large kettle. Pour in boiling water till it covers ¾ of the sides of the molds. Bring

Christmas Sweets

FROM AROUND THE WORLD

water back to boiling point and cover the kettle. Then reduce heat and simmer for 8 hours, adding water as needed to keep the level in the kettle constant.

When the puddings are done, take them out of the water, remove the covers and cool to room temperature. Replace the covers (or cover with foil) and refrigerate for at least 3 weeks. (Plum puddings used to be made a year in advance and kept in a cool place until Christmas!)

Before serving, place molds on trivets in a large kettle and pour in boiling water as before. Cover the kettle, bring to a boil and simmer for 2 hours. Then loosen the sides of the pudding from the molds with a knife and invert pudding on a serving plate. Decorate the center of each pudding with red and green cherries and sprigs of holly. Serve with chilled brandy hard sauce or hot rum sauce.

BÛCHE DE NOEL

Bûche de Noel or French Yule Log is a melt-in-your-mouth sponge cake richly filled and frosted. This lavish dessert, a tradition with the French at Christmas, is as delicious to look at as it is to eat!

INGREDIENTS:

    6 eggs, separated
    ¼ teaspoon salt
    ½ cup sugar
    1 teaspoon vanilla
    ½ cup flour

    1 recipe Continental Butter Cream
        (recipe below)

    1 recipe Creme Chantilly
        (recipe below)

Beat the eggs whites with the salt until

they stand in soft peaks. Add 4 tablespoons of sugar, one at a time and continue beating until meringue is very stiff. In a separate bowl, beat the egg yolks with the remaining sugar and vanilla until fluffy.

Gently fold about ¼ of the meringue into the egg yolk mixture. Then pour back into the bowl of meringue. Sprinkle with 2 tablespoons of the flour and fold. Repeat this until all the flour is blended. Be careful not to overmix!

Finally, pour into buttered 11" x 16" jelly roll pan that has already been lined with buttered wax paper. Bake 10 to 12 minutes in a 400° oven until golden.

PROCEDURE:

Sprinkle a tea towel with ½ cup confectioner's sugar. As soon as the sponge sheet has finished baking, take it out of the oven and invert it on the towel so the wax paper is on top. Do not remove wax paper. Roll the cake tightly in the towel to a 16" long cylinder. Cool carefully, unroll and peel off the wax paper. Trim off the crusty edges and spread the cake with a thin layer of Continental Butter Cream (chocolate-flavored), then with a thick layer of Creme Chantilly. Reserve the rest of the butter cream. Then reroll the cake and refrigerate for half an hour.

After refrigerating, cut a small piece off each end of the cake, diagonally, and place on either side of the "log" with the diagonals against the cake.

Put the rest of the chocolate butter cream into a pastry bag fitted with a star tube, and pipe long lines over the "log" to resemble bark. Then pipe the white butter cream you set aside earier in a spiral over the "log's" cut ends. Trim with green icing leaves and red icing berries. Refrigerate until serving time.

CONTINENTAL BUTTER CREAM

    ⅓ cup water
    ⅔ cup sugar
    ⅛ teaspoon cream of tartar
    5 egg yolks
    1 cup soft butter
    5 ounces melted semi-sweet chocolate
    4 tablespoons extra-strong coffee
    3 tablespoons cognac

Mix sugar, water and cream of tartar in a saucepan. Stir over low heat until sugar is completely dissolved. Raise heat and boil without stirring until syrup tests 238°.

Meanwhile, beat the egg yolks in a bowl until fluffy. Then pour the hot syrup in a thin stream into the egg yolks, beating constantly. Set aside till completely cooled and then beat in the softened butter, a little at a time.

Now set aside a small amount of white butter cream, and then beat the melted semi-sweet chocolate, coffee and cognac into the remaining butter cream.

CREME CHANTILLY

2 tablespoons sugar
½ teaspoon vanilla
1 cup heavy cream
1 teaspoon gelatin

Add the gelatin to 2 tablespoons cold water in a metal or pyrex cup. Set in a pan of boiling water and heat until gelatin dissolves and appears clear. Do not stir! Beat this mixture into the heavy cream just as the cream begins to thicken. Then add the sugar and vanilla to the whipped cream and chill.

STOLLEN

German Stollen, or Christmas cake, is a jelly-roll shaped sweetbread with bits of candied fruit, sliced almonds and rum-soaked raisins scattered throughout its rich buttery dough. Delicious anytime of the day, so you can serve it with afternoon tea, after dinner or with coffee late in the evening. And, like fruitcake, its taste improves with age and can therefore be made well in advance of the holidays.

INGREDIENTS:

1½ cups golden raisins
½ cup mixed candied fruit
½ cup preserved orange peel
2 tablespoons rum or brandy
½ cup sliced almonds
1 cup milk
2 sticks butter, cut up
⅓ cup sugar
½ cup flour
2 packages dry yeast
grated rind of 1 lemon
1 teaspoon vanilla extract
½ teaspoon almond extract
½ teaspoon orange extract
½ teaspoon salt
4½ cups flour

PROCEDURE:

Mix raisins, candied fruit, orange peel and rum (or brandy) in a bowl. Cover and let stand overnight, or at least for one hour.

Then scald milk and put in large mixing bowl. Add the butter and the sugar. Stir until the butter is melted. Mixture will be lukewarm. Next, mix the ½ cup flour with the dry yeast and add to the lukewarm

mixture. Set in warm place until mixture becomes bubbly.

Then add the vanilla, almond and orange flavorings along with the lemon rind and remaining 4½ cups flour to the bubbly mixture. Cover and put in a warm place until mixture has doubled in bulk, (at least one hour or more.)

After the mixture has doubled, knead in the almonds and liqueured fruit. Form 2 rolls about 8″ long and 3″ in diameter. Place on a buttered baking sheet in a warm place and let double in size. Then bake at 375° for about 40 to 45 minutes.

HOW TO COAT THE STOLLEN:

Have a pan of boiling butter (one stick or more) ready and a pan of melted apricot jam (½ cup jam and 1 tablespoon water.) When the Stollen comes out of the oven, pick off any burnt raisins and with a fork poke holes all over the cakes. Paint the cakes with melted butter first, then paint with melted apricot jam. Roll the cakes in granulated sugar and set on racks to cool. When cool, dust heavily with powdered sugar and wrap in plastic. Store the finished cakes in tightly covered containers or in the refrigerator.

PANETTONE

Italian Panettone, a fruit-filled sweetbread, is a treat served in Italy only at Christmas. You'll find it so delicious you may want to make it all year round for breakfast, tea or a late evening snack!

INGREDIENTS:

1½ pounds flour
5½ ounces sugar
½ pound butter
½ ounce salt
10 egg yolks
8 ounces white raisins
4½ ounces candied citrus fruits
     (diced into small pieces)
4½ ounces candied orange peel
     (diced into small pieces)
1½ ounces yeast
grated rind of 2 lemons
½ cup lukewarm milk

PROCEDURE:

Dilute yeast in the ½ cup lukewarm milk. When yeast is thoroughly diluted, mix with **some** of the flour into a sponge-like consistency. Then add the rest of the flour along with the egg yolks, sugar, salt and butter.

Mix all these ingredients well until they loosen from the edge of the bowl, adding

just enough milk so the dough becomes soft, but not runny. (This additional milk was not mentioned in the list of ingredients because the amount is usually too small a portion to be measured.)

Now add the candied citrus fruits, candied orange peel and grated lemon rinds to the dough mixture and blend well. Then let the dough rise 2 times, kneading it down after each time.

Fill into buttered Gugelhupf mold or an empty #2½ fruit can. Let the mixture rise to fill ¾ of the mold and make several cuts across the top of the dough with a buttered knife.

Bake at 350° to 375° for about 45 to 55 minutes. Let cool, turn out of the mold and spread on a coating of hot melted butter.

BASLER LEKERLI

Swiss Basler Lekerli, glazed cakes of candied fruit and nuts spiced with just the right touch of cherry brandy, is truly a dessert as delightful as Christmastime itself. And it's a sweet you can make and store in advance, so when the busy holidays arrive you're ready with an interesting surprise for your friends!

INGREDIENTS:

2¼ pounds of Lebkuchen Ground Dough
     (Recipe below)
2 ounces chopped white almonds
2 ounces chopped candied citrus fruit
2 ounces chopped candied orange
     rind
2 tablespoons cherry brandy
¾ ounce allspice
⅛ ounce powdered ammonium
     carbonate (may be purchased
     at a drug store)
a pinch of baking soda
part of a whole egg

PROCEDURE:

First dilute the powdered ammonium carbonate and baking soda with part of the whole egg, using as little as possible. When the powder is diluted to a smooth, but not runny consistency, add to the Lebkuchen Ground Dough and mix well.

Then, add the allspice, almonds, fruit, brandy and blend well. Roll out the dough to finger thickness and place on a baking sheet. Bake in a moderate oven (about 350°) for approximately 20 to 25 minutes.

Let cool in refrigerator overnight and the following day glaze with powdered sugar lemon icing. (Recipe below.) Cut in rectangles and store in tightly covered container.

Continued on page 92

POWDERED SUGAR LEMON ICING

Mix powdered sugar with fresh lemon juice into the consistency of mashed potatoes. Heat to 90° on a candy thermometer and then spread over cooled Basler Lekerli.

THORNER LEBKUCHEN

Polish Thorner Lebkuchen are spicy fruit-filled cookie shapes all deliciously decorated to entice your holiday guests. These festive Christmas sweets have a habit of disappearing quickly, so make enough of them to last through all the season's happy get-togethers.

INGREDIENTS:

    2¼ pounds Lebkuchen Ground Dough
        (Recipe below.)
    ½ ounce candied citrus fruit
    ½ ounce candied orange rind
    1 teaspoon allspice
    ½ teaspoon cinnamon
    1⅓ ounces ground white almonds
    ¼ ounce powdered ammonium
        carbonate (may be purchased
        at a drug store)
    a pinch of baking soda
    part of a whole egg

PROCEDURE:

First dilute the ammonium carbonate with part of a whole egg using as little as possible. When the powder is diluted to a smooth, but not runny consistency, add to the Lebkuchen Ground Dough and mix well.

Then put candied citrus and orange rind through a meat grinder and add to the Lebkuchen Ground Dough, along with almonds, spices and baking soda. Blend and roll out into a smooth dough that can be cut into desired shapes—hearts, stars, circles. If you wish, you may roll the dough out into one sheet pan and decorate with whole almonds and candied fruit.

Bake in a moderate oven (about 350°) for approximately 20 to 25 minutes. Let cool in refrigerator overnight and the following day frost or decorate with nuts, chocolate or color sprinkles. Store in a tightly covered container.

LEBKUCHEN GROUND DOUGH

    1 pound flour
    7 ounces honey
    1½ ounces light corn syrup
    2 ounces brown sugar
    5 ounces water

Heat honey, sugar and syrup well, but do not boil. Let cool, then add flour to make dough mixture.

Cover dough with wax paper and let rest in a cool place for at least a full week. Then it's ready to use.

It's a good idea to make up several batches of this dough before the holidays.

COLOR FLOW TIPS

Color Flow is the easy way to "draw" with icing. It's really quite simple once you get the knack of it—basically you just outline, and fill in.

Step one — tape down design and cover with wax paper or clear plastic wrap, making sure to smooth and tape tightly to remove all wrinkles.

Step two—outline design. Mix Color Flow icing according to package directions. Set electric mixer at low speed to avoid whipping in too much air. Add color at this point, dividing batch if necessary. Then keep covered with a damp cloth to prevent crusting. For outlining, use icing straight from the batch and number 1, 2 or 3 tube. Outline design carefully, keeping lines clean and smooth, then set aside to dry for at least an hour (to prevent colors bleeding). Overpipe lines that seem too thin.

Step three—fill in. Place a portion of icing in a small container and add water, a few drops at a time, stirring by hand (never beat!) to soften icing so it flows out of bag slowly. To test flow, spoon out icing and let a "blob" drop back into bowl. When it takes a full count of ten for the "blob" to sink into the mixture and disappear completely, icing is ready to use. Do not use tube for filling in, but instead cut a small opening at tip of bag. (A tube might break the outline.) Then fill bag half full of icing—no more or it might "squish" up and drip on design. Fill in outline, pressing gently and doing areas closest to outline first. If you have more area to fill than can be covered by one half-full decorating bag, have a second filled and ready. Color Flow icing crusts quickly and crust lines will show if icing begins to dry before you finish filling in. If you are using two or more colors, let one dry completely before flowing in another. If tiny bubbles appear, "pop" with pin while icing is still wet.

Step four—let dry 48 hours (or design will crack!) Then and only then, peel off paper and attach design to cake with dots of royal icing. *To make a stand-up design that is visible from both sides, outline and fill with icing on both sides. Allow front to dry at least 48 hours, then peel off paper, turn over, outline and fill in back same way. (Be sure to dry front thoroughly first, otherwise wet icing on back will seep through to soften front.) After doing back of design, allow to dry another 48 hours.*

HOW TO MAKE A CHRISTMAS VILLAGE
Shown on page 81

Do Color Flow Pieces. Use Christmas Village patterns from CELEBRATE! Charter Pattern Book. Outline required number of each pattern piece with tube 2 and fill in outlines with Color Flow. See Color Flow tips above.

Make snowy setting. Cut a piece of styrofoam, 24x24" square. Cut a second piece about 15" long x 9" wide. With a sharp knife, carve smaller piece so front is some-what crescent-shaped, top has natural curves and sides slope slightly. (Leave enough room for buildings and trees.) Tie a string of tiny Italian lights into several clusters (one for each house and largest for church). Punch holes in styrofoam and push lights up through them. Lead cord off back of base and attach smaller piece of styrofoam to one end of larger with lines of royal icing. (Lights for house on bottom of "hill" can be concealed under icing.) Cut 9x6" oval of shiny Mylar aluminum foil, or use a mirror, and attach to lower part of base as shown with icing. Cover entire base with thick coating of white boiled icing, swirling here and there. Build up "snowbanks" around pond and work with spatula for a "shoveled look". Sprinkle all with edible glitter.

Make trees and bush. Use tree-former to make large and small trees and a standard marshmallow cut in half for bush. Pull out tiny leaves with tube #75.

Assemble buildings. Use unsoftened Color Flow icing in colors to match outline of pieces. Pipe tiny line along edges, then put buildings together. Assemble chimneys before attaching to roofs. Dry an hour.

Put scene together. Place buildings over lights and position trees. Pipe a little extra icing around base of houses to secure them and add to "real" look. Top buildings, trees with sifted powdered sugar.

WHAT TO DO WITH EGG YOLKS

Many of our readers have asked us for recipes to use the egg yolks remaining after they have made icing. Here is a marvelous one!

ENGLISH LEMON CURD*
A fine filling for tarts or cakes.

    5 egg yolks
    ½ cup sugar
    2 large lemons (juice and grated rind)
    ¼ cup butter

Grate the lemon peel, then squeeze out the juice and strain. Combine egg yolks and sugar in the top of a double boiler. Add lemon juice and grated peel, then butter little by little. Stir constantly until thick. This will keep in a covered jar in the refrigerator for months.

A wonderful filling for cakes and delicious in tarts with a garnish of whipped cream. The English even spread it on toast!

From the Wilton Book of Classic Desserts.

VOLUME TWO

Celebrate!®

JANUARY / FEBRUARY

Decorating directions for the
Celebrate! Birthday Cake on page 104

Every day brings a birthday for someone, perhaps someone dear to you. Between your family, parents, friends and co-workers, you may find yourself celebrating from 12 to 20 birthdays this year. We think this makes the birthday cake the queen of cakes, around which more happy laughter is heard and more good wishes given than any other. The gay array of birthday ideas on these and the pages that follow is our way to help you to say "Happy Birthday" more beautifully than ever to everyone you know!

Sixteen's a sweetheart of a cake with Color Flow hearts and flowers making a brilliant show and 16 candles blazing brightly all around. Since 16 is the birthday that traditionally turns a young girl into a young woman, it is frequently celebrated with the kind of party that calls for a large and lavish cake. One like the 3 tiered Sweetheart Cake at left that serves 55.

Use Heart and Flower patterns from CELEBRATE! II Pattern Book. Tape small hearts to Cake-Side Formers, outline with tube 2 and fill in with Color Flow. Tape clear plastic wrap over cake-top and corner patterns and again outline with tube 2 and fill in with Color Flow.

Then prepare cake tiers, making one 12″ square and 4″ high, another 10″ round and 3″ high and a third, 6″ round and 3″ high. Ice tiers in colors shown and edge with shell borders, doing base of square cake with tube 32, top of it with tube 21. Use 21 again for top and base of center cake, 19 for base of top cake. Do all stringwork garlands with tube 2, about 2 inches apart on top cake, one inch apart on square cake. (For upside down garlands, draw string along surface.) Attach Color Flow designs with dots of icing, push in "16" pick with candle at top and add 16 candles to square cake in Garden Step candle-holders.

A BIRTHDAY'S NEAR
...LET'S CELEBRATE!

Directions on page 104

A hit at home plate. Serve up a thrill for your lively "Little Leaguer", with a cake that's crowned with baseball caps and circled with icing baseballs! Take party guests to the ball game, home for cake and ice cream after. This cake's so easy to do, you can decorate it while they're doing an "instant replay" of the game.

Here's how: bake, fill and ice a 10″ round, 2-layer cake at least 4″ high. Pipe large balls around base in various colors of icing, using tube 12 (add red "stitching" to white balls with a paintbrush and red paste food color). Frame top of cake with shells, using tube 19. Do lettering with tube 2 and top cake with ring of baseball cap favors. Attach candles to caps with melted wax or royal icing.

MAKE SOMETHING

Tee off for a treat. Your golfer will say it's great! Have a "banquet" in his honor with guests making speeches about his golfing ability and presenting him with a mock "trophy." Have everyone bring golfing equipment gifts and serve our "Duffer's Cake" for a final treat.

To do it, bake, fill and frost a cake 10″ round and 4″ high. Top with green-tinted coconut and border with shells, doing the double row at top with tube 17 and the single row of puff shells at base with tube 32. Trim with real golf tees, attaching all around sides of cake as shown with dots of icing. Use more tees for candle holders, attaching candles with icing, also. Set "Duffer" figurine in center and let the party begin!

Light a super candle for your superman! Set it in the center of a flower-wreathed ring cake made in his favorite flavor. Then prepare the foods he loves best, invite just a few of your closest friends and celebrate. The large candle's a dramatic and different touch—and it won't tip off the number of years he's seen.

Making the cake couldn't be easier. Do it all ahead, so you can concentrate on the meal. Pipe icing nasturtiums, violets and leaves far ahead using flower-making directions from "The Wilton Way of Decorating", Volume I. Just before party day, bake a large ring cake, using the recipe he likes most. Drizzle a white glaze icing on top as shown, set large round candle in center surround with flowers and leaves.

Match the cake to the gift wrap—for a sweet bit of fun! He'll like the bold, masculine colors and think you're clever as well as thoughtful. Give him a gift of many parts (such as a chess or table tennis set) and wrap each separately in the same wrap.

To make the cake, just bake a two-layer cake 10″ round and 4″ high. Fill and frost in light blue buttercream and mark off in tenths at edge. Use a toothpick to outline a smaller circle at top center and pipe "ribbons" outward from it as shown. Do beige center ribbon with tube 48, brown ribbons on either side of it with tube 46. Circle top center of cake with bold white shells, using tube 105 and do borders to match. Push appropriate number of blue candles inside top circle and light up!

FOR THE BOYS!

CLOWNS 'N' ANIMALS FOR CIRCUS FUN!

You just can't miss with a circus party, for every kid loves clowns, elephants, lions and giraffes—as well as all the color and gaiety that goes with a circus. Have peanuts in the shell, popcorn, hot dogs and lots of brightly-colored balloons and streamers. Hire a local high-schooler to dress up as a clown, hand out favors and run the games. And center the table with our stupendous, colossal high-rise circus cake!

Start ahead of time. Do sugar animals, Color Flow letters and candles in icing rosettes several days (or weeks) before the party. Then putting it all together later will be quick and easy. Mold sugar animals using sugar mold animal set and directions that come with it. Trim with icing as shown, using tube 2. Do Color Flow letters, out-

lining, filling in and drying on curve of cake pans. (Use directions that come with mix.) Pipe rosettes on wax paper with tube 21 and push in birthday candles.

Just before party, bake and ice three tiers —one two layers, and 10" square, another one layer and 6½" round, and a third, one layer and 5" round. Assemble as shown with mini-tier separator set at top and clown separator set at center. Attach letters, then circle all tiers with white bulb borders, using tube 9 for square tier, tube 7 for round tiers. Add more bulbs at corners of square tier, also, for "frame" effect. Push a number candle holder (child's age) with candle into cake top. Add candles in rosettes to square tier. Let the guests parade to the party table!

LITTLE CAKES MAKE A BOUQUET OF Wild FLOWERS

The wildest flowers you'll ever see—in colors gay as a midsummer garden! They'll never fool Mother Nature, but are charming fun for a luncheon, shower, garden show or party—a conversation piece your guests will talk about long after the party is over. The "blossoms" are actually little cakes, baked in new individual flower-shaped cupcake pans. Make one blossom for each guest or use the "bouquet" of five flowers for your centerpiece—and make extras for each guest who attends. Pick up the colors in your table decorations and try to match at least one color with fresh flowers, too!

To make them bloom: bake 5 (or more) cakes in Blossom Pans. Place cooled cakes on a rack and pour over softened fondant-type icing. Then decorate as shown.

For yellow and orange curved petal flowers, begin at base of cake and work to top, using tube 103. For aqua and rose pointed-petal flowers, pull out tiny pointed petals around and around with tube 74. For lavender flower, do lots and lots of little "dot" flowers all over (pipe one dot at center, then five dots around it with tube 3). Center all flowers with a large dot of contrast color icing, using tube 5 and add artificial stamens.

To arrange on serving tray, first cover with paper doily, then pipe spray of stems with tube 7. Where stems meet, pipe a rosy bow with tube 104. Position flowers and add leaves with tube 70.

MAKE TIME FOR LOVE

Bake a rose-decked valentine that says "Be Mine" and spark a romantic February 14th celebration!

First bake a 9″ x 3″ heart cake and a 12″ x 3″ square cake. Ice the heart a pale pink, and the square a deep pink. Make the rose and rosebud trims in advance using various shades of pink icing and tubes 101, 103 and 104. Set the flowers aside to dry so they'll be ready to add on the cake.

Next, pipe the cake borders, again using pale pink icing for the heart and deep pink icing for the square. The circular shell bottom borders are made with tubes 19 for the heart and 22 for the square. The ruffled top borders are made with tubes 67 for the heart and 69 for the square.

Before you begin adding your floral blooms, secure the cupid figurine with icing on a small styrofoam circle. Then place the cupid atop the heart and attach various size and color roses and buds with icing till you've formed a cluster of flowers on each cake corner and on the heart top. Decorate the blossoms with bright green leaves using tubes 65 and 69, then add flower stems and write your romantic message with tube 3. Now your cake of pretty valentine pinks is ready to honor cupid's special day! Serve it with scoops of ice cream topped with cherry sauce for a treat that's truly complete!

Spell out your wishes for Valentine's Day, the new year or just any day you'd like to make special with a bright yellow cake of "love" in blooms!

To start, make a variety of icing flowers—so when you're ready to bake your cake, your colorful floral trims will be ready too! Use a number 9 Flower Nail and tubes 102 for petite pink roses and buds, 104 for larger pink roses and white wild roses and 103 for daisies. Attach artificial stamens to wild roses and dot daisy centers with tube 4. To give daisies a pollen effect, dab your finger in yellow-tinted sugar and touch it to the flower centers. Next, make the tangerine-tinted nasturtiums with a 1⅝ Lily Nail and tube 103. Add tube 6 centers and attach artificial stamens. To complete your garden, make several drop flowers with tube 199. Set all flowers aside to dry and place daisies on a curved Flower Former.

Now for the cake! Bake a 9″ x 13″ x 2″ rectangle and carve out your "love" letters using pattern from CELEBRATE! II Pattern Book. Ice the cake a sunny yellow and outline the letters using tubes 20 for bottom shell border and 18 for top shell border. Then with icing, attach your "ready-made" flowers to the letters "l" and "v" and set out for all to admire!

This is one cake you'll want to make again and again for so many occasions. Perfect for a bridal shower or an anniversary, you can vary the cake-flowers to match the bridal bouquet or the anniversary corsage! Or just trim the cake with any floral assortment you like!

BAKE A VALENTINE!

DESSERTS* FROM THE DAYS OF AMERICA'S YOUTH

Washington and Abe Lincoln too, may well have enjoyed these two well-loved American desserts. They are simple, satisfying and unadorned, and come from a time when most of what graced the table was the product of the diner's own labor and skill. Serve them to your family on a blustery February evening—see smiles come to their faces.

INDIAN PUDDING
(Hasty Pudding)

Maize, or corn meal, the gift of the American Indians to the Pilgrims, is the important ingredient of this delicious pudding. A hearty dessert for a winter evening.

- ⅓ cup yellow corn meal
- ⅓ cup cold water
- 1 quart milk
- ½ teaspoon salt
- ½ teaspoon cinnamon
- 1 teaspoon ginger
- ¾ cup dark molasses
- ¼ cup butter

Stir corn meal and water together. Scald the milk and stir in the corn meal mixture. Cook over very low heat, stirring constantly, for about 20 minutes or until thick. Add the rest of the ingredients and mix well. Pour into a buttered 1½ quart casserole and bake in a 325° oven about 1½ to 2 hours.

New Englanders serve this pudding with ice cream. It is also good with cream.

PERFECT RICE PUDDING

The very best rice pudding, with a rich, caramel-like flavor. If you remember it from childhood, you will be anxious to make it yourself. If you have never tasted it, prepare for a treat! The proportions may seem unusual, and the baking time amazingly long, but there is no more worthwhile occupation for a winter's day than the preparation of this delicious dessert.

- 8 cups milk
- 4 tablespoons rice (not the quick-cooking variety)
- ⅔ cup sugar
- 1 teaspoon salt

Combine all the ingredients and pour into a large oblong baking dish. Bake in a very slow oven, 225°, for about six hours. Stir the mixture every half hour or so until the rice is completely dissolved and the pudding thickened. Toward the end of the baking, you may add ½ cup of currants or raisins, but the flavor is just as fine without them. Serve warm with cream.

From The Wilton Book of Classic Desserts

SALUTE GEORGE WASHINGTON

Washington, who led the revolutionary army as its general, and the nation as its first president, was known for his great courage and integrity. This probably

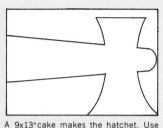

A 9x13" cake makes the hatchet. Use left-over pieces for an after school treat.

inspired the familiar legend of the young George's brave confession to his father that it was he who cut down the family cherry tree. To make a cake that looks like the hatchet he did it with, is very simple. First, model "cherries" of marzipan and roll out and cut marzipan leaves to go with them, using leaf-shaped cookie cutter (mark veins with toothpick and dry on Flower Former to curve). Bake 9x13" sheet cake, chill and cut into hatchet shape using pattern from CELEBRATE! II Pattern Book. Cover handle with wax paper while you ice blade blue, cover blade while you ice handle brown. Attach cherries and leaves as shown. (Note: if you're pressed for time, you can probably find marzipan cherries ready-made in any food specialty shop. To make your own, see page 74.)

CELEBRATE
FEBRUARY'S
HEROES

In a single month, come the birthdays of two of the most honored men in American history! Plan a special dinner or party around each, with early American dishes and a patriotic cake. Play charades inspired by 1776 or the Civil War. The kids will learn a little history . . . and love it!

REMEMBER LINCOLN

While Washington is remembered for what he did, Lincoln is remembered chiefly for what he said. With a few clear, simple words, he brought light and truth to a confused, war-torn nation. Honor his words then with this special book cake. **To make it:** first mold stars of blue-tinted sugar using star shape from Candy Mold Set. For letters, use Color Flow icing, technique and pattern from CELEBRATE! II Pattern Book. Outline, fill in and dry letters on book cake pans in exact position they will have on cake itself, so they will fit curve of "pages." Bake and ice a 9″ x 13″ x 4″ cake. Also bake a cake in Book of Beauty pans and ice top cream, sides gold. Use fork to define "pages." Assemble cakes on foil-wrapped board and pipe blue cord of icing around bottom of book cake with tube 9 to simulate hard cover. Then pipe overlapping book-mark ribbons with tube 45 and attach letters. Drape red, then white icing ribbon garlands at top edge of sheet cake with tube 104, attach sugar stars between. Edge cake base with tube 21 shells for a handsome finishing touch.

HOW TO DECORATE THE CELEBRATE! FIRST BIRTHDAY CAKE
Shown on page 93

It's the one we designed especially for our readers on the occasion of this magazine's first birthday! A pink and petal shaped confection, it's draped with flowers and dainty lace—a most feminine tribute to a young lady on her birthday or, with candles exchanged for an ornament, a most romantic cake for her spring wedding!

It will also make a breathtaking centerpiece for a gala reception. The design, though simple, takes time and care, but we think it well worth the effort.

First, do flowers, lace. Pipe many drop flowers of royal icing in pale and slightly deeper pink, using tubes 193 and 224. Add same-color centers with tube 3 and pipe small pink leaves with tube 65. Then trace lace hearts in three sizes, large, medium and small, using Lacy Hearts pattern from CELEBRATE! II Pattern Book. Use tube 2 for large and medium hearts, tube 1 for small heart and tiny scroll. Do lace pieces in royal icing also for extra strength and make more than you need as they're very fragile at best. Push the appropriate number of birthday candles into some of the larger drop flowers while icing is still wet and reserve for cake top.

Prepare cake tiers, using petal-shaped wedding pans, in sizes 6", 9", 12" and 15", all in two layers for a total height of 4 inches each. Ice tiers pale pink and assemble with 5" tall Iridescent Pillars, using 7" round cardboard circle cut in petal shape (to match cake pan) and covered with pink foil, for top separator plate, and 18" circle of cardboard cut into petal shape and covered with foil for base plate.

Then decorate. Pipe neat shell borders on all tiers, using tube 21 for bottom of 15", 12" and 9" tiers, 16 for both bottom and top of 6" tier. Use tube 19 for top of 15" tier, tube 17 for top of 12" and 9" tier. Attach lace pieces and flowers in garland fashion, curving round each petal of cake. (Draw guideline with toothpick first, if desired.) Use three large flowers at center of garlands, two small ones at ends and finish with tiny leaves using tube 65 at points. Do lace garlands same way, but finish with tiny scrolls and join together with a single drop flower. Do more flower garlands on cake board, finishing these with scrolls as shown.

For center ornament. Attach some of reserved drop flowers with dots of icing to florist's wire that has been tinted pink. When dry, push into a small circle of styrofoam, also iced pink and secure between pillars with more icing.

HOW TO DECORATE BIRTHDAY CAKES
Shown on page 95

Dotted swiss cake—most feminine centerpiece ever fashioned for a little girl's birthday! Dress her to match, and have a dotted swiss tablecloth, ruffly nut cups and napkins. And—for a nice extra touch—put pink and white fresh flowers on the table, too!

So simple to do! Just bake a mini-tier cake, ice it pink and pipe white dots in random fashion on sides with tube 2. Frill tiers with white ruffles, using tube 104, then top ruffles with shell-motion and tube 7. Push birthday candles into icing rosettes made ahead with tube 21 and add to cake top.

Make a cake that's "everything nice" —just like her!

Birthday Clown cake. Absolutely certain to thrill any child, from first to tenth birthday! Sets the scene for a happy circus party—with animal favors and circus games. Large enough to treat grandparents, aunts, uncles and family friends after!

Prepare two tiers, one 10" round and 4" high, the other 6" round and 3" high. Ice and assemble as shown. Pipe "spokes" all around top of base cake with tube 47 and edge with string using tube 4. Circle both tiers with bright bulb borders, using tube 7. Attach "Happy Birthday" letters, done with Color Flow technique and dried on curve of cake pan. Add candles in Push-In Candle Holders, let Jolly Clown tip his hat to the birthday girl!

Dancing Child Cake. Merry little girl whirls in a garden setting—atop a garland-draped party cake. Sure to charm child and grown-up alike! Make many pink drop flowers ahead with tube 225. Make tube 21 rosettes, push in candles, dry. Then ice a two-layer cake, 8" square, 4" high, pale yellow. Frame base with border of puffy shells, using tube 21. Drop stringwork guideline all around top edge, then attach drop flower garlands with dabs of icing. Add tiny green leaves with tube 65. Follow garlands all around with widespaced dots, using tube 2. Place Dancing Child figure on cake top, add flowers at her feet. Add fence and candles.

HOW TO MOLD A SHOW-STOPPING CANDY ELEPHANT
Shown on page 140

Here's how to mold that magnificent elephant parade! Drop coupler into large 18" plastic decorating bag (just coupler base, not ring) and fill with 3 pounds of tempered chocolate or summer coating. Make sure elephant mold is absolutely clean and dry without a trace of grease inside, then clamp together. Prop upside-down in large saucepan with elephant's legs up, trunk tipped down. Insert decorating bag into second leg and press. Watch through first leg until trunk is filled, then tap it against table to clear air bubbles. Now prop elephant so legs are level and fill even with bottom of "feet". Tap whole mold against table several times to clear any air bubbles that might be left. Place in refrigerator, putting upside-down onto rack and propping sides with crumpled aluminum foil. Let chill several hours or until firm. As it sets, chocolate shrinks away from sides of mold, and unmolds easily. After unmolding, remove any excess chocolate or coating with a knife.

TEMPERING CHOCOLATE

To make an elephant of light or dark chocolate, the chocolate must first be tempered. To do this, heat water in bottom of a 1½ quart double boiler to about 175 degrees F. Remove from heat and place cut up chocolate (one cup at a time) in top half of double boiler to melt. Stir every 10 minutes until melted chocolate reaches 110 degrees F. Remove from heated water and cool until almost a stiff state.

For light chocolate, reheat tempered chocolate to between 85 and 88 degrees, fill decorating bag and mold.

For dark chocolate, reheat tempered chocolate between 90 and 92 degrees, fill decorating bag and mold.

SUMMER PASTEL COATING

Since this is a chocolate substitute it need not be tempered. Pastel colored chocolate coatings may be purchased from most commercial candy stores. Break up 3 pounds of coating and place in top of double boiler. Bring water to a rolling boil, turn heat off and let stand 30 minutes. Stir to blend. When it has a liquid look, it is ready to fill the elephant mold.

HOW TO DRESS UP THE ELEPHANTS

Dust rolling pin and board with powdered sugar. Roll out marzipan (use your favorite recipe) to about ⅛" thickness. Cut out shapes for saddle blankets, headpieces and "boots". Put on elephants and trim with royal icing.

VOLUME TWO

Celebrate!

MARCH / APRIL

Decorating directions for
Garden Wedding Cake on page 122

lily of the valley

A garden gazebo houses a kissing couple atop triple tiers of floral scrolled cake! Serves 290.

Decorating directions, page 113.

rambling rose

Petalled roses of velvety icing   cling to a cake

as green as a spring garden!

Serves 142. Decorating directions on page 113.

petunias

spark a spring shower

A perfect match . . . the cake, ice cream and sandwich loaf you serve at the bridal shower or announcement party! Garlands of pink petunias bring them together, for the prettiest display in many a day.

The sandwich party loaf is filled with three different and delicious fillings, so all you need to add are crispy shoestring potatoes, a fresh green salad and a sparkly punch! And, if you make the petunias well ahead and the party loaf, cake and ice cream mold the day before, you can do all the decorating shortly before the party begins.

First, make the petunias. Use a two-piece lily nail in the 1⅝" size and line bottom half with foil. Then, with deep pink royal icing and tube 102, held so wide end is down, narrow end up, begin to press out petals. Start them down inside nail, moving up to outer edge. Keep pressure steady and turn nail, jiggling hand slightly as you go, to form ruffled petal edge. Then move down inside nail again to complete petal. Repeat for a total of five petals all around. Let dry in foil cup, then mix powdered sugar and a few drops of water into a thin paste, or use thinned royal icing and brush it lightly into center and about ⅔ of way up toward petal edge for a feathery effect. In center of each flower, brush some yellow icing, then in very center pipe a single yellow dot for stamen with tube 2.

Then do bell cake. Bake a cake in a two-piece Gourmet Bell Mold, using a single cake mix. Cool and pour on pale pink fondant to ice. Use tube 2-D, stabilized white whipped cream and a shell motion to pipe the rich, ruffled border around bottom. Use tube 104 for white bow at top. Pipe a bulb of green icing for each flower and place in garland circling bell as shown. Add green leaves with tube 67.

Do ice cream bell, essentially the same as cake, except pack chilled halves of mold with softened vanilla ice cream, clamp mold together and freeze. Decorate with border and bow just as bell cake, changing bow from white to pink. Return to freezer until serving time. It's best to add petunias just before serving, propping with toothpicks as needed. Then quickly pipe green leaves. A petunia can be removed to garnish each serving.

Directions for sandwich loaf on page 122.

morning glory

For the most glorious morning of their lives!
For how to do the cake and the morning glory
flowers, turn to page 113. Serves 155 guests.

blue
bell

Fresh as springtime . . . heaped
with heavenly bell-shaped blooms!
Decorating directions, page 114
Serves 72.

May basket...

filled with good wishes to shower on the bride and groom
Read how to decorate on page 114. Serves 98.

HOW TO DECORATE LILY OF THE VALLEY

Shown on page 106

A couple of wedding charmers steal a kiss on a tower of cake tiers decorated as freshly as the flower garden surrounding them. The cake, covered with its own bell-shaped lilies of the valley, eagerly awaits to ring out the happy news that a gala spring wedding is about to unfold!

To make: First bake three cake tiers, a hexagon shape, a 14″ round and an 18″ round. Be sure to cut wooden separator plates in advance to hold six 5-inch pillars. (Plastic separator plates hold four pillars only.)

To decorate: Edge base of 18″ tier with tube 4B shells and pipe tube 22 shells around the tier's top. For the 14″ middle tier, pipe a row of upright tube 22 shells at base and drop a double row of tube 3 stringwork directly over them. Edge the middle tier's top with a tube 19 shell border.

To add the scrolled floral side trims, first pipe a curved vine of icing around both round tiers with tube 4. Then pipe the bell-blossomed lilies of the valley with tube 79 and the long, slender leaves with tube 67.

To decorate the hexagon-shaped top tier, pipe tube 17 rippled borders around the top and base. Then with icing, position a white Angelino trim on each of the cake's six sides and frame with scrolls of icing using tube 15. Crown the center tier with a Twin Cherub ornament and the topmost tier with "A Kiss in the Garden" gazebo.

HOW TO DECORATE RAMBLING ROSE

Shown on page 107

As its name suggests, this most delicately shaped flower is the acrobatic artist of the rose family. Clinging and climbing to show off its beautifully colored petals and bring a freshness to anything it touches, it's a perfect choice for trimming a garden-green cake for a spring bridal shower!

First bake a two-layer 14″ round cake and a

hexagon cake. Ice and assemble, placing the round cake on a foil-covered cardboard cake circle. Make up tube 102 and 103 roses, and tube 103 rosebuds and set aside to dry. Then decorate the round cake tier by first piping tube 19 zigzag garlands around the cake base, and then adding a tube 14 rippled trim around each garland. Next edge the top border with tube 32 shells; then pipe a tube 3 curved vine around the cake attaching rosebuds with icing and trimming with tube 67 leaves.

To decorate the hexagon-shaped cake, edge all borders, (top, sides and bottom) with tube 18 shells. Then arrange a cluster of roses to each of the six cake sides by attaching the flowers with icing. Place a larger tube 103 rose in the center of each floral cluster, then top with a trio of tube 102 roses. Trim all the floral arrangements with tube 67 leaves. Top the cake with a fresh-as-springtime ornament, "Petite Double Ring Fantasy," and your shower showpiece is ready to glorify any gaily decorated table setting—whether indoors or out on a garden patio surrounded by fresh roses!

HOW TO DECORATE MORNING GLORY WEDDING CAKE

Shown on page 110

Garlands of morning glories for the most unusual wedding cake of the season! Prettiest part of it—the three-dimensional effect of the beautiful icing blossoms!

First do morning glories. Do most in medium size, using a 1⅝″ two-piece lily nail and tube 103 for outer edge. Do a few for center of separator in larger size, using a 2¼″ nail and tube 104. Line nails with foil cups, then fill two decorating bags with white icing, putting a long stripe of pale blue icing in one cone first, from tip to top, in line with the narrow edge of the tube. In all white cone, use tube 127, placing wide end down into cup of one of the lily nails. Press out icing as you turn nail until a hollow cup of icing is formed, then ream out excess icing carefully with a toothpick. Use blue-striped

cone fitted with tube 103 or 104 to pipe a ruffle all around the edge. Smooth inside with a damp artist's brush. Add dot of yellow icing with tube 2 for stamen. Remove foil cup with flower, dry thoroughly. For the morning glories that will attach to vine on center and top tiers, add calyx and florist wire "stem." Add calyx only to others. To add calyx, pipe a bulb of green icing with tube 7 to back of dried flower, brush into cone shape. To add stem, push green florist's wire into bulb before it dries, brush up onto wire to secure. Turn flower upside down to dry. Reserve.

Then prepare cake. Bake, fill and ice 3 tiers white—one 6″ round, 3″ high, a second 10″ round, 4″ high and a third, 14″ round, 4″ high. Assemble with 5″ square Lacy-Look Columns and 12″ separator plates. Ring base cake with pale blue Tuk-n-Ruffle.

And decorate! Do garden fence border at bottom of 14″ tier, using tube 32 for regular and upright shells, tube 3 for stringwork between them and tube 16 for rosettes at top of each. Do shells for all other borders, using tube 21 for bottoms of center and top tiers, 19 for tops of bottom and center tiers and 16 at top of top tier. Pipe vines across front of top tier, all around center tier and across top of bottom tier, all with tube 3. Push morning glories on stems into sides of tiers as shown, and pipe a "branch" from vine to calyx of each flower to make joining look natural. Add other morning glories with icing, and pipe leaves with tube 70. Finish with Vanity Fair ornament, adding a few morning glories to it, too.

113

HOW TO DECORATE
BLUEBELL WEDDING CAKE

Shown on page 111

A tower of flower cakes decked with Bluebells to complement the chimes of a blissful wedding day! A beauty in blue that's easy to decorate because you can make your flowers weeks in advance. The rest—all simple one-step borders.

For the flowers: Place a square of aluminum foil in the bottom half of a 1½" lily nail, then press in the top half to form a foil cup to pipe a flower in. Next with tube 66 and bright blue icing, press out three ¾-inch petals. Start from down in the center of the nail, and as you squeeze out a petal move up and out towards the nail's edge. To finish, pipe three more petals between the spaces of the first three. Dot the center with icing, attach artificial stamen and remove foil and flower to dry. Follow the same procedure to make lots of Bluebells.

For the cake: Bake three cake tiers in the 6", 9" and 12" Wilton Petal Pans; then ice all a snow white. Assemble the tiers using a blue foil covered board as a base, and 10" and 8" separator plates with clear plastic twist legs. Pipe shell base borders around all three tiers using tube 17 for the 12" tier, and tube 16 for the 9" and 6" tiers. Edge the tops of all tiers with tube 87 zigzag borders. Then by placing a mound of icing on top of each curved petal of the two lower tiers, attach clusters of Bluebells, draping some down over the sides. Next, top the 6" tier with a new Circles in Lace ornament, and with

dabs of icing position flowers all around the ornament and cake tier's base. Trim all flowers with tube 67 leaves and the cake's ready for the celebration!

HOW TO DECORATE
MAY BASKET CAKE
Shown on page 112

Under a floral umbrella, a proud bride and groom stand encircled by cake the color of a fresh spring garden. Lacy baskets filled with blossoms add to the lush springtime setting and express the hopes for love and happiness to bloom in abundance!

To make this eye-catching cake covered with congratulatory wishes for a spring shower, bake two round cake tiers, one 8" x 3" and the other 12" x 4". Ice both tiers a light green and position on a foil covered board or cake tray.

Next, make lots of tube 224 drop flowers with tube 2 centers in a variety of bright spring shades and set aside to dry. Then decorate the bottom tier with puffy zigzag garland borders, using tube 18 for the base and tube 17 for the top. For the top tier, edge the base with a tube 15 rippled border and trim the tier's top with a tube 16 zigzag garland border.

Now with dabs of icing, attach tiny clusters of pretty petalled flowers in between the puffed garland borders, and also to the cake ornament's umbrella and base. Then trim the flowers with tube 65 leaves and pipe your good luck wishes to the couple on the cake side with tube 4.

To decorate the daintily laced plastic baskets, first pipe a good-sized mound of icing in each one. Then position lots of multi-colored drop flowers, overlapping blossoms so every basket is filled to the brim with petals. Then decorate the floral arrangements with tube 65 leaves, tie up the baskets with tiny ribbons and place them round the cake for a finishing touch as fresh as a field of flowers!

HOW TO DECORATE
MOTHER'S DAY CAKES
Shown on opposite page

Make this Mother's Day an extra special one for your mom by preparing a meal that includes her favorite dishes along with a dreamy dessert surprise—a rose trimmed cake that you've made and decorated yourself! Both of these cake beauties are as fun to decorate as they are to present to mom!

Dance of Spring: Three merry children dance on Mother's rosy cake! Bake a two-layer, 12" round cake and ice a pale gold. Make two-toned pink and gold petalled Tiffany Roses with tube 104 and set aside to dry. Next, edge the cake top with a flat band of curved icing ribbon using tube 103 and trim each curve's peak with a dot of tube 5 beading. Then pipe zigzag curves of icing using tube 16 under the ribboned border, and frame with tube 2 beading.

For the cake's decorative bottom edge, pipe a tube 16 zigzag border around the base and drape curves of tube 103 icing ribbon above it; again adding a tube 5 bead to each curve's peak. Now, with dabs of icing, position roses around the cake's top and base, trimming each with tube 67 leaves. Crown the cake with a circle of Dancing Child figurines, place icing roses at their feet and ring with tube 15 border. Completed, you not only have a cake for mom to enjoy on her special day, but a trio of figurines for her to remember and treasure all year long!

Basket of Roses: Ice a two-layer 9" round cake and trim cardboard cake base with Tuk-n-Ruffle. Then make about a dozen large icing roses with tube 127 and set aside to dry. To achieve the basket weaving effect around the cake, first fit two decorator bags, (one with white icing, one with yellow) with tube 48. Then with the white icing, pipe a vertical line from cake top to bottom. Next, beginning at the top of the white vertical line, pipe a ½" long horizontal band of yellow icing. Pipe another one about ⅜ of an inch under the first and so on all the way down to the cake's base. When you've completed this first row, pipe a second vertical line of icing where the bands end and repeat the band piping procedure, working between the spaces in the first row. Continue basket weaving around the entire cake, then edge the top with star puffs and the base with a rope border, both piped with tube 4B. To finish, pipe icing on cake top, attach roses and trim the flowers with large green cloth decorator leaves.

Decorator Tip

A neat easy way to tint coconut. Place the coconut in a plastic bag and add a few drops of food coloring. Twist bag closed and knead for a few minutes until coconut is evenly tinted.

make
every
thing
rosy

FOR MOTHER ON HER DAY

Directions on opposite page.

115

Too pretty not to keep as elegant Easter mementos, these exquisite eggs of sugar and filigree make decorative table accents that can be displayed long after Eastertime. Arrange them on a shelf or special showplace, or gather several in a bow-tied wicker basket to present as a thoughtful spring gift!

FLOWER EGGS

A bouquet of pastel sugar shapes, each crowned with spring flowers . . . daisies, poppies, bluebells, sweet peas and more . . . make a lovely centerpiece that lasts long after Easter!

Mold sugar eggs using 2 cups granulated sugar and 4 teaspoons water. Blend ingredients by hand, divide in batches to tint with food color and pack mixture into Egg-Shaped Cupcake pan. Scrape off excess sugar, unmold immediately and set aside to dry for use later.

Next, tape flower patterns from CELE-BRATE! II Pattern Book over the center curved backs of the egg-shaped pan. (Be sure to cut several slits around the edges of each pattern so it can be taped over curves as flatly as possible.) Brush over taped patterns with a coating of shortening, then outline patterns with tube 2 and fill in with assorted Color Flow icings. When dry, remove color flow flower designs one at a time by heating the underside of each cupped egg with a candle. Hold the candle under each design just long enough to loosen it from the pan, then very carefully slide it off from the bottom up with your thumb.

After you've removed all the color flow trims, scoop out a little sugar from the hardened egg mold halves and assemble with icing. Then position a floral color flow design on top of each egg with icing and pipe a tube 13 rippled border where egg-halves meet.

PLACE CARD EGGS

Use sugar mixture recipe given for Flower Eggs; and again tint and pack Egg-Shaped Cupcake pan to mold. Unmold, dry and assemble egg halves with icing, then prop in small paper cups to decorate. Pipe on eyes with tube 7, cheeks with tube 11, hair with tubes 2 and 13, and mouths, noses and glasses with tube 2.

For place-card egg holders, use plastic egg cups or construct your own cardboard holders. Pipe outlines for collars and ties with tube 2, then fill in with Color Flow. Pipe beaded necklace with tube 2, flowers with tube 103 and spell out name places with tube 3. Now place your egg faces in the decorated cups and you're ready to seat some happy guests with a take-home holiday favor!

FILIGREE EASTER EGGS

A new look in Easter eggs! They're lacy see-through filigree, piped in pretty pastel icing to set off the brightly-colored jelly beans inside. So delicate, so different—yet they're not really that difficult to do. Here's how:

Mix up a batch of egg white icing, using 6 egg whites and 2 lbs. of confectioners sugar. Blend at low speed for 5 minutes, then divide batch and tint various pastels. Keep covered with a damp cloth while you work to prevent drying. If icing seems too thin, blend in a bit more sugar.

Pipe designs on plastic egg-shaped sugar molds. Coat top half of mold with shortening first, then put fingers inside mold to prop while you pipe a string of icing with tube 2 all around outside of it, following the inset edge (the line about ⅜" above the actual edge). Then place mold on flat surface at eye level and pipe filigree design all over top. Make up designs as you go along, using dots, "I's", cornelli lace, circles or lines. Just be sure everything is joined, so completed design is all in one piece. Set aside to dry at least 4 hours and do bottom half of mold. Do exactly the same as top, except before doing filigree design, lay a spiral string of icing on flat oval at top of mold's curve. This will provide the "base" for your egg.

To remove filigree designs from molds, place in pre-heated oven (250°) for 30 seconds. (This will melt shortening, loosening designs.) Carefully turn molds over, so design rests in palm of your hand and gently push outward with thumb. Design will release from mold. Let dry a bit longer to harden a little more.

To join halves, pipe a couple of lines of icing (one atop the other) on back part of bottom half, then press back of top gently into it, prop with 2 cotton balls to dry in open position. Let dry for at least 4 more hours, then **very gently** fill completed filigree egg with multi-color jelly bean eggs. Bring everyone in to admire your handiwork!

keep
sake
eggs
for
Easter

EARLY GOTHIC CHURCH
Dresden, Germany
Designed in 1864
MADE FROM CUBE SUGAR & ROYAL ICING
by
LUTZ OLKIEWICZ
PASTRY CHEF DRAKE HOTEL

Easter whimsey for decorators

For Chicagoans, and those visiting the city, Easter brings a very special treat. A visit to The Drake Hotel near the lake front gives an opportunity to view several enchanting bits of Easter whimsey all decorated by Lutz Olkiewicz. Each year the artistry varies.

As you step into the Raleigh Room you are greeted by a giant Easter egg. Five and a half feet tall, and more than a yard in diameter, Chef Olkiewicz constructed the egg on a wood base, entirely covered with yellow marzipan. Shining flowers, and rosettes of ribbon are made of pulled sugar. The graceful sprays of pussy willows and forsythia are royal icing.

As you step down to the lower lobby you'll get your first glimpse of a marvelous sugar cathedral. This is a scale replica of the Dresden Cathedral destroyed in 1945. Though constructed on a wood frame, the exterior is constructed of entirely edible materials—thousands of meticulously stacked sugar cubes form its walls, the gothic "carving" and roof slates are made of royal icing, and the shining crosses are gilded pastillage. The glowing "stained glass" windows are parchment paper, brightly painted with food colors. Walk slowly around the cathedral to see the perfect architectural detail of the back (near left). The cathedral is 54 inches high, 55 inches long and 40 inches wide.

In the International Club is another of Chef Olkiewicz's fanciful creations—a marzipan coach drawn by six bunnies with a bunny coachman and three bright-eyed ducklings riding on top. The "roadway" is strewn with icing flowers and all the trim is royal icing.

The coach is 54 inches long, 32 inches wide and 35 inches tall.

HOW TO MAKE
CAKES PRETTIER

The easiest, no-time-involved way to make a cake pretty and appealing is to give it the charm of COLOR.

The beauty of a garden, the appeal of a painting, the attractiveness of a costume is based to a great degree on its color.

Decorated cakes, too, depend on color to be beautiful. Of course, all decorating should be as neatly executed as possible. And any serious decorator willing to practice can attain near-perfection.

But the use of color is a more joyful, more personal, more challenging art, yet one that is given scant attention in most books on decorating. Here are 3 easy, effective ways to use color, based on experience in the CELEBRATE! Decorating Room.

Use the simplest color scheme when pressed for time to experiment, or in doubt as to choice of colors for cakes. Of course the very simplest is a cake in all white, or just one pale color. For such a true monochromatic effect, keep borders and trim quite heavy and sculptural so that the play of light and shade will give drama and interest. Many of the most beautiful cakes are decorated in just one color.

Varied intensities of one color can give a lovely effect. A pale pink wedding cake decked with deeper pink roses and deep pink rosebuds. A creamy shower cake heaped with yellow and gold daisies, with a base border in the deepest gold. A pastel green cake trimmed with borders and stringwork in deeper shades of green. The possibilities are great, the effects always pleasing and artistic.

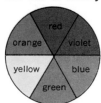

The use of closely related colors is fun and effective. To plan such a scheme, a simple color wheel is helpful. Using related colors is more challenging, yet more exciting than the first two color plans. Choose two colors next to each other on the color wheel, perhaps red and orange. Mix two bowls of icing in these hues. Now make a number of drop flowers in orange, and some in red.

Add a little red icing to a larger amount of orange and produce red-orange flowers. Do the same in reverse proportions and make flowers in a new soft-red hue.

Then add a little white icing to both red and orange icings and make flowers in deep pink and apricot. A larger addition of white will make new pastels.

When all the flowers are dry, ice a cake in pale apricot or pink. These pale colors will serve as a background for the bright colored flowers.

Then trim the cake with the flowers, arranging them in garlands, clusters, bouquets and borders according to your taste.

You'll feel a true sense of pleasure when you view your creation, and so will everyone else.

Of course, this method works just as well for other related colors. Choose orange-yellow, yellow-green—the results will be equally pretty, but very different.

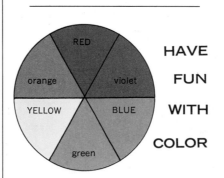

HAVE FUN WITH COLOR

One-color effects and schemes using two related colors make beautiful cakes. Now let's try more daring color plans using opposite or complementary hues.

The three basic or **primary** colors are **red, yellow** and **blue.** From these three colors all others can be made and by mixing the two primary colors closest to each other on the color wheel, we achieve the secondary hues of green, violet and orange.

Red and yellow mixed in equal proportions will make orange; yellow and blue, green; blue and red, violet. The color directly opposite a primary color on the color wheel is its complement.

Here is an interesting color phenomenon. Stare fixedly at an area of red for several moments. Now quickly shift your eyes to a white surface. You will see green—the complement of red.

An easy way to experiment with color
Get out several white cake circles or pieces of white cardboard. Make a small batch of boiled icing and have at hand jars of paste colors in the three primary hues, red, lemon yellow and sky blue.

Now mix yellow and blue together to make green, using as much color as possible so that the green is at its fullest intensity. Color a little of the icing red, again making the red as intense, or bright, as possible.

With a spatula, put a little of the red icing on a cake circle, and next to it, some of the green. All kinds of exciting cakes come to mind. Red roses with green leaves. Poinsettias and their foliage. Christmas cakes with red lettering and green holly.

Now mix a little more white icing into your red and green, so that you have bright pink and medium green. Put these two colors next to each other on the white surface. The effect will be very pretty, and not quite so exciting as the bright red and green combination.

Finally, mix more white into the pink and green icings, so that the pink is pale, and the green pastel. Put these two colors next to each other on the cake circle. There is a whole new feeling to this color scheme. It is dainty, charming and pastel and makes one think of cakes for bridal or baby showers, or very feminine cakes.

Notice too that the white background sets off the two brighter color schemes and makes the colors appear even more vivid. Bright colors appear brightest against white.

The pastel pink and green look well against white too, but do not really need this neutral background. A pale green cake decked with pastel pink flowers would be very pretty, or a pink cake with green borders.

From this little experiment we see too, that complementary colors should be used together at equal or near-equal intensity or brightness.

We can repeat this experiment with a violet and yellow combination, and with blue and orange. Somehow, at their full or brightest intensity, these combinations do not call to mind pretty cakes. Pale violet and light yellow is a very attractive cake combination, but purple and bright yellow is not. Pastel apricot and pale blue would make a pretty cake, but bright orange and blue would look un-appetizing.

Some colors not appropriate
Rules are made to be broken, especially in the use of color, but one rule that should always be observed is to make the cake look as delicious as it is pretty. Purple and bright blue are not very appetizing colors, so we use them with great care on our cakes. Lavendar and pale blue, on the other hand, can be quite attractive when used with discretion. A pale yellow cake heaped with pastel violets, or a light apricot cake with light blue flowers would be pleasing to both the eye and the appetite.

One color that we do not use in the CELEBRATE! decorating room is black. Black is just not an appetizing color for food. Nor is any shade of gray. Even for Color Flow outlines, we find we can achieve a cleaner, prettier effect by using a deep tint of one or more of the colors used in the design. If we want a deep color for a special effect, we simply tint the icing as deeply as possible, but never add black. This keeps the colors clean and fresh-looking.

Once you've experimented with mixing and coordinating primary colors, it's time to move on to multiple color combinations for cakes that are truly eye appealing.

The challenge of decorating with multiple colors

Decorating a cake with three or more colors is a joyful challenge to the artistic cake decorator, and when your efforts are successful, the results are stunning. After all, our homes, clothing and automobiles all sing with color, so decorated cakes can be just as bright and colorful.

Perhaps it's a little more difficult to combine several colors on a cake than it is to use them in your wardrobe, because a cake must first of all appeal to the appetite. Here are some ways to make your cakes look tempting as well as beautiful.

It's a good idea to experiment before icing an important cake. Get out some white cardboard or cake circles, mix some white icing and tint small amounts in the colors you plan to use. Place them next to each other with a spatula on the white cardboard. Then judge if the effect is pleasing, and correct your colors to improve the scheme.

Nature is a perfect guide

Most decorators first turn to nature's own schemes for inspiration. Here are some examples of beautiful color combinations.

The dainty, realistic tints in this tray of flower cupcakes are copied from nature as closely as possible. All the colors are pastel, none overwhelms the others.

The brilliant violet, yellow, orange and pink of tulips copy the real flowers' colors. Each hue is at its fullest intensity.

Here subtle, rich tones of gold, russet red and warm violet are set off against pale gold.

In all three cakes, the colors are varied, but all are at equal or near-equal intensity. Use pastels with pastels, brights with brights, rich colors with others just as rich.

A white or neutral background will display bright or deep colors at their best, as we see in the tulip and mum cakes.

HAVE FUN WITH Color

Dare to use vivid hues

The marigold cake uses a complementary color scheme. Bright blue bachelor buttons make yellow-orange and red-orange marigolds even more vivid.

The gay red and blue borders on the drum cake are posed on a yellow background for this happy, primary color scheme.

Bright little gingerbread people in vivid pastels dance around a pale green cake.

The same rules of keeping colors at equal intensity and backgrounds quite neutral were used in decorating these three cakes.

Don't be afraid to be original

It's not necessary to use the hues that nature planned for all your cakes. Picture a white cake heaped with bright blue petunias and trimmed with apple-green lattice. Try pale green roses tied with violet ribbons on a pastel yellow tier cake. And whoever saw turquoise and yellow elephants, or chicks in rose and orange? Yet they sail together quite happily on this bright pink Noah's Ark. Just follow the rule of keeping colors at equal intensity, and experiment before you start decorating the cake.

"Stage" your beautiful cakes

Your decorated cakes are works of art, and deserve a harmonizing background to show them at their best. Silver and crystal add sparkle to cakes for formal occasions. Brass and copper give glow to cakes using a warm color scheme. Bright china and plastic trays are good choices for gay-colored cakes.

Tablecloths, too, should flatter your centerpiece cakes. Usually a cloth that repeats the color of the basic icing is best, but try contrasting hues too. Even prints, plaids and polka dots can set off your cakes—just be sure the pattern is not so busy that it competes with the decorations.

Sandwich loaves are old-fashioned favorites finding new popularity today. And no wonder—they can be made ahead, serve easily, they give the hostess an opportunity to express individuality in her choice of fillings, and nothing looks prettier than a nicely decorated loaf. Here is an especially tempting one.

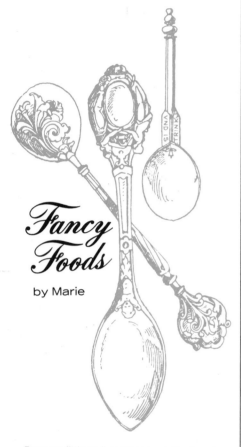

Fancy Foods
by Marie

Prepare fillings first (recipes follow) and refrigerate while you get the bread ready.

You'll need a two-pound loaf of bakery bread sliced horizontally into ½-inch slices. (Most bakeries will do the slicing for you.) If you want thicker slices or can't find a bakery that will do the slicing, mark the fresh bread with a string where you want to slice it, then freeze before slicing with a serrated or electric knife. Discard top and bottom slices and use the 4 or 5 slices between. Cut off crusts and you're ready to fill. We've given enough filling for a loaf made of 4 slices, make an extra recipe of the chicken salad or substitute minced cooked shrimp if you want to use 5 slices. You can also use two types of bread as we did, if you like—white and whole wheat. Order two loaves and use two or three slices from each. Assemble loaf while bread is still frozen. If it is defrosted by the time you've completed it, you can simply refreeze it to serve later, if you're not serving it immediately. (Be sure to keep completed loaf refrigerated until serving, otherwise decorations will soften and fillings spoil!)

To assemble loaf, butter bottom slice, place on cardboard base covered with foil and spread with ham salad filling. Butter both top and bottom of next slice, place on top and spread with chicken salad. Butter third slice on both sides again, place on top and spread with egg salad. Butter bottom only of top slice and place in position. (Buttering slices prevents filling from soaking into bread; you just need a very thin coating.)

Frost loaf next with cream cheese that has been brought to room temperature, tinted and softened to spreading consistency with a little milk or cream. Mark hearts on sides and top with toothpick, then outline with white cream cheese that has been brought to room temperature, using tube 16. Overpipe hearts with same tube and "e" motion. Border loaf with shells, using tube 20 for top, tube 32 for bottom. Pipe petunias (using tube 103) and leaves as directed above, using tinted cream cheese instead of icing. For center, use softened white cream cheese, then yellow-tinted cheese over that and for stamen. Important: keep flowers and leaves frozen until just before serving, as they soften very rapidly. Then place on loaf and serve immediately. Garnish loaf with fresh endive and lettuce leaves. You'll need approximately six 8-ounce packages of cream cheese for frosting, flowers, leaves and borders.

Egg Salad

8 hard-cooked eggs—shelled and put through food mill
4 teaspoons soft butter
¼ cup mayonnaise
⅛ teaspoon garlic salt
⅛ teaspoon seasoned salt
Pinch of cayenne pepper
1 teaspoon vinegar
½ teaspoon prepared mustard

Mix ingredients gently with fork until blended, but not paste-like. Refrigerate until ready to use.

Ham Salad

2 cups ground cooked ham
½ cup chopped sweet pickle
⅓ cup mayonnaise

Combine all ingredients and refrigerate.

Chicken Salad

2 cups cooked chicken diced fine
½ cup minced celery
¼ teaspoon salt
¼ teaspoon white pepper
¼ cup mayonnaise

Combine ingredients, mix well, refrigerate.

Shrimp Salad

Make same as chicken salad, but substitute minced cooked shrimp for chicken.

HOW TO DECORATE GARDEN COVER CAKE
Shown on page 105

A wedding wonder in white, this cake is made up of 4 tiers, (a 16", 12", 10" and 6") separated by 5" Grecian Pillars. Each pair of tiers is topped with an enchanting Twin Cherub ornament.

To start: Make up lots of leaves with tube 70, pull out leaf points with an artist's brush and set on curved Flower Formers to dry.

To decorate the 16" tier: Frame the circular edges with shell borders using tube 4B for the base and tube 32 for the top. Then drape tube 17 fluted garlands around the entire tier and overpipe with double rows of tube 4 stringwork. Between every other garland attach a cluster of leaves (made in advance) with icing and add several tube 8 berries. Fill in garlands with sugar bells.

To decorate the 12" tier: Edge both top and bottom borders with tube 32 shells; then using tube 5, drop a single curved guideline around the entire tier. Overpipe this guideline using a back and forth hand motion with the same tube. Cover the curved garland with a single row of tube 4 stringwork; then pipe double rows of tube 4 stringwork above and between each garland. Trim garland tops with leaves and berries.

To decorate the 10" tier: Pipe star borders using tube 21 for the base and tube 19 for the top. Overpipe the base border of stars with tube 3 string; then, using tube 4, pipe curved guideline and rippled garland side border like you did for the 12" tier. Trim garland tops, alternating sugar bells with leaves and berries.

To decorate the 6" tier: Pipe tube 21 stars around the base and a tube 16 reverse shell border around the top. Drop a double row of tube 4 stringwork and add a few leaf and berry trims for a grand finish! Serves 250.

VOLUME TWO

Celebrate!

MAY / JUNE

Decorating directions for
Citrus Slice Cakes on page 137

CALIFORNIA poppies, bright as the west coast sunshine, reflect the radiance of all the sun-kissed cakes and icing flowers in this issue of CELEBRATE!

Whether it's a garden party in the sun, a surprise shower for a June bride, a daisy-strewn summer wedding, a special after-dinner dessert for Father's Day, a fireworks Fourth of July or a glorious graduation day—you'll find a CELEBRATE! cake to make it memorable . . . aglow with every color under the sun!

So as the months of May and June arrive with blue skies and balmy breezes, welcome them in with cake and celebration. Let their sun shine in on all your summer fun!

Decorating directions for California Poppy Cake are on page 132.

sunshine yellow...

pure gold...

GOLDEN RAYS spread their glow on a cake and show off the brilliance of the face of the sun! What a cheery summer send-off for vacationing friends or a treat for a fun family fiesta!

This cake is easy to decorate, because you make the Color Flow sun in advance, whenever you have time. Just tape wax paper over the patterns from CELEBRATE! II Pattern Book and trace the features with red icing and tube 2. Then fill in the sun rays and face with yellow and orange Color Flow and set aside to dry. Ice a two-layer, 10″ cake white on top, yellow on sides. Attach the Color Flow sun to the cake top with icing, and trim some of the rays with tube 3 red beading. Next, edge cake with bead borders using tube 12 for the base and tube 10 for the top. Now drape two rows of tube 104 orange icing ribbon around the cake sides and summer's all ready to center the table and brighten the faces around your hacienda del sol!

Summer—the season filled with happy wedding celebrations is prefaced with fun to shower on the bride-to-be. A fresh way to convey your best wishes is to preview the wedding on a cake decorated to show off the bride's pick of colors and flowers! Here we chose the summer wedding favorites —sunshine yellow and daisy bouquets.

To decorate the bridal party cake, make the icing daisies first using tubes 101, 102 and 103. Dot flower centers with tube 4 and yellow icing, press flat with finger and sprinkle with edible glitter. With the exception of a few small daisies for the bridesmaid bouquets, dry all the flowers on a curved flower former. Next, cut several short lengths of florist wire, ice green with tube 3, pipe on tube 65s leaves and set in styrofoam to dry.

To make the wedding party, use doll picks and small Wonder Molds. Ice the bridal attendants' dresses and pipe tube 102 hem ruffles. Then ice bodices, decorate with tube 2 beading and trim neckline with tube 102 ruffle and tube 1 bows. With icing, position several daisies on each skirt and place one daisy in each bridesmaid's hands. For the bride, ice skirt and bodice, then swirl on tube 1 cornelli lace designs, leaving a v-shaped opening for a front panel. Fill this panel with tube 1 heart-shaped icing lace designs that have been piped and dried on wax paper. Use Heart Lacework patterns from CELEBRATE! II Pattern Book. Attach the designs with icing; then make a two-layer fine net tulle veil and trim with tube 2 beading. The bouquet, also made of fine net, is made with small daisies and tied with a tiny ribbon. Attach with icing to doll's hands.

When the wedding party is ready and waiting, ice and position cakes—a 14-inch, 2-layer square, and a 9-inch 2-layer heart. Frame both base borders with beading using tube 9 for the square and tube 4 for the heart. Pipe tube 104 ribbon borders above beading, and with icing attach daisies. Next with a toothpick, trace curves on the square cake top and sides. Do the same for the heart's sides, but outline the top in a heart shape. Swirl designs of tube 1 cornelli lace between toothpick outlines, then pipe over tracings with tube 2 beading. Now with icing, arrange a spray of assorted size daisies from the heart top to the square cake top, and trim with sprigs of your ready-made icing leaves. Position the wedding party and present your breathtaking shower surprise!

Color Flow daisies spread their sunshine on a 9x13" cake—a perfect party size for a summer buffet dessert or an outdoor patio get-together with friends! Do the Color Flow designs first using the Daisy Patterns from CELEBRATE! II Pattern Book. Outline all the flowers, stems and leaves; then fill in with Color Flow icing and dry. Next outline the outside edges of the cake top and side-frame designs and fill in backgrounds and flower centers with orange Color Flow icing. When dry, position the Color Flow top with icing, using a few soda straws to elevate the daisy frame and extra icing to elevate the daisy pair center. For the cake sides pipe a mound of royal icing on each underside corner and center of the four designs; then push toothpicks in the icing mounds. Dry and push toothpicked Color Flow into appropriate cake sides. Frame the cake top edges and side corners with tube 13 zigzag borders. Finish off base with tube 21 zigzag border and tube 16 zigzag row above.

daisies
take
the cake

FATHERS are the special men in our lives so tell them so on their day! Whether dads, grand-dads or great-grand-dads, let them know how much they're loved. Prepare a dinner in their honor, include their favorite dishes and for a grand finale serve them a cake fit for a king!

For dads who are avid western fans, round up a mini-tier cake and decorate it cowboy style! All you need are round Mini-Tier Pans and one cake mix to make a happy Father's Day memory.

First, make the large cactus pieces using plastic soda straws. Cut the straws into the lengths of cactus you desire; then insert one of these straws into a bag of green tinted icing fitted with tube 1E. In one steady motion, squeeze and pull out the iced "cactus" straw. Do the same for the other two cactus pieces, then make the smaller cactus sprouts using tubes 32 and 17 and thin wires in place of straws. Stick all the cactus parts in styrofoam and when dry shave off the bottom of the smaller sprouts and attach to larger pieces with icing. Once again, push assembled cactus in styrofoam to dry and get the cake ready for decorating!

Continued on page 137

tell him he's tops!

128

Decorating directions on page 137.

sunlit cakes for

SUMMER SWEETS for those you love all aglow with sunlit icings and other decorations just as bright generate good times for all sorts of parties!

Birthday sweets for a sweet little girl or boy and their favorite friends! Fun to make and decorate and even more fun for the children to eat with the yummy cookie trims!

Cut the cookies from a roll-out dough recipe using the Alphabet, Daisy and Gingerbread cookie cutters. Cut lots of smaller gingerbread "people" and one large gingerbread doll. Then outline the "Happy Birthday" letters and daisies, and "dress" your cookie people with the following icing mixture: one-half recipe royal icing, one-quarter recipe boiled icing and one tablespoon clear corn syrup. (The syrup gives the icing the proper texture so it adheres to the cookies.) Divide the icing into batches and tint a variety of warm colors; then place assorted icing colors into decorating bags and cut the tips to pipe cookie shirts, skirts, dresses and trousers. When the cookie "clothes" have dried, pipe on faces, hair, buttons and bows with tubes 101s, 1 and 2. For the larger cookie "doll" pipe on hearts, bow, hair and face with tube 2, ruffled sleeves with tube 102. Edge the cookie flowers and letters with tube 2, then pipe flower centers with tube 3 and drop flower trims with tube 225. When all the cookies are dry, attach toothpicks to the bottoms of the "Happy Birthday" letters and to several cookie daisies and dolls, including the large doll representing the birthday girl, with royal icing.

Now, also in advance of decorating the cake, make sugar mold hearts using the plastic Heart Candy Molds and a mixture of two cups sugar and four teaspoons water. Mix the sugar and water by hand, tint with pink food coloring and pack into the molds. Scrape off the excess, unmold immediately and set heart shapes aside to dry.

Using the Long Loaf Pan, bake a cake, ice it a sunshine yellow and place it on a foil-covered rectangular cake board. Edge the cake with bright yellow tube 8 beads around the top and multi-color tube 10 beads around the bottom. Push the toothpicked "Happy Birthday" letters into the cake top along with a daisy trio and the large girl

cookie doll. Then, with icing, attach several cookie "people" to the cake sides along with sugar hearts, cookie daisies and the birthday girl's cookie name. With tube 12 pipe enough candle holders for the birthday age and while icing is still wet push in candles. Use the tiny toothpicked cookie people to decorate scoops of ice cream. Make place cards for each party guest and place one in the hand of each cookie boy and girl, "glue-

ing" with icing.

When the children see what you have for them—cake, cookies, ice cream, all their favorites—they'll really be anxious to sing out the birthday wishes so they can enjoy all the goodies!

Sweet Hearts pictured above described on page 137.

summer parties

HOW TO MAKE A CALIFORNIA POPPY

Mix a batch of orange-tinted royal icing, slightly stiffened for added petal strength. Then place a piece of aluminum foil into the bottom half of a 1¼-inch lily nail and partially press in the top half so the foil liner does not quite fill the entire cup. Now with tube 103 and a decorating bag of orange icing you're ready to make a flower!

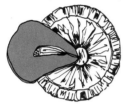

Touch tube's wide end to nail center, squeeze a petal out over the nail's edge, bring it across and back to the center.

Form three more square-shaped petals exactly the same way, with each having a slight opening in their center as shown.

Fill these petal openings by smoothing the icing with a dampened art brush. Then pipe a small mound of icing in the flower center.

Now, remove the colored heads from several artificial stamens, and push stamens into the poppy's center while icing is still wet. Brush the tips of the stamen stems with thinned orange icing, remove flower and foil from cup and set aside to dry. Now using white, lemon yellow and orange icings, make about 100 poppies and you can make a cake like the one on page 124.

HOW TO DECORATE THE CALIFORNIA POPPY CAKE
Shown on page 124

A two-tiered petal cake iced in sunshine yellow is covered with bright-white, hot-orange and lemon-yellow poppies. What a refreshing way to treat the girls at a summer garden party or club luncheon!

To decorate, first make the pretty petalled flowers following the procedures and pictures shown at left. When all your flowers are made, then ice several florist wires green, pipe on tube 2 leaves and stick in styrofoam. When poppies and leafy stems are dry, you're ready to trim the cake!

The 6″ and 12″ petalled cake bases are first edged with zigzag borders of icing, using tube 17 for the large tier and tube 15 for the small tier. Next, on the side of the 12″ tier, drape a tube 14 curved garland of icing over each petal curve. Drop strings of tube 2 latticework from this tier's top edge to the curved garlands, first slanting all the strings in one direction, and then crossing over by slanting strings in the opposite direction. Now with tube 14, overpipe all the garlands and frame the tier's top edge with zigzags of icing to hide any uneven latticework edges. Fill all the vacant spaces between latticework garlands with tube 14 zigzag puffs of icing.

For the top tier, pipe the same latticework and garlands using tube 14 for the zigzag curves and top border and tube 2 for the drop strings of lattice. When you've finished all the borders, pipe mounds of icing around the bases of both cake tiers at the curved edge of each petal. While the icing is still wet, arrange clusters of six poppies around the bottom tier and clusters of three poppies around the top tier. For the cake top, once again heap a mound of icing using it as a base for attaching assorted-color poppies.

For finishing touches, trim flowers on tier sides with tube 2 fern-like leaves and place your ready-made leaf-strewn wires among the poppies clustered on the cake top. Set your cake out for a dazzling dessert display and if you have any extra icing poppies use them as garnishes for scoops of ice cream or as decorations for other serving platters.

The pretty poppies are decorative trims so very appropriate for summer, and a cake as dazzling and delightful as this could serve for so many occasions—birthdays, showers or just a-glad-summer's arrived party. One thing for certain, for whatever occasion you make this attractive cake, it's sure to be one that's remembered.

here comes the sun!

And right along with it come flowers, leaves and tree-ripened fruits! So celebrate this sunniest of seasons with a cake just as radiant and bright!

Using your favorite cookie dough recipe, cut out cookie flowers, trees and smiling sun-beam faces. Ice all the cookie shapes in assorted colors of softened royal icing; then pipe on the gay decorations. Use tube 2 for the sun-beam outlines and face features, and tubes 65 and 74 for the tree leaves. Use a 199 tube to stroke on ribbed tree bark icing, then decorate trees by attaching tube 59° violets (made in advance) with icing and piping on tube 4 icing balls for lemons and oranges. To decorate cookie flowers, use tube 101 for flat ribbon outlines, tube 14 for ribbed outline and tube 2 for string outlines. Pipe stamens and dot decorations with tube 2; then pipe over all cookie leaves with a 70 tube, adding leaf "veins" with tube 2.

While cookies are drying, ice a 10″ round cake and frame the base with tall blades of tube 2 icing "grass." Edge cake top and base with tube 8 beading, then pipe more tube 2 "grass" on cake top. With icing, attach cookie trees and sun-beam faces to cake sides. Then with more icing, attach toothpicks to the decorated cookie flower stems and when dry push into cake top.

If you have any extra decorated cookies you can place them on festive serving plates or attach toothpicks to them as before and push them into scoops of ice cream.

STAR SPANGLED

CELEBRATION CAKES

A FLAG SALUTE

For a patriotic Fourth of July celebration, offer a salute to the nations of the world with a trio of cake tiers displaying brightly decorated Color Flow flags!

You can make the flags days in advance to save time on cake decorating day! Cover Flags-of-Nations patterns from CELEBRATE! II Pattern Book with wax paper, outline with tube 2 and fill in outlines with appropriate shades of Color Flow.

When flag decorations are thoroughly dry, bake three square cake tiers—a 14x4″, a 10x3″ and a 6x3″. Frost all in white. Assemble tiers with 11″ and 7″ square separator plates and 5″ Grecian Pillars. Attach flags with icing to all four sides of each cake tier. Next edge the 14″ tier using tube 105 for the shell base border and tube 21 for the circular "i" motion shell top border. Frame the other two tiers with the same borders using tube 21 for both the base and top of the 10″ tier, and tube 19 for both the base and top of the 6″ tier.

Now decorate all three tier tops by first edging the base and middle tier's separator plates with a zigzag hand motion and tube 16. Next cut three styrofoam circles, one 4″ in diameter and two 3″ in diameter. Push American Flag picks into the large styrofoam circle, assorted International Flag picks into one of the small styrofoam circles and place on lower and middle tier tops as shown. Frame the circular styrofoam

edges with rows of tube 16 zigzag. Use the other small styrofoam circle for the cake top. Push a red candle in the circle's center, surround with American Flag picks and decorate foam base with tube 16 zigzag, overpiping with elongated tube 20 shells. Now set the top tier's candle ablaze for the grand finale to your patriotic neighborhood picnic or after-the-parade community celebration!

AUNT AMERICA

Completely covered with stars of creamy icing and shiny Color Flow, this cake is a perfect patriotic tribute to serve after your Fourth-of-July back yard barbeque or the evening's sky show of fireworks!

To start, make Color Flow trims using the Star patterns from CELEBRATE! II Pattern Book. Tape wax paper over patterns, outline with tube 2 and fill in outlines with Color Flow. Next, make your very favorite cake in the large Wonder Mold pan, push a

doll pick in the cooled cake's top, place the doll cake on a pretty party plate and you're ready to decorate!

To make the doll's apron, first outline the outer edge with tube 2. Then ice the entire apron white and overpipe with alternating double rows of red and white tube 16 stars. Note: the last apron "stripe" contains four rows of tube 16 white stars.

Now pipe Aunt America's blue skirt and blue/white dress top with more tube 16 stars; and frame the skirt with a tube 104 ruffled hem. With icing, attach the blue Color Flow stars to the apron's bottom stripe and position white Color Flow stars all over the skirt.

To make the doll pick's hat, ice a plastic top hat white and glue on red and blue ribbon "stripes." With a little more glue place an American Flag pick in her hand and call the gang around for a star of a treat!

A wedding cake sweetly strewn with bright-eyed daisies and dainty rosebuds! Serves 165. (Decorating directions page 137.)

HOW TO DECORATE CITRUS COVER CAKES
Shown on page 123

Fresh as the fruits they represent these lemon, lime and orange citrus cake slices are a novel way to announce the arrival of summer! The cakes are easy to decorate so you can make several to complement scoops of cool citrus sherbets as a refreshing finale to a summer party!

To decorate, bake 8″ and 10″ round cakes, cutting the 10″ rounds in half to represent citrus wedges. Ice the cake tops in light shades of lemon yellow, lime green and tangy orange, draping the icings down onto the straight side of each half-cake wedge.

Next, using deeper shades of the same icing colors, frost all around the curved cake sides, letting some of the icing overlap onto the edges of the cake tops and over onto the straight edges of the cake-halves. With white icing, pipe the outer circular edged fruit "segment" outlines with tube 102 and the inner wedged "segment" divisions with tube 44. Use tube 12 to pipe the fruit slice centers, then press flat with finger.

To make the citrus seed marks, fill decorating bags with deeper icing shades, cut tiny holes and pipe short seed lines by dragging the bag across the cake top. Complete, your cakes are ready to slice and serve!

FATHER'S DAY CAKES
Continued from pages 128, 129

Ice and stack your three round mini-tier layers on a foil-covered board and edge the bottom of each with shell borders using tube 18 for the large tier and tube 17 for the two smaller tiers. Pipe triple-row zigzag garland puffs around the tier tops trimming them with icing stars. Use tube 17 for the bottom tier's garlands and stars, and tube 15 for the two smaller tiers.

Push one cactus into the cake top and attach the others at the base with icing. Then write your birthday message with tube 3, position a cowboy figure on the top tier and call in the dad who's the best in the west, north, east and south!

A great way to make dad a cake fit for a king is do just that—decorate a cake that sweetly crowns him king for a day! Make the sugar trims in advance using the Ball-Shaped Mold and Writing Set alphabet letters. Fill molds with sugar mixture using 2 cups

granulated sugar and 4 teaspoons water. To make dad's face tint some sugar flesh with food colors and pack into mold halves. Scrape off excess and unmold immediately. Do the same for the "Happy Father's Day" message using green-tinted sugar. After the ball mold halves have dried for about two hours, hollow out the centers and assemble with royal icing. When dry, pipe on "dad's" features using tube 8 for the eyes, tube 10 for the nose, tube 3 for the smile and tube 2A for the rosy cheeks pressed flat with your finger. Pipe the ears with tube 12, the hair and moustache with tube 16 and set the soon-to-be "king" aside to dry while you ready the cake!

Ice a 9 x 13 x 3″ cake a soft yellow and place it on a foil-covered board. Edge the top and bottom with bright yellow bead borders using tube 10 for the base and tube 8 for the top. Pipe curved zigzag garlands around the cake sides with tube 16 and decorate with upright shells using the same tube. Now position your sweet-faced "father" and a Collar and Tie Set on the cake top, and trim the tie with tube 4 beading. Attach the sugar mold letters with icing, crown the king and all four cake board corners with candle holders and light up your royal decorations for the grand presentation!

Show him he's a prize catch for a dad. Outline Fish and Bubble patterns from CELEBRATE! II Pattern Book with tube 2 and fill in with Color Flow. Ice 12″ round cake white and use a toothpick to trace scrolls around sides of cake. Cover scroll outlines with tube 16, then edge cake base and top with tube 16 reverse shell borders. Position Color Flow fish and bubbles on cake top with icing, adding tube 2 fins to fish and tube 16 scroll-like waves to base of fish. Write tube 2 "Hi Dad!" to finish off cake top.

HOW TO DECORATE SWEET HEARTS CAKE
Shown on page 131

Summer sweethearts stand atop tiers of hearts and flowers and spread more sunshine for summertime parties! The pretty pansies are made first using tube 103 and a flower nail. Add decorative floral "veins" with an art brush and pipe centers with tube 2. Set pansies aside, drying several on a Flower Former to gently curve petals.

Bake the three-tiered cake confection using

one cake mix and the Heart Mini-Tier Pans. Cool cakes, ice all three tiers yellow and assemble on a heart-shaped golden foil-covered board. Frame the tiers with ruffles and shells as shown using tube 70 for the base and tube 67 for the top of the large heart, tube 16 for the base and tube 67 for the top of the middle-sized heart and tube 16 for the base and tube 65 for the top of the small heart.

With icing, drape two rows of flowers down two sides of the cake and attach a few more pansies around the base. Trim the flowers with tube 66 leaves and with a dampened art brush, touch each leaf at several points to make a scalloped edge.

Top the cake with a pair of Teen Sweethearts and serve your tiered hearts at a cake-coffee-and-conversation social or at a party for a newly engaged young couple!

HOW TO DECORATE SUMMER BLISS
Shown on opposite page

Daisies and rosebuds on the palest beige cake—a sweet setting for a summer celebration and a striking cake that's relatively easy to decorate!

Make all the flowers in advance using tubes 103 and 104 for the rosebuds and tubes 102, 103 and 104 for the dainty daisies. Dot the daisies with tube 3 centers, then press flat and sprinkle with edible glitter. Set all your flowers aside to dry, placing your daisies on a Flower Former to curve the petals.

Now using 11″ square separator plates and 3″ square filigree pillars ice and assemble three square tiers—a 14 x 4″, a 10 x 4″ and a 6 x 3″. Edge all three tiers with shell borders in white using tube 30 for the bottom and tube 20 for the top of the 14″ square, tube 20 for the bottom and top of the 10″ square and tube 18 for the bottom and top of the 6″ square. Attach arrangements of daisies and rosebuds to all tier sides with icing, trimming with tube 3 stems and tube 66 leaves. Arrange another floral cluster atop the 14″ tier's separator plate again attaching blooms with icing and trimming with tube 3 stems and tube 66 leaves. Top the cake with "The Celestial Twins" bearing garlands of flowers and appropriately decorate the ornament base with a few icing rosebuds and daisies. Now fete the bride and groom with your bouquet of icing blossoms. Serves 165.

make a happy cake!

Bright sun, blue skies and a table full of sweet smiling-faced graduates—what a thoughful way to spread happiness among family and friends!

Fun to make and decorate, you don't have to wait for a special occasion to tell someone

"HAVE A NICE DAY"

Just make the Color Flow clouds, sunshine and letters in advance using the "Have a Nice Day" patterns from CELEBRATE! II Pattern Book. Tape clear wrap over the pattern pieces, ouline the designs with tube 2, then fill in between outlines with appropriate shades of Color Flow icing.

When all your Color Flow designs are dry, ice a 10" square cake pale blue, marking off one third of the cake top to ice a bright green. Pat green icing with a damp sponge to effect a "grassy" appearance; then attach all the Color Flow trims with icing.

Finish your trims as brightly as you started by edging the cake with bead borders using tube 12 for the base and tube 10 for the top.

SMILING GRADUATES

After the commencement ceremony, honor your graduate at home with a party prepared expressly for him! Smiling sugar-capped cake faces are a sure way to reflect this proud moment for your happy student; and what's more they're table decorations that double as delicious-tasting treats!

Make the sugar graduate caps first, using two cups granulated sugar and four teaspoons water. Mix by hand, and tint some of the sugar if you like for added color appeal. Then pack molds, scrape off excess sugar mixture and unmold immediately. After two hours, carefully pick up the "cap" parts of the molds and hollow out the damp sugar inside to a thickness of about ¼ inch. When thoroughly dry and hard, assemble "caps" mortorboards and tassels with royal icing and once more set aside to dry.

Ice all the Small Wonder Mold cake faces flesh, then pipe on "hair" using tube 3 for string locks, ringlets and bangs, tube 14 for thicker ribbed locks and bangs and tube 18 for braids. Pipe eyes with tube 7 and cheeks with tube 2A, pressing flat with finger. Add sweet smiles with tube 3, position caps and march the graduate in for the surprise!

VOLUME TWO

Celebrate!

JULY / AUGUST

Decorating directions for
3-Ring Circus on page 148

CIRCUS PARTY

WHAT'S more fun than a circus—that marvelous combination of pageantry and ballyhoo? Its appeal is as basic as baseball, so ageless it attracts grandparents and grandchildren too. So let's give a circus party, one that's just as colorful and jolly as the circus itself. We've planned our party for children—but the circus makes a good party theme for guests of any age.

"Half the fun is in the planning," and we know you'll enjoy every minute you spend putting this show on the road. Here's the blueprint:

ADVANCE BALLYHOO. Send out really spirited invitations. Buy big balloons, blow them up, and print "Greatest Show on Earth" and the date, time and address on them with black magic marker. On the other side of the ballon print "come as a clown" or "acrobat" or "bareback rider." Deflate the balloons and send each off in an envelope to an honored guest.

PLAN THE MAIN ATTRACTION. Make a really smashing centerpiece. The children will be thrilled with this circle of candy elephants caparisoned in spangled marzipan blankets trudging trunk to tail in a brown sugar "sawdust" ring. A jolly clown stands on an icing-trimmed ornament base to direct them. Make the "ring" from a strip of light cardboard taped together and trimmed with seals. Directions for molding the elephants are on page 104.

The winner of each game can be given an elephant as prize, with one lucky guest carrying off the clown.

Leaf through the pages of this issue for other circus centerpieces, just as spectacular.

STAGE THE SHOW. It's easy to bring circus color to the party. The best place to have it is in your back yard. In case of rain, a swept-out garage, porch or play room will do nicely. Tack up big circus posters (obtainable at many book, stationery and gift shops) to fences and walls of house and garage. Tie bunches of balloons to tree limbs. They'll be

Continued on page 154

THE CIRCUS IS ALIVE AND WELL IN BARABOO

ANY cake decorator who has ever aspired to working on a project of really monumental proportions should make the opportunity to visit the Circus World Museum in Baraboo, Wisconsin, this summer. Why? Because here you will see the work of artisans who a half century or more ago designed and decorated the lavishly-embellished wagons that once rumbled down the streets of towns all over America, giving the thousands of curbstone spectators an enticing preview of the fun to be had at the outdoor circus that very day.

Here, well-protected under the roof of the four hundred foot long Circus Parade Pavillion, are over 100 handsomely-carved and decorated circus wagons. All have been painstakingly restored to mint condition by craftsmen in the Museum's shops. The collection is valued at one and one-half million dollars, and this may well be highly conservative.

The wagons, though frequently massive, often display the decor of richly decorated cakes, an observation we believe most CELEBRATE! readers would be quick to make.

The two wagons immediately below are fine examples of circus rolling stock that should delight anyone interested in using a pastry tube to achieve classic designs. The treasured vehicle in the lower left hand corner is the Swan Bandwagon, which weighs in at 8,240 pounds. Built in 1905, it is 23 feet long and was designed to carry a band of eighteen to twenty musicians. Such handsome equipage was

normally drawn by six to eight matched dray horses, handled by a driver of extreme skill.

To the right of the Swan Bandwagon is a "picture frame" cage. It is the only wagon in the growing collection, the precise origin of which is unknown. It can only be assumed that any animal put on display in such elegantly-bordered quarters must have been regal in appearance.

The exact date when the "Dolphin Tableau" (upper right) made its appearance as a parade spectacular is not known; but it is known to have been built either during or slightly before the Civil War in America. It was built in England and, with its wood carved dolphin on the top platform, is considered a typical English parade vehicle. It was generously presented to the Museum by Bailey and Mary Fossett.

The Columbia Bandwagon, at the lower left, was built in 1897 for Barnum & Bailey and served to carry both band on its top platform and cargo in its voluminous inner room. Its ornamentation consisting of arches, scrolls, plumes, shells, cherubs, classic columns and heraldric devices should be a source of pleasure to any cake decorator who feels that nothing worth putting on display should be understated!

The "Cinderella" (lower right) is one of seven nursery rhyme floats built in the 1880's for the Barnum & Bailey Greatest Show on Earth. It was built for parade use only. Of the original seven, only this one,

Continued on page 154

YES, you can make a tiger jump through a ring of flame—and create the most talked about birthday cake ever! Or just make this spectacular cake for your favorite "tiger" or any special occasion.

Each guest at the party receives his own clown cupcake to take home—and the birthday child can keep the tiger himself as a lasting memento. Outline Tiger pattern from CELEBRATE! II Pattern Book with tube 3 and fill in with Color Flow. This can be done weeks ahead to spare preparty jitters. Make the yellow Color Flow circle too.

The day before, or morning of, the party, ice and decorate the cakes in buttercream. Place five or six flat sugar cubes on the yellow circle, and carefully position the tiger on top of them. Before the cake is cut, he can be lifted off and saved for another tiger cake or framed for a lasting wall decoration.

To frame the tiger. First, obtain a masonite or hardboard circle or square about 14″ across. Paint it red or any bright color and attach a wire across the back for hanging. Position the paper tiger pattern on the hardboard and mark outlines with a pin. Pipe small mounds of Color Flow

Continued on page 154

HOW TO TAME

A

TIGER

144

INVITE a menagerie of animal friends to your house and watch a party turn into a circus! The cakes and cupcakes are just the right size to serve an avid group of young circus fans, and all the animals are piped in easy-to-do icing stars, which is a bonus for a busy mom!

Patterns for all three animal cakes on the opposite page as well as the tiger cupcakes are included in the CELEBRATE! II Pattern Book.

PRANCING PONY. To make, just tape wax paper over pony and ponytail patterns and outline the different color areas with tube 3. Fill in these outlines with tube 15 icing stars, piping the stars closely together for added pattern strength. Let star-studded pony and tails dry overnight, then ice an 8″ x 3″ square cake and you're ready to decorate. Carefully peel wax paper off pony trims and attach pony to cake top with icing. With more icing, position pony tails on all four cake corners. Outline all tail trims, including the pony's tail on the cake top, with tube 3; then frame the cake with more stars using tube 18 for the top border and tube 16 for the base border.

LOVABLE LION. To decorate, tape wax paper over pattern and outline with tube 2 and roaring red icing. Fill in outlines with tightly piped tube 15 stars. When lion is dry, ice a 10″ x 4″ round cake and place on a foil-covered board. Pipe vertical stripes around the cake with tube 45, then border the cake top and bottom with tube 18 zigzag garlands. Decorate base border with tube 45 ribbon, then ornament vertical cake stripes with tube 18 rosettes. Carefully peel wax paper off of starry lion and place him on cake top with a few dots of icing.

ELEPHANTS ON PARADE! As before, tape wax paper over pattern, outline with tube 3, then fill in with tube 16 icing stars. Overpipe the outlines for stronger definition. Set elephant aside to dry overnight. Also in advance, bake cookies cut into elephant shapes and "paint" with thinned down icing. Outline cookies and pipe features with tube 2.

When cake trims are ready, bake and ice a 10″ x 4″ square cake and place on a foil-covered board. Carefully peel wax paper off elephant and position on

Continued on page 154

ANIMALS ARE SUCH WELCOME GUESTS

3-RING

CIRCUS

Now it's time to ready your 3-ring circus acts! Using Floral Scroll ornament bases as "stages," add icing stars, swirls, garlands, upright shells and all other trims with tube 14; then position the star acts! For the clown, use tube 4B to figure pipe him right on the ornament "stage" base. Hold tube perpendicular as you apply maximum pressure to squeeze out body. As icing mounds to desired height, stop pressure, push in plastic soda straw for support and clip level with top of body. Next tuck tube 32 into sides and base of body and squeeze to pull out arms and legs, adding stars for feet with the same tube. Pipe wrists and ankle trims with tube 101s, hands with tube 3. Push in plastic Clown Head pick and set on cake top. On the other two "stages" attach elephant and panda with icing, and place on the cakes.

Pipe tube 3 icing stripes in the grooves of 10¼" Roman Column pillars. With iced pillars dry, assemble the circus cakes. Set out popcorn and peanuts and call in the children for the biggest party surprise they've ever had! And whether you make just one of these spectacular cakes or all three, they'll be the starring acts of the day!

HERE'S a sure way to capture some of the fun and excitement of the real Big Top performance. These 3-ring circus cakes put clown and animal acts right before admiring eyes. Such an appropriate theme for a children's summer party, you could have the little guests dress as their circus favorites, award prizes for the best costumes and celebrate with cake and ice cream!

To create a circus show like this one, bake and ice three 12" x 4" round cakes and three dome-shaped cakes made in large Wonder Mold pans. Place the round cakes on assorted-color foil-covered boards, topping each with a 10" separator plate. Position the iced Wonder Mold cakes on 10" separator plates also, and you're ready to decorate!

To trim each Wonder Mold cake, mark off guidelines for stripes with a toothpick, then overpipe with tube 16. Ring each dome-shaped cake base with tube 18 rosettes, then pipe a large tube 32 rosette at the peak and push in a toothpicked construction-paper flag while icing is still wet.

To decorate the 12" round cake pictured at the far right below, first edge base with tube 32 stars. Next, pipe the side garlands, using tube 17 and a circular motion; then, using the same tube, frame the cake top with stars and trim the separator plate with a ruffled edging of icing using tube 16.

To decorate the 12" round cake pictured below at center, pipe tube 32 star base borders and star side garlands. Add a single row of tube 3 stringwork underneath garlands, then pipe a tube 47 ribbed line of icing from garland points to cake top. Trim cake top with tube 18 stars and decorate separator plate edges with tube 16.

To decorate the 12" round cake pictured at the far left below, pipe wide 1D ribbed stripes around cake sides; then border cake base with tube 32 stars and cake top with tube 18 stars. Pipe large tube 4B rosettes at stripe tops, and once again decorate separator plate edges with tube 16.

HOW TO LEAD A PARADE

Decorate a bright circus wagon pulled by a team of sweetly starred ponies! Make the ponies first using pattern from CELEBRATE! II Pattern Book. Tape wax paper over pattern, outline different color icing areas with tube 2, then fill in areas with tube 16 royal icing stars. Pipe the stars tightly together for added strength. Let both circus ponies dry over night; then carefully peel off the wax paper, turn ponies over and lay toothpicks on rear legs with about one inch extending beyond legs. The picks will help ponies stand up right. Repipe with stars, piping right over toothpicks. Set ponies aside to dry.

Next, prepare cakes for assembling the circus wagon. Bake and ice two 5″ square cakes, one small loaf cake and one blossom cake, using pans from the Little Loafer and Blossom pan sets. Position the loaf cake in front of one of the 5″ cake squares on a board cut to the exact size of both cakes. Now using dowel rods for support, position the other 5″ cake square on top of the first. Clip two dowels level with cake top, leaving the

other to be inserted in the blossom cake for support. Decorate the assembled circus wagon with tube 14 star borders and tube 16 icing swirls and curliques. Add a few more tube 14 stars to the sides of the wagon cake.

Pipe tube 15 upright shells on the petals of the blossom cake, then frame with tube 3 beading. To complete, drape a tube 101 icing ribbon around cake sides; then ornament with tube 14 stars, adding large tube 10 beading at top of cake. Position the decorated blossom cake atop the wagon, securing it on the protruding dowel rod.

With the wagon assembled, you're ready to make the cake base. Ice a 16″ x 18″ x 1″ styrofoam rectangle and pat with a sponge to effect grassy appearance. Place iced rectangle on a foil-covered board and frame with tube 10 beading. Place the wagon cake on the styrofoam base, using stacks of sugar wafer cookies as supports and placing them where wheels will be added. The wagon's wheels are iced cookies that have been

Continued on page 154

HOW TO BUILD

IKE a magic vision to delight a child's eye, this gaily striped Big Top cake rises from a cloud of cotton candy, pennant flying high, a smiling tiger at the entrance.

You don't need to be a circus hand to build it—its construction is just as much fun as eating it!

First bake a cake in a hexagon pan, using one cake mix or your favorite recipe. Chill the cake. Split and fill to achieve added height—and extra flavor!

Now make a pattern for the top of the tent. Fold a piece of paper in half, matching edges exactly. At the lower edge of the folded paper measure 2½″ from the fold and make a mark. Now measure from the lower edge of the folded paper and make a mark 5″ from the bottom on the folded edge. Join the two marks. Cut the closely folded paper along this line. Open, and you will have a triangle. Trace this shape six times on light cardboard (shirt cardboard is good). Draw a line on each cardboard triangle to show its center. (The same as the fold on your paper pattern.) Tape all the triangles together, matching base and points. Presto—the roof of the big top!

Cut a wedge out of the center of one side of the cake in a pointed "doorway" shape, using a paring knife. Ice the inside of this wedge green, then set the cake on a 12″ foil-covered cake board and ice all over in white icing. Now you may write a surprise message on the cake top. Set the cardboard "roof" on the cake, matching the six sides, and press gently into position. Now decorate!

Fit two decorating bags with tube 16—fill one with white icing, the other with red. Decorate the roof first. Pipe two lines of red icing at the edge of one triangular section. Then pipe two lines of red on the opposite edge. Now pipe two lines of white icing against the red stripes. Continue in this fashion until triangle is completely covered with stripes. Always start the stripes on the center line of the triangle, and keep all lines very close together so that no space shows between them.

Cover the cake sides with the same technique, matching the colors of stripes. As you approach the bottom of the cake, increase your pressure to compensate for the slight flare of the cake shape.

Make a border of tube 21 stars at the base of the cake, using alternating colors. Pipe a tube 104 ruffle at the top edge of the cake, then just above it a border of tube 8 balls.

Fashion a pennant from a colored paper triangle glued to a toothpick. Pipe a rosette at the very peak of the roof and set the pennant into it. Finally figure-pipe the rolled "curtain" at the doorway with tube 8.

Now set a smiling tiger (from the Animal Cartoon Set) in the Big Top entrance and circle the cake with a circus train hauling a load of animals. Display your Big Top to delighted guests!

To serve the cake, run a spatula under the ball border and lift off the cardboard roof. Now the guest of honor can read your secret message! The circus train and animals are little gifts to take home. The Big Top Cake serves 12.

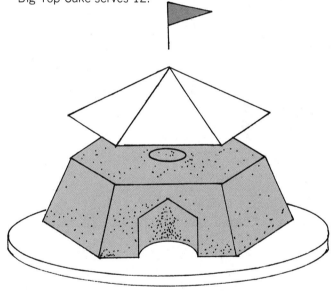

YOUR OWN BIG TOP

HOW TO TRAIN A TEDDY BEAR

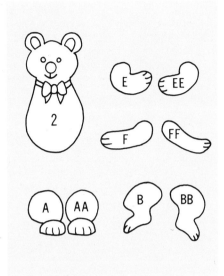

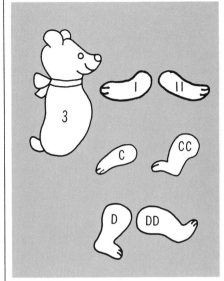

Three adorable little cakes for a toddler's birthday, each trimmed with a teddy bear, his favorite toy, each bear in a different action pose. Part of the charm of these tiny cakes is their size—they're baked in 5″ round pans, two layers for each. But most of the fun of creating them comes from Jointed Teddy Bear patterns found in CELEBRATE! II Pattern Book.

At first glance, the pattern looks confusing—just a collection of legs and torsos, with not a complete teddy bear on the sheet. The way you put the parts together makes every teddy bear "custom made." By selecting various combinations of front and back legs and torsos you can make Teddy dance, kick, sit, march, and possibly stand on his head! The children will be enchanted with these unique "toys."

To help plan the poses of your bears, trace parts of the pattern and put them together to form a complete figure. Then make the Color Flow pieces by outlining the patterns with tube 2 and filling in the usual way. Set aside to dry thoroughly.

Then ice and decorate the cakes. All are identical except for color. Pipe a ruffle at

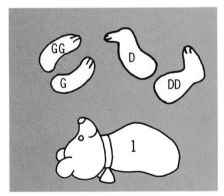

base with tube 104, then make a bulb border above it with tube 6. Use tube 6 again for a curved garland at top of cake. Drape tube 2 stringwork in contrasting colors over the garland, and finish with a tube 6 bulb border.

Now assemble the teddy bears on top of each cake, attaching with dots of icing. Each cake serves 6.

Teddy playfully kicks a flower. Make pattern G and GG front legs, D and DD back legs and torso number 2 in Color Flow. Following the sketch you've made by tracing the pattern pieces, first put legs GG and D on the cake top with dots of icing. Then put torso on top of them and add legs G and DD on top of torso. The "layering" of Color Flow pieces gives a realistic 3-dimensional effect. Add a drop flower for Teddy to kick.

Teddy reposes or jumps for joy. For reposing Teddy make front leg patterns E and EE, lower leg patterns A and AA and torso 1. Put pieces together in this order—first torso, then front and lower legs. Jumping Teddy

uses the same torso, patterns F and FF front legs and patterns B and BB lower legs. Attach the two sets of legs to the cake top and place the torso on top of them.

Teddy marches and sits. Use torso number 2, front leg patterns I and II and lower leg patterns C and CC for the marching Teddy. First position legs I and C, then the torso, last, legs II and CC. For sitting Teddy make torso 3, front legs I and II, lower legs D and DD. Assemble in a similar way.

Train some Teddy Bears to do tricks! Give each little cake to perform on or let them mingle on a larger cake. They'll win every child's heart with their fun-loving ways!

PARTY PLAN (con'd from page 141)

used later for games. Stretch a line of bright plastic or cloth banners from tree to tree. Hang them over your front door too, with a boldly painted cardboard sign proclaiming "Greatest Show on Earth" to welcome guests as they arrive. Let a member of the family dressed as a clown escort them to the party. And have a record player playing calliope tunes to get everybody in a circus mood.

MAIN ATTRACTIONS. Give everyone a cone of cotton candy as they enter the party. This puts the guests in the spirit of the occasion and gives them something to do while other guests arrive. Then start the games!

A relatively quiet one to begin with—PIN THE TAIL ON THE LION. Tack up a big picture of a lion drawn on wrapping paper. (Use the lion cake on page 146 as a guide.) Have ready a rope "tail" attached to a hat pin, blindfold each child, spin him around and watch his efforts to pin the 'tail' in the right place. Good for a lot of laughs.

PASS THE PEANUT. Divide guests into teams. Teams line up. First member receives a teaspoon with a peanut in it—walks to a designated spot and back, without dropping the peanut, then passes the spoon to the next team member. First team finished is the winner—each team member receives a bag of peanuts to take home.

BALLOON BREAKING. Choose teams. Tie a balloon to each child's ankle. Set a time limit, ten minutes. Everyone tries to break other guest's balloons and protect their own. Team with most balloons left at sound of whistle wins. Remove balloons and award as prizes, giving one to each of the winning team members.

Time for quiet play! Make this an individual-winner game. Each guest receives a blown-up balloon. At a signal, each sits on his balloon and tries to break it. The first one to succeed wins—a candy elephant! Second and third-prize winners receive elephants too. A paperback book on games will give you many more ideas. Just adapt the games to the circus theme.

THE GRAND ENTRY. Games finished, now's the time for the big circus parade. Stepping in time to a calliope record tune, children parade to show off their costumes. A select group of parents are judges—prizes can be as many as you wish, preferably one to each guest. Most Beautiful, Funniest, Most Realistic, Most Original. The parade proceeds to the REFRESHMENT TENT.

Really a table or counter draped with a gay cloth and sheltered by a golf umbrella! Hot dogs with all the trimmings are handed to each child who then goes to a brightly covered picnic table. Tie a balloon, marked with the child's name, to each chair. Bowls of potato chips line the table, and pink lemonade is set at each place. Serve ice cream in paper cups, and of course, a slice of the centerpiece cake.

CLEAN-UP DETAIL. Ask the children to help with cleaning up. Paper plates and table-cloths can be thrown into plastic bags, peanut shells picked up, leftover food carried to the kitchen. Banners and posters taken down and given to the willing workers. In just a few minutes everything is neat and orderly as before—and the circus spectacular is over!

BARABOO (con'd from page 143)

"Mother Goose" and "The Old Woman in the Shoe" remain. All are on display at Circus World Museum. All are very worth seeing.

But the impressive collection of one-of-a-kind circus wagons is just one of many attractions at Circus World Museum. There are 6 huge buildings on the colorful fifteen acres and each is packed with all of the paraphanelia that goes with the romantic lore of the circus. There are live performances each day; together with goat cart rides for little tots and rides on a real circus wagon for circus buffs of any age. Each day, too, a circus train is unloaded with the use of huge draft horses, a procedure that was a familiar sight 50 years ago in practically every whistle stop in the nation.

There are also frequent concerts on the una-fon, the band organ and the steam calliope. The steam calliope (pronounced kalē ŏp) lays rightful claim to being the loudest of all musical instruments and anyone who has been near the Circus World's "America" while it is in operation under a full head of steam would not be likely to dispute this. The noise factor is aptly described by one of the Museum's officials as being the same as that which might be achieved by lining up 32 steam locomotives and having them somehow blast out a simple tune. It is said to have been first used in 1857 by a show billed as Nixon and Kemp.

The Circus World Museum is owned and efficiently operated by the State Historical Society of Wisconsin and is open 7 days a week from mid-May to mid-September. Admission is $2.50 for adults, $1.00 for children. A terrific value!

The site of this spectacular institution is easily reached from many mid-America locations, since Baraboo, Wisconsin, is just 100 miles from Milwaukee, 40 from Madison, 175 from Chicago and 260 from St. Paul.

Needless to say, the Circus World Museum staff has not forgotten the other pleasures associated with the circus. Hot dogs, hamburgers, popcorn, peanuts, cotton candy and pink lemonade are all close at hand. What more could anyone ask?

TAME A TIGER (con'd from page 144)

icing within the outline and gently press the Color Flow tiger on the mounds. Dry thoroughly, then hang on the wall!

To decorate the cakes. Ice cupcakes and pipe a tube 16 zigzag border around each. Center each with a clown head.

Ice a two-layer 12" round cake and place in center of a 20" foil-covered cake board. Position the yellow Color Flow circle (made ahead) in center of cake on mounds of icing so it rises about ¼" above surface of cake. Angle a tube 19 zigzag border around the circle. Divide cake into twelfths and pipe tube 17 points all around sides of cake. Surround base of cake with tube 4B red stars and pipe a tube 16 star between each. Pipe a tube 4B star at bottom of each zigzag point.

Then pipe a tube 17 garland around top edge of cake. Drape tube 3 string and pipe twelve tube 4B stars on top of cake.

Place Color Flow tiger (made ahead) on sugar cubes on circle. Put candles in crystal candle holders and insert in cake around circle. Ring cake with cupcakes. Center your creation on the party table and light the candles. Ahhh!

ANIMAL CAKES (con'd from page 147)

cake top with icing. Outline elephant with tube 4, overpiping tail, ear, front tusk and eyes. Next, attach cookie elephants to cake sides with icing and with tube 2 pipe tails to connect elephant trunks. Edge cake with bead borders, using tube 7 for the top and tube 10 for the base. Now set out your cake for all to see the parade of elephants holding hands!

TINY TIGERS. A tray of tigers make sweet treats for circus party goers. Make faces, using the Heart Cupcake pans. For ears, cut large marshmallows to size and toothpick to cupcake face. Do the same for the mouth, using small marshmallows. Outline tiger stripes and all other features with tube 2, then fill in with tube 14 icing stars. Add white whiskers with tube 2, then "paint" on eyes, using thinned down icing and an art brush. When your cupcake tiger cubs are finished, display them on a party plate and watch them quickly do a circus disappearing act to the delight of the party guests.

CIRCUS WAGON (con'd from page 149)

decorated with tube 101 ribbon borders, tube 15 shells, ribbed "spoke" designs and rosettes, and tube 3 beading. Attach the brightly trimmed cookie "wheels" to the wagon with icing, placing them so as to conceal the stacks of sugar wafers.

Now with wagon cake and wheels in place on the iced styrofoam, attach plastic animals with dabs of icing. (Note: fill the pink elephant with some icing to prevent him from being top heavy, then trim him with thinned icing and tube 3 beading.) Hook up the prancing pony team by carefully inserting each toothpicked hoof into the styrofoam and securing it with a tiny bit of icing. Hitch up the pony team with gold-colored cord, attaching reins to elephant's trunk. The circus wagon is ready to lead a parade of eager children to the party table! What a grand and glorious way to finish off a day filled with circus fun and games!

VOLUME TWO

Celebrate!®

SEPTEMBER / OCTOBER

Decorating directions for
Patchwork Quilt Cake on page 172

Traditional Quilt Designs inspire quaint Early American Cakes

*E*ver since the seventeenth century when homes were first established in America, people have been designing and making quilts—friendship quilts, wedding quilts and even family quilts in which every patchwork is a picture block depicting a memorable family event. Now with a quaint quilt cake, you can recapture this lovely ancestral art of Early America.

Inspired by actual Early American quilt patterns, each of the quilt cakes pictured here and on the cover were decorated as close to the original patchwork designs as possible. The brilliant quilt cake featured on the cover of this CELEBRATE! issue is a copy of the "Wild Goose Chase" patchwork which was first quilted around 1830. We colorfully reproduced the diamond-shaped patchwork design which gave this quilt pattern its trademark and made it one of the most admired and treasured quilts of its time!

The star-studded quilt cake pictured on the facing page is a close copy of the "Star of Bethlehem" patchwork, first quilted around 1855. The red and blue fabric stripes and pinwheel-like stars which make up this quilt's famous patchwork pattern were reproduced in icing and sugar mold stars to create a cake coverlet as stunning as the original design.

The colorful cake quilt pictured above was patterned after the popular "Double Wedding Ring" patchwork designed around 1920. Like the rings of

Continued on page 172

Facing page: a 19th century pieced quilt is the background for Early American pewter and copper, and a cake inspired by the "Star of Bethlehem" pattern. Above: "Double Wedding Ring" cake glows before blooming marigolds.

PATTERN A CAKE WITH A

Pennsylvania Dutch Motif

As bright as the traditional designs the Pennsylvania Dutch painted on their homes, barns, dishes, cups and other housewares, a cake displays a vividly colored pattern taken from this popular American folk art. Originally from the German Rhineland, the Pennsylvania "Dutch" settled in America throughout the 17th and 18th centuries and brought with them their distinctive art style which reflects in so many homes today. And since these colorful patterns are enjoyed so much, why not display them on something else everyone enjoys—a cake!

To decorate a cake like the one above, use the Pennsylvania Dutch patterns from CELEBRATE! II Pattern book. Tape wax paper over the pattern, outline all pattern sections with tube 2 and fill in with softened Color Flow icing.

When the trims are completely dry, ice a 10" x 4" high square cake and place on a foil-covered board. Carefully peel the wax paper off the Color Flow rooster and position on top of the cake with icing. Decorate the rooster with tube 1 string lines on the wings and body and tube 3 beading. Pipe the rooster's legs and feet with tube 4 and you're ready to attach the other Color Flow patterns.

Again carefully peel the wax paper off the side trims and position a flowery design and a pair of hearts on each cake side with icing. Frame all four designs with tube 1 icing beads and all you need add are the cake borders. Edge both cake top and base with shell motion bulb borders using tube 9 and serve your Pennsylvania Dutch treat to 20 cake-eating enthusiasts! It's a sweet surprise they won't forget!

HOW TO DECORATE
A KATE GREENAWAY
PAPER DOLL CAKE

Kate Greenaway lived only one year of the twentieth century, but her delicate, flower-like portrayals of children and the delightful verses that accompany them are as fresh, appealing and popular today as they were in the days of Queen Victoria.

Miss Greenaway was born in London in 1846, the daughter of an engraver. Her art studies gave her the knowledge of costumes that lends so much charm to her drawings. She became known first for her Christmas cards, Valentines and magazine sketches, and it wasn't until later that she began illustrating books and writing verse.

Although she never married, her love for children and her perceptive understanding of their ways and feelings shine forth in all her works. Perhaps that is why they are so cherished by children, even today.

TO DECORATE CAKE

Make the doll figures first. Use the clever Paper Doll patterns from CELEBRATE! II Pattern Book to do 3 basic doll figures, 2 dresses and 2 bonnets. (Patterns for little boy dolls are included.) Cover patterns with wax paper, outline designs with tube 2 and fill in areas with softened Color Flow icing. When thoroughly dry, add features to doll faces, "c" patterns and cornelli lace to dresses, trim to bonnets and umbrellas with tube 1. Add ruffles with tube 101s. Pipe tube 225 drop flowers with tube 2 centers.

Then ice a two-layer cake baked in oval cake pans and place on foil-covered cake board, a little larger. Pat green icing on top of cake with damp sponge for "grass" effect. Attach dolls and flowers with icing, add leaves with tube 65 and "put on" doll dresses and bonnets with more icing. Next, circle top and bottom of cake with tube 103 standout ribbon garlands. Pipe bottom ribbons almost flat on cake board. Then fill with tube 20 white zigzag puffs—half ones at top, full ones at bottom. Position flowers at garland points, add a leaf under each. Serve to 12 enchanted children.

Polly's, Peg's and Poppety's
  Momma was kind and good;
She gave them each, one happy day,
  A little scarf and hood.

A bonnet for each girl she bought,
  To shield them from the sun;
They wore them in the snow and rain,
  And thought it mighty fun.

But sometimes there were naughty boys,
  Who called to them at play,
And made this rude remark–"My eye!
  Three Grannies out to-day!"
                    —KATE GREENAWAY

Delight any little girl with a Kate Greenaway cake

Now you can capture the quaint charm of Kate Greenaway drawings and the
fun of paper dolls on a cake top! Special Color Flow patterns make them easy to do.

Bow knots and dainty embroidery trim Love Song

Decorating directions on page 172

Parasols and Posies express Sweet Shower Wishes

Decorating directions on page 172

Send a good-to-eat greeting....

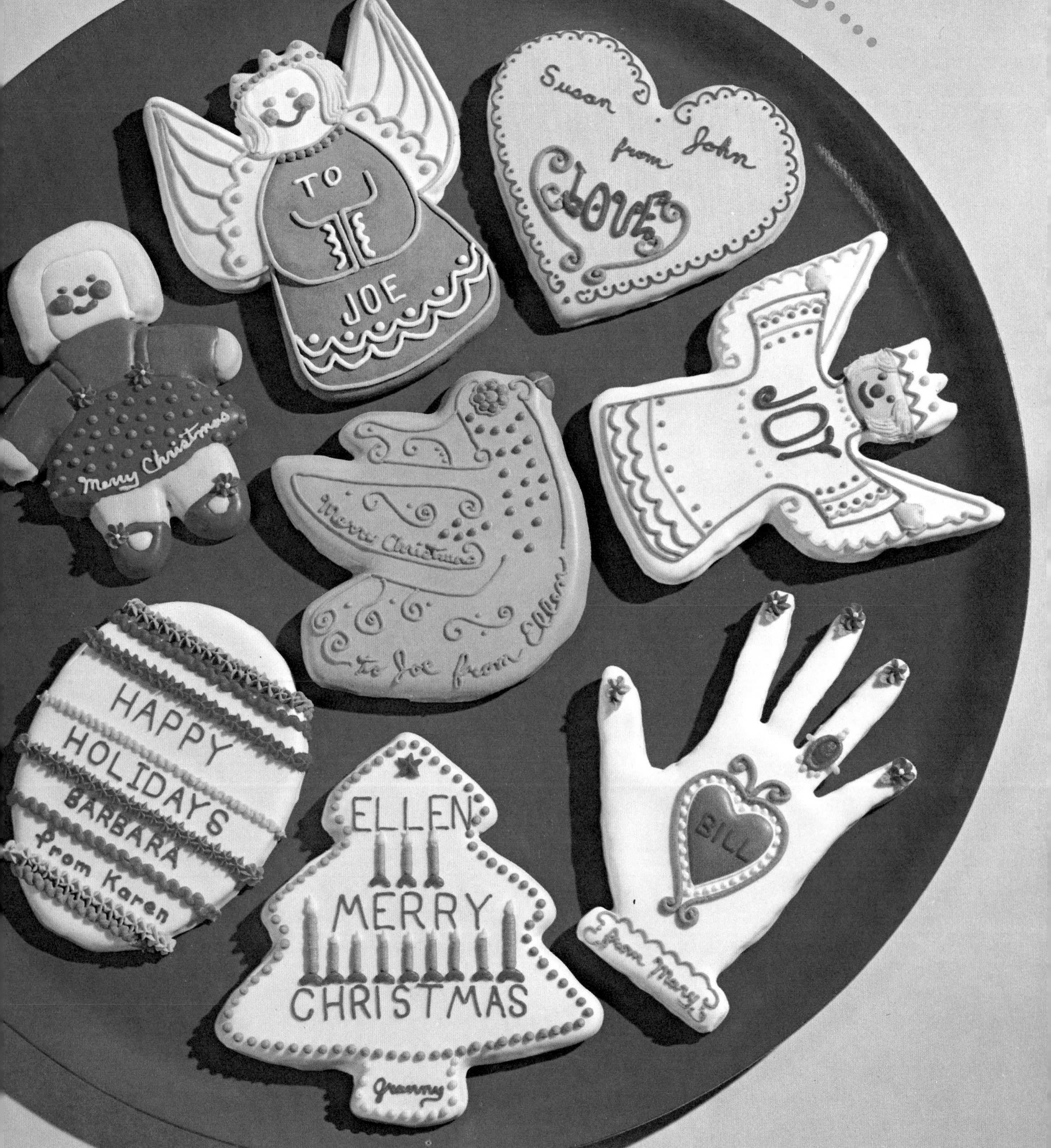

TO
JOE
Susan from John
LOVE
Merry Christmas
JOY
Merry Christmas
to Joe from Ellen
HAPPY HOLIDAYS BARBARA from Karen
ELLEN
MERRY CHRISTMAS
Granny
BILL
from Mary

Decorating directions, page 172

"Hard by a great forest dwelt a poor wood-cutter with his wife and his two children. The boy was called Hansel and the girl Gretel. Once when he could no longer procure even daily bread, he said to his wife: ". . . how are we to feed our two children?" Answered the woman, "early tomorrow morning we will take the children out to the forest . . ."

Model enchanting fairy-

Little Jack Horner
Sat in a corner,
    Eating a Christmas pie;
He put in his thumb,
    And pulled out a plum,
And said, What a good boy am I!

Little Miss Muffett
Sat on a tuffet,
    Eating her curds and whey;
There came a big spider,
    Who sat down beside her
And frightened Miss Muffet away.

Directions for all figures on following page.

tale figures from Marzipan

Marzipan is the traditional Christmas confection that's actually fun to shape—like working with modeling clay! Here CELEBRATE! shows how to fashion it into delightful figures on pages 164 and 165.

RECIPE

1 cup almond paste (8 ounce can)
2 egg whites, unbeaten
3 cups confectioners sugar
½ teaspoon vanilla or rum flavor

Knead almond paste by hand in bowl. Add egg whites, mix well. Continue kneading as you add sugar, 1 cup at a time, and flavoring, until marzipan feels like heavy pie dough. Separate dough to tint into various colors. Knead color into dough, working in one drop of liquid color at a time until desired shade is reached.

TO MODEL, PUT TOGETHER AND GLAZE

Bodies, heads, limbs and trims of figures must be modeled separately, then put together. Pinch amounts needed off tinted portions as directed for individual figures and model. This is easiest done if you hold both arms up and roll pieces between heels of hands.

To put marzipan pieces together, touch each to a sponge soaked with egg white, then fix to second piece with a turning motion. After figures are assembled, lightly brush on glaze solution (mix ½ cup corn syrup, 1 cup water, bring to boil). This gives a soft shine. For tools, you will simply need an orange stick, sharpened at one end, and a small kitchen knife with pointed blade.

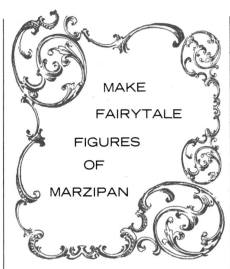

MAKE FAIRYTALE FIGURES OF MARZIPAN

bend for legs, two 1″ long cylinders for boots, a ball, 1¼″ diameter, for head, small pieces for pie (done in two parts), hands, belt, collar and hair (roll last three flat). It is best to begin with ball shape for everything, then model into cone, dome, or whatever is needed from that. Secure head, hands, pie with toothpicks. Pipe on features and buttons with tube 1.

Jack Horner, complete with pie, plum and amazed look. To measure off amounts of dough needed for various parts of figure, you must use your judgement, taking diagram and dimensions given here as a guide. You will need enough dough for a cone-shaped body, 2¼″ high and 2¼″ wide at base, two 2½″ long cylinders for arms, a single cylinder about 5″ long, ½″ thick to

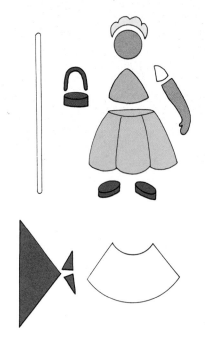

Gretel. This little lady takes the largest amount of dough. Her body is made up of two cones, one set atop the other. For larger cone, 2¼″ tall, 2¼″ wide at base, mark in folds with orange stick. Make smaller cone, 1″ high and 1½″ wide at base. Sleeves of dress are ½″ cylinders, modeled separately from arms, which are 1½″ long. Apron, babushka and hair are rolled out, and a thin cylinder of dough is used for belt. Basket is small ball, flattened, then shaped into 1″ diameter bowl with thumb. Attach string of dough for handle. Gretel's hands are cut into end of arm cylinders. Put together and glaze. Add features and trims with tube 1. Trim ornament base with drop flowers.

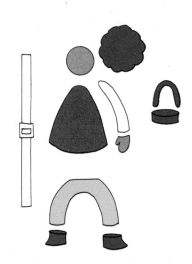

Hansel. The intrepid destroyer of witches himself. Use the largest amount of marzipan dough for his cone-shaped body, 2¼″ tall, 1¾″ wide at base, a smaller amount for the two 2″ long cylinders that form the two arms, less for curved 1½″ long cylinder that forms his legs and two 1″ long cylinders that form his boots. Use next smallest piece for his 1″ diameter ball-shaped head and remainder for hands, belt, hair and basket. Roll a rope shape for belt, then flatten. Roll hair flat, and notch. Put all together, glaze, then add other details with tube 1 and royal icing. Fill basket with brown sugar.

Miss Muffet. With curds and whey, but happily the spider is not yet beside her. For Miss M., divide marzipan dough as follows: use largest amount for cone-shaped body, 2¼″ tall, 2″ wide at base; next largest for the single 5″ long, ½″ thick cylinder that forms her legs, a slightly smaller amount for the two 2″ long cylinders that form arms and 1″ diameter ball that forms head. Use remaining amount to roll out for hair bow and shoes, and a small ball to model into 1″ wide bowl. Model all pieces and put together with egg white. Glaze, then pipe ruffle for bonnet, dress and sleeves with white icing and tube 103. Pipe tube 1 buttons, features and dots on dress. Use sugar for "curds and whey".

An Old World Treat for Christmas

Here is the recipe used by Master Pastry Chef Larry Olkiewicz for a delicious German candy called "Kirschwassertropfen". It's a very superior confection that you can make quite easily at home for an extra-special holiday treat.

These liqueur-filled chocolates were first created by the patissier of the House of Lower Saxony in the 19th century. They were such a sensation among the royalty that the recipe was soon pirated by cafés and candy shops, where they became the rage of all candy-loving Europeans, who realized they were well worth their high price. "Kirschwassertropfen" are still just as popular in Germany, still very expensive, and, because of their fragility, never exported. Truly a deluxe confection!

Here is the picture recipe of "KIRSCH-WASSERTROPFEN", the recipe used by Chef Olkiewicz. It makes about 150 pieces.

First assemble your ingredients:

13½ ounces of cubed sugar
4½ ounces of water
1½ ounces of kirschwasser, rum or brandy (or any other 80 to 90 proof liqueur)
4 or more pounds of cornstarch
1½ pounds tempered* chocolate (Chef Olkiewicz recommends fine imported milk or semi-sweet pure chocolate bars.)

Have at hand a clean soft brush, a Heart Candy Mold, a candy thermometer, square or oblong pans, and a ruler or other straight-edge. A bent fork for dipping, a small wire sieve.

Fill the pans to over-flowing with cornstarch, then draw the ruler across it so the cornstarch has a flat, smooth surface. Carefully press the Candy Mold into the cornstarch, then remove it, leaving clear heart-shaped depressions. Since this recipe makes about 150 candies, you will need sufficient surface of cornstarch to press in the mold six times. (The mold has 25 impressions.) Leave in a warm place (about 100°).

Bring the sugar and water to a boil and continue boiling for about 2 minutes until it reaches a temperature of 224°. Remove from heat, mix in the liqueur and cover with a damp cloth. (This prevents the liqueur from evaporating.) Let stand about 5 minutes, then pour into a pitcher with a very small spout. Syrup will still be hot.

Carefully pour the syrup into the heart-shaped depressions in the cornstarch, filling completely. Gently sift more cornstarch over the syrup to completely cover. Let stand in a warm place (100° to 110°) for about 4 hours. The syrup will have formed a thin, crisp crust. Then turn the candies over very carefully in the corn starch, so rounded side is up, using a fork, and let stand again in a warm place for about 4 hours.

Lift the candies out of the cornstarch carefully, and brush off the loose cornstarch with the brush. Then place each one on the bent fork, dip in tempered chocolate and lay on a wax paper-covered tray to harden. Do this very gently. Do not tap the fork on the side of the chocolate dish—this may break the delicate crust. After they are hard to the touch (in just a few minutes), place in the refrigerator for a few moments to give them a final "snap".

In the picture above, the uncoated candies are ready for chocolate dipping.

Chef Olkiewicz adds: "Hide from your friends, or they won't leave your house until they are all gone!" Another note of caution: Warn everyone to put the whole candy in his mouth at once—otherwise the delicious syrup will dribble out.

---

*How to Temper Chocolate

Heat water in bottom of a double boiler to about 175 degrees F. Remove from heat and place cut up chocolate (one cup at a time) in top half of double boiler to melt. Stir every 10 minutes until melted chocolate reaches 110 degrees F. Remove from heated water and cool until almost a stiff state. *For light chocolate,* reheat tempered chocolate to between 85 and 88 degrees. *For dark chocolate,* reheat tempered chocolate to between 90 and 92 degrees.

If chocolate becomes stiff before you are finished coating the candies, reheat very gently until it is liquid again.

Heap big fun's in store for your family tribe this fall if you decorate a cake Indian style! This time of year displays a harvest of hues and a surprise of warm weather, so what better time to plan a party and reflect on the pleasure that summer has brought, while awaiting the new season yet to come.

A TOWERING TOTEM POLE is a great offering for guests at a party powwow. Tape wax paper over Totem Pole pattern from CELEBRATE! II Pattern Book, outline with tube 2 and fill in with Color Flow. When thoroughly dry, peel off wax paper, turn over and decorate the other sides the same way. (Note: Position toothpicks at the base of the nose and the feathered headpiece before decorating the opposite sides. These toothpicks will be used to support these decorations on the cake.)

When you've completed these Color Flow trims, bake four 6″ x 3″ round cakes, icing the top and sides of one cake, and the *sides only* of the other three cakes. Place two cakes, iced on sides only, on a foil-covered board, positioning one atop the other. Insert three dowel rods into both these cakes (as shown in the diagram above), then top with a cardboard circle cut to the same diameter as cakes. Now take the third cake, with sides iced only, and cut a slit across the top center. Make this slit deep enough so you can position the center of the Color Flow wingspan, but not too deep as to sever the cake. (It would be advisable to chill the cake before slitting it.) Before inserting the Color Flow wings into the cake,

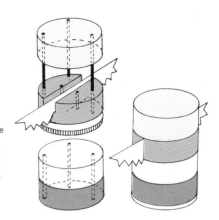

Position top cake, push in 3 dowel rods that extend into second cake below.

Insert wings into second cake before placing it on totem pole

Place cardboard circle in center of totem pole

Push 3 dowel rods into both base cakes for proper support.

wrap the center support span with clear plastic wrap so Color Flow icing does not absorb moisture from the cake and break. Carefully place wings upside down into the cake, then invert cake and position it on the totem pole. Push two dowel rods into the center of this cake, on each side of the wingspan within, as shown in the diagram above. These give added support to the decorative Color Flow wings. Finally, position the remaining cake on top of the totem pole and insert three dowel rods that extend to support the winged cake below. (See diagram above.)

Now you're ready to decorate! Pipe star designs and shell borders with tube 16, string trims with tube 3, smile with tube 7, ruffle borders with tube 104 and large beads of icing with tube 9, small beads with tube 3.

Continued on page 191

Witches ride tonight on a pumpkin-colored cake. To make, place an iced 8″ x 4″ cake on a foil-covered board, then trace a crescent moon with tube 3 and smooth in icing. Now you're ready for figure piping fun. Use tube 4 for the witch and start by squeezing out a hook-shaped nose. Pipe the chin by moving tube around in a comma-like stroke. For the forehead, begin above the nose and in one continuous motion, squeeze and move tube down to meet chin; then pipe a vertical row of overlapping tear shapes for hair. To pipe the witch's body, use tube 4 again and a heavy, even pressure to squeeze out a thick slanted torso. Squeeze out a thick icing line in the opposite direction for the thigh, then add calf and shoe. Tuck tube behind knee to squeeze out back leg and shoe. Next, tuck tube into side of torso and pipe inside arm, long broomstick strings and finally front arm. Still using tube 4, pipe short strings for broomstraw and long wavy strings for the witch's skirt. For the hat, pipe a triangle and fill in with icing; then add the brim and several long strings for flowing hair and scarf. Dot eye. Frame the cake top with tube 8 shells and the base with tube 67 leaves. Top leaves with cornstalks piping tube 5 strings, tube 67 leaves. Outline pumpkin shapes with tube 5 comma-like strokes, then fill in and add stems. Serves 10.

Bake a teacher a cake with a bright shiny apple and get the school year off to a rosy start! To decorate, use Blackboard pattern from CELEBRATE II Pattern Book. Tape wax paper over the pattern, outline each section with tube 2 and fill in with Color Flow icings. While the Color Flow decoration is drying, ice a cupcake into a round shape; then brush on tinted piping gel to give it a shiny red glow. When the apple and blackboard are done, ice an 8″ x 3″ high square cake and edge the base with a tube 18 shell border, the top with a tube 8 rope border. Pipe scallops of icing beads around the cake sides with tube 4, then add green dots between and on cake corners using the same tube and a heavier pressure.

With the cake borders piped, position the Color Flow blackboard with popsicle sticks and attach the shiny cupcake apple with icing. Trim the apple with a tube 5 stem and a tube 65 leaf, then pipe a row of rosy red icing apples around the cake base with tube 12. Top off these apples with ready-made marzipan decorator stems and leaves, or pipe your own stems with tube 2 and leaves with tube 65s. Your back-to-school set will be proud to present this cake to the teacher—in fact they may want to eat it themselves! Serves 12.

A B C's spell out fun when they're on a yummy back-to-school cake. To decorate, use School Girl pattern from CELEBRATE! II Pattern Book. Tape wax paper over the pattern and outline each section with tube 2, filling in with Color Flow icings. When your Color Flow trim is done, set it aside to dry and make the cookie numbers, letters and symbols using the Alphabet and Number Cookie Cutter Sets and a roll-out cookie dough recipe. When cookies have baked and cooled, brush on Color Flow icing and decorate with tube 3 borders, beads and tiny dot flowers. Set cookies aside to dry with Color Flow trim while you ready the cake.

For the cake, bake and ice an 10″ x 4″ high square cake and place on a foil-covered board. Carefully peel wax paper off the Color Flow school girl and position her on the cake top with icing. Next, frame the cake with bead borders using tube 11 for the base and tube 9 for the top. To finish, attach cookie letters and numbers with icing and call in the children to show them how sweet going back to school can be! This cake is a fun way to get little ones in the school spirit, and you can make the Color Flow and cookie decorations in advance to save time. Serves 20.

Witches ride tonight

170

Bake teacher a cake

A B C's spell out fun

TRADITIONAL QUILT DESIGNS (con'd)

printed fabrics which gave this pattern its name, rings of icing entwine on a cake top to capture this quaint quilt's beauty.

All of these quilt cakes are fun to make—and what better way to bring the family and close friends together than with a cake patterned after an American tradition that brought families together in fellowship years ago. So with the arrival of cool, crisp fall weather, tell your family you're spending a cozy evening at home and serve them a sweet spread you've quilted in cake!

To make the "Star of Bethlehem" quilt cake pictured on page 156, bake a 9" x 13" x 3" high sheet cake and cut it to a 9" x 12" size. Shape the stars with candy sugar molds using 2 cups granulated sugar and 4 teaspoons water. Mix ingredients by hand and pack into molds, scraping off excess sugar. Invert immediately to unmold stars and set aside to dry until hard. Next, cut a scalloped paper pattern for the cake's sides and toothpick in place so you can ice the bottom half of each side red. Remove pattern, ice remaining sides and cake top white. (Note: rough edges where icing colors meet will be covered with the decorative ruffle border.) Now trace the appropriate pattern from CELEBRATE! II Pattern Book, on the cake's top and pipe over these tracings with red and blue stripes using tube 13. When all the stripes are piped, secure a sugar mold star in each patchwork square with icing. Add the side borders next, using tube 104 to pipe a scalloped ruffle around the entire cake. Top the ruffle with alternating red/blue, blue/red ribbed scallops using tube 13. To finish, pipe a tube 21 star border around the cake's base and decorate the cake top with tube 18 white icing stars. Completed, this cake truly reflects the tradition of a treasured American art!

The "Double Wedding Ring" quilt cake, pictured on page 157, is made with a 9" x 13" x 2" high sheet cake, cut to 9" x 12". Trace the appropriate ringed pattern on the cake top with a toothpick, then overpipe the intersecting rings with tube 18 and a circular motion. At all points where four icing rings meet, pipe eight tube 21 stars; and at all points where two icing rings meet, pipe four tube 21 stars. Decorate the cake base with a tube 21 star border, then decorate your coffee table with your quilted ring cake!

Our glorious cover cake on page 155 features the dazzling **"Wild Goose Chase"** pattern in icing stars. To decorate, outline the pattern on a 12" square, 4" high cake with tube 3. Fill in all the outlined pattern sections with tube 17 icing stars, piping the stars closely together so all of the cake is colorfully covered. Edge the entire cake base with a tube 17 rosette border and another brightly quilted cake is pieced together in icing to complement coffee

and conversation.

After you've tried your hand at one of these cakes, you may want to quilt your own favorite pattern in icing! Any design you choose is sure to make a sweet spread that's as memorable as the quilt it represents!

HOW TO DECORATE PARASOL SHOWER CAKE
Shown on page 161

Parasols and posies trim an old-fashioned cake in blushing pink for the bride-to-be.

To decorate, make the frilly feminine parasols first. Use the umbrella shape from the Sweetheart Cookie Cutters to fashion rolled out cookie dough into party parasols. Bake cookies and when cool, decorate. Ice the handles pink and pipe the parasol tops with ruffles of white icing using tube 101s. Start at the base and work up, overlapping rows of ruffles. Pipe tube 2 icing bows on the parasol handles and set aside to dry.

Make lots of tiny tube 101s roses and rosebuds in advance also. When dry, attach most of the posies to florist wires with icing and decorate with tube 65s leaves. Position a rose atop each cookie parasol with icing. Ice the inside of the miniature sprinkling cans white for an opaque effect, then insert a small round piece of styrofoam into each. Push the wired flowers into the styrofoam, then tie a ribbon bow on each handle.

Bake a 10" round 2-layer cake and ice in a pretty pink. Pipe the base border first, starting with the two outer rows of icing ruffles. Use tube 102 and pipe a single row of curved ruffles about an inch out from the cake. Pipe the next ruffled row within and overlapping the first. Now to connect these borders to the cake, pipe tube 18 zigzag garlands within the rows of ruffles. (Note: the ruffled borders are piped directly on the cake board or plate; they do not touch the cake itself.) Above these frilly borders, pipe scallops of icing using tube 3 and an "i" hand motion. Finally to complete this base border, pipe tube 65s leaves in between each garland of ruffles and attach tiny made-ahead roses with icing. For the cake top, make a tiny paper heart pattern, or toothpick trace hearts freehand around the entire cake's edge. Overpipe these hearts with tube 16, then use the same tube to pipe zigzag garlands on the cake sides. Once again, as for cake base, pipe tube 65s leaves in between each garland and decorate with pink roses, attaching with icing.

Attach decorated cookie parasols around the cake with icing and arrange the sprinkling can bouquets on the cake top. Then watch the guests' delighted expressions! Serves 14.

HOW TO DECORATE "LOVE SONG"
Shown on page 160

A quaint "embroidered" sweet that's appropriate for many occasions—an anniversary celebration, a bride-to-be's shower, even an intimate wedding!

To decorate, ice and assemble 12" x 4" and 6" x 3" cakes on a foil-covered board. Use a toothpick to divide the large cake into sixteenths, and the small cake into tenths. Indicate these divisions about an inch above each of the cake bases, and about an inch in from each of the cake tops. Using the divisions as a guide, pipe a double row of zigzag garlands around both cake bases. For the large tier pipe the first garland row with tube 21, the second with tube 16, and for the small tier pipe the first garland row with tube 16, the second with tube 14. Pipe upright shells between each garland scallop, using tube 16 for the 12" tier, tube 14 for the 6" tier. With the same tubes, edge the bottom of both cakes with large and small scallops. Then drape all rippled garlands with double rows of tube 3 stringwork, tying up each garland point with dainty icing bows.

For the cake tops, use the marked divisions as a guide to pipe graceful crescents of icing around each tier. Use a circular hand motion and tube 16 for the 12" cake, tube 14 for the 6" cake. Add a rosette between each crescent of icing with tube 16.

For the delicate finishing touch, use tube 3 to pipe the "dotted swiss" icing embroidery around the sides of both cake tiers. Position a sweet songbird on top. Serves 30.

HOW TO DECORATE GINGERBREAD GREETING CARDS
Shown on pages 162, 163

Fun way to send your holiday wishes and a delicious treat at the same time! The cookie letters are an American adaptation of an old Dutch tradition. In Holland, the initials of the person who will receive the greeting are baked of pastry. We've chosen gingerbread to box and mail, or give in person. The other shapes are CELEBRATE!'s own—for cards that will never be forgotten!

To make them, follow your own ideas. Just mix up a big batch of your own favorite spicy gingerbread cookie dough. Roll out and cut out! Use letter patterns from CELEBRATE! II Pattern Book (patterns are half-size, but easy to enlarge). Cut the other Merry Christmas shapes with Really BIG Cookie Cutters. Bake, cool and paint some with softened Color Flow icing, tinted as you wish. When thoroughly dry, pipe on greetings with gay colored icings and tubes 1, 2 and 3. If you wish, pop on a drop flower here and there. Then send to your surprised and delighted friends and relations.

Celebrate!

NOVEMBER / DECEMBER

Decorating directions for
Gingerbread House on page 188

Holi day Treats

TO OUR READERS

Here are the prize-winning recipes from CELEBRATE!s 1974 Holiday Treat Contest. They've all been tested by the Culinary Arts Institute—all are delectable and well worth the effort. So pick out your favorites and treat your family and friends at Christmas time or anytime that's special.

SUGAR PLUM RING

This rich glazed coffee cake, ideal for holiday entertaining, was the winning entry of **Mrs. Frank Slater** of Sherman, Texas. It breaks into colorful, bitesize "plums."

    1 package active dry yeast or 1 small
      cake compressed yeast
    ¼ cup warm water
    ½ cup milk, scalded
    ⅓ cup sugar
    ⅓ cup shortening
    1 teaspoon salt
    3¾ to 4 cups all-purpose flour
    2 eggs, beaten
    ¾ cup sugar
    1 teaspoon ground cinnamon
    ¼ cup butter or margarine, melted
    ⅓ cup whole blanched almonds
    ½ cup red candied cherries
    ½ cup green candied cherries
    ⅓ cup dark corn syrup

1. Dissolve yeast in warm water.
2. Combine scalded milk, ⅓ cup sugar, shortening, and salt in a large bowl; stir until shortening is melted. Cool to lukewarm. Add and beat in 1 cup flour. Beat in dissolved yeast and then eggs. Beat in enough remaining flour to form a soft dough.
3. Put dough into a greased bowl and turn dough to grease top. Cover bowl. Let rise in a warm place until dough is doubled in bulk.
4. Punch down. Let rest 10 minutes.
5. Mix ¾ cup sugar and cinnamon. Divide dough into 4 portions. Cut each portion into 10 pieces and shape into balls. Coat balls with melted butter, then with cinnamon-sugar; arrange a third of balls in a well-

greased 10-inch tube pan. Sprinkle with some of almonds and both colors of cherries. Repeat with 2 more layers.
6. Mix corn syrup with any butter remaining from dipping; drizzle over top. Cover and let rise in a warm place until doubled in size.
7. Bake at 350°F 35 minutes. Cool 5 minutes; invert coffee cake on a platter.

SCHNITZ BREAD

Mrs. Donald Brause of Bucyrus, Ohio, sent us this old German recipe, now adapted to modern techniques and baked in 1-pound coffee cans. You'll like this fruity, spicy combination.

    ¾ pound prunes, pitted
    ½ pound dark raisins
    ⅔ cup dried apples
    ½ cup dried apricots
    ⅔ cup diced candied mixed fruits
    ⅔ cup chopped pecans
    ¾ teaspoon ground cinnamon
    2 packages active dry yeast
    1 cup warm potato water
    ⅓ cup mashed cooked potato
    ½ cup sugar
    1 teaspoon salt
    ⅓ cup butter or shortening, melted
    2¼ pounds (about) warm all-purpose
      flour

1. Put prunes, raisins, apples, and apricots

into a large saucepan and add water to cover. Cook, covered, until fruit is soft. Cool slightly. Stir in candied fruits, pecans, and cinnamon. Turn into a large bowl and cool to lukewarm.
2. Dissolve yeast in warm potato water.
3. Stir potato, sugar, salt, and melted butter into fruit mixture. Mix in dissolved yeast. Beat in enough flour to make stiff dough.
4. Put dough into a greased bowl large enough to allow dough to double in bulk. Cover bowl. Let rise in a warm place until dough is doubled in bulk.
5. Punch dough down. Divide in 5 equal portions. Shape into loaves and put into 5 greased 1-pound coffee cans. Cover with lids. Let rise in a warm place until dough is doubled in size.
6. Remove lids from cans. Arrange cans on low rack of oven.
7. Bake at 350°F 45 minutes. Remove loaves from cans and cool on racks.

Continued on page 176

Above: three tempting holiday cakes. Fresh Apple Cake (at top), Prune Tart (at left) and Carrot Cake.

Opposite page: holiday breads. At top, Sugar Plum Ring and Schnitz Bread. On the cutting board, Banana Bread, Mother's German Sweet Braid, and at right, Kalachy. On the blue plate, Bohemian Roll-ups, and ready to wrap for giving, the Christmas Loaf.

BANANA BREAD

Everybody loves Banana Bread, and this is an excellent one, light, moist and tender. It's the winning entry of **Mrs. Dorothy N. Garrison** of Valley Station, Kentucky, who says it keeps at least 3 months frozen.

½ cup shortening
1 cup sugar
2 eggs
3 fully ripe bananas, peeled and crushed
2 cups all-purpose flour
1 teaspoon baking soda
1 teaspoon salt
½ teaspoon ground cinnamon
½ cup chopped pecans (optional)

1. Cream shortening, sugar, and eggs thoroughly. Add bananas; beat well.
2. Blend flour, baking soda, salt, and cinnamon. Beat into banana mixture until blended. Mix in pecans (if using).
3. Divide batter equally in 2 greased and floured 9x5x3-inch loaf pans.
4. Bake at 350°F about 1 hour, or until a cake tester comes out clean. Cool slightly, then remove from pans and cool on rack.

BOHEMIAN ROLL-UPS

From **Mrs. Edward Vlk** of North Royalton, Ohio, comes this yeast bread with poppy-seed filling, a favorite with old-world Bohemian cooks. Or try date or almond filling.

1 package active dry yeast or 1 small cake compressed yeast
¼ cup warm water
¼ cup sugar
¼ cup butter or shortening
2 teaspoons salt
⅔ cup milk, heated to warm
2 eggs
4 cups (about) all-purpose flour
Prepared poppy seed, almond, or date filling (about 2 cups)
Cream

1. Dissolve yeast in warm water.
2. Put sugar, butter, salt, and milk into a large bowl; stir until butter is melted. Beat in the eggs, then the dissolved yeast. Add and beat in flour until a soft dough is formed.
3. Cover, let rise in a warm place 30 min.
4. Punch dough down and divide in half. On a lightly floured surface, roll each half into a 12-inch square. Spread with desired amount of filling. Roll up jelly-roll fashion. Seal ends and place, seam side down, on a greased cookie sheet. Brush top with cream. Cover. Let rise in a warm place until doubled in size.
5. Bake at 350°F about 25 minutes. Serve warm. Makes 2 roll-ups.

MOTHER'S GERMAN SWEET BRAID

Mrs. Adolph Carlson of Jacobson, Minnesota, sent us a well-worn family recipe translated from a German original. The basic dough can be used many ways; we baked a braid to serve with festive meals.

2 packages active dry yeast
½ cup warm water
¾ cup milk, scalded
¼ cup butter
½ cup sugar
1 teaspoon salt
2 eggs
5 cups (about) all-purpose flour

1. Dissolve yeast in warm water.
2. Combine scalded milk and butter in a bowl; stir until butter is melted. Cool to lukewarm. Mix in sugar, salt, eggs, and then yeast. Add and beat in enough flour to make a soft dough.
3. On a lightly floured surface, knead dough until smooth and elastic.
4. Put dough into a well-greased bowl and turn dough to grease top. Cover bowl. Let rise in a warm place until dough is doubled.
5. Punch dough down. Divide into 6 equal portions. On lightly floured surface, roll each portion with hands into a long roll. Braid 3 rolls together for each loaf. Tuck ends under and place loaves on greased cookie sheets.
6. Bake at 350°F about 25 minutes, or until well browned. Makes two 1¼-pound loaves.

CHRISTMAS LOAF

The Amish are famous for good food, so it's no surprise that this delectable Amish bread from **Darlene Bitner** of Mt. Pleasant, Pennsylvania, is among our winners.

2 cups milk
½ cake compressed yeast (about 1 oz.)
¼ cup warm water
3 cups all-purpose flour
1 teaspoon salt
1 cup milk
1 cup butter
1 cup sugar
3 to 5 cups all-purpose flour
½ pound raisins, chopped
½ pound currants
¼ pound citron, chopped
½ cup almonds, blanched and sliced

1. Scald 2 cups milk, pour into a large bowl, and cool to lukewarm. Crumble yeast over warm water and stir until dissolved; mix into milk. Add 3 cups flour and salt; mix well. Cover. Let stand in warm place until bubbly.
2. Scald 1 cup milk; add butter and stir until melted. When lukewarm; stir into yeast mixture along with sugar. Add and beat in enough flour to form a soft dough.
3. On a lightly floured surface, knead dough until smooth and elastic; use more flour if necessary. Combine fruits and sprinkle with some flour. Knead fruit mixture into dough.
4. Put dough into a greased large bowl and turn to grease top of dough. Cover bowl. Let rise in a warm place until dough is doubled.
5. Punch dough down. Shape into small loaves and put into greased small loaf pans (such as nine 3¾x4⅞x1½-inch Little Loafers or seven 7½x3¾x2¼-inch loaf pans). Sprinkle tops with sliced almonds. Cover pans. Let rise in a warm place until doubled.
6. Bake at 400°F 20 minutes. Remove loaves from pans and cool on racks.

KALACHY

This luscious walnut-filled coffeecake submitted by **Mrs. Walter Schultz** of Lewiston, New York, was an annual "old-country" treat in her husband's Czechoslovakian family. It makes six loaves, which freeze very well.

2 packages active dry yeast or 1 large cake compressed yeast
¼ cup lukewarm water
2 cups milk
½ cup butter
¾ cup sugar
1 teaspoon salt
6 to 7 cups all-purpose flour
2 eggs
Walnut Filling (see recipe) or a prepared filling such as poppy seed or almond

1. Dissolve yeast in lukewarm water.
2. Scald milk and pour into a large bowl. Add butter, sugar, and salt; stir until mixed. Blend in dissolved yeast. Add 3 cups flour gradually, mixing well. Add eggs and mix well. Add and beat in enough of the remaining flour to form a soft dough.
3. On a lightly floured surface, knead dough until smooth and elastic.
4. Put dough into a greased large bowl and turn dough to grease top. Cover bowl. Let rise in a warm place until dough is doubled.
5. Prepare Walnut Filling.
6. Punch dough down and divide into 6 portions. On lightly floured surface, roll each portion into a 12-inch square. Spread dough with a sixth of filling. Roll up and place, seam side down, on greased cookie sheet.
7. Bake rolls at 375°F about 20 minutes, or until browned. 6 coffee cakes.

WALNUT FILLING

1 pound walnut halves or pieces
1 package (12 ounces) vanilla wafers
½ to ¾ cup sugar
1¼ teaspoons ground cinnamon
¾ to 1 cup corn syrup
½ cup butter, melted
½ cup milk

Crush walnuts and vanilla wafers in an electric blender. Turn into a large bowl. Add sugar, cinnamon, corn syrup, butter, and milk; mix well, adding more milk, if necessary, until good consistency to spread. Makes about 5 cups.

STRAWBERRY DIVINITY

Christmas wouldn't be Christmas without candy, and CELEBRATE! received many confections as contest entries. **Mr. Richard Kelly** of Brandonville, West Virginia offered a light, luscious Strawberry Divinity.

3 cups sugar
¾ cup light corn syrup
¾ cup water
2 egg whites
1 package (3 ounces) strawberry-flavored gelatin
1 cup chopped nuts (optional)

1. Lightly butter a 9-inch square pan.
2. Combine sugar, corn syrup, and water in

a heavy 3-quart saucepan. Cook over medium heat, stirring until sugar is dissolved. Bring to boiling; if using a candy thermometer, set in place. Cook to the hard-ball stage (252°F).

3. Meanwhile, beat egg whites with electric mixer until stiff but not dry. Beat in gelatin.

4. When syrup is 252°F, pour in a thin stream over egg whites, beating constantly. Beat as long as possible; use a wooden spoon if mixture becomes too stiff for mixer. Mix in nuts (if using). Turn into buttered pan.

5. Cool until firm. Cut into 36 pieces. 2 lb.

FIVE POUND FUDGE

Holiday time or any time, fudge is a favorite.

This generous recipe comes from **Darla Anderson** of Des Moines, Iowa.

 2 packages (6 ounces each) semisweet chocolate pieces
 2 bars (8 ounces each) milk chocolate
 16 large marshmallows, quartered, or 160 miniatures
 1 cup chopped pecans
 1 tablespoon vanilla extract
 1 can (13 fluid ounces) evaporated milk
 4½ cups sugar
 ¼ cup butter

1. Combine chocolate, marshmallows, pecans, and vanilla extract in a bowl.

2. Put evaporated milk, sugar, and butter into a dutch oven. Stir and bring to a rolling boil. Cook over medium heat **exactly** 5 minutes.

3. Remove from heat and add reserved ingredients; mix well. Turn into a buttered pans. Cool. Cut into squares.

Continued on page 186

Clockwise from the top: Strawberry Divinity, Five Pound Fudge, English Walnut Toffee, Darlene's Christmas Candy, Caramel Divinity Roll, Triple Layer Delight, Holly Wreath Clusters and Peanut Brittle.

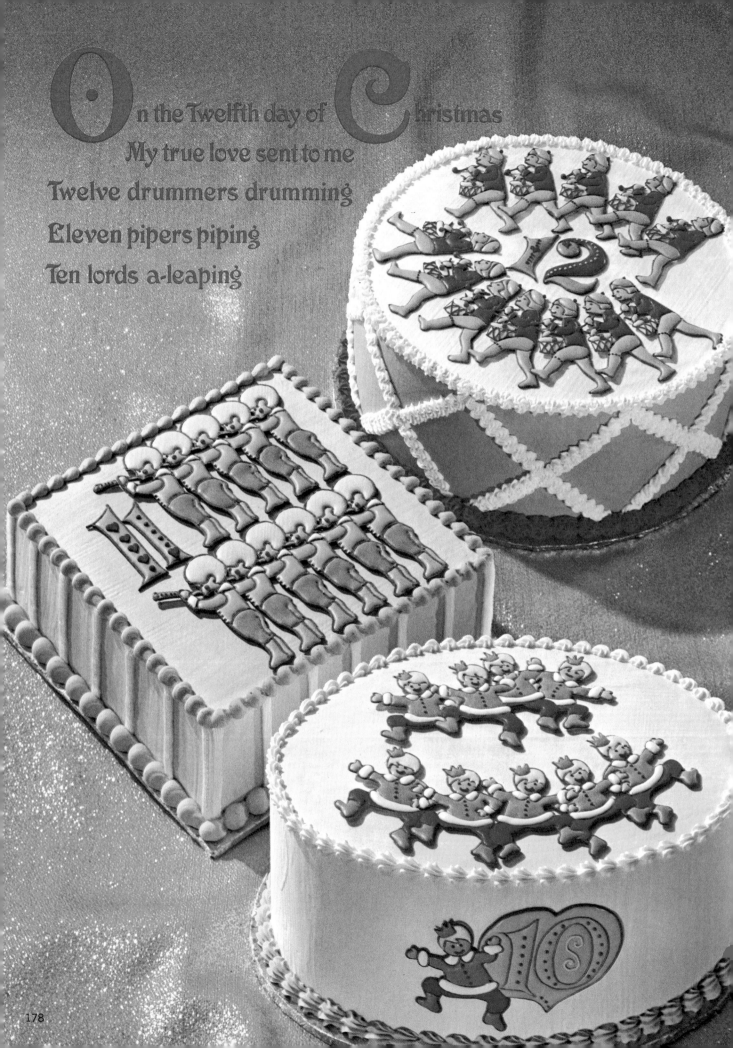

On the Twelfth day of Christmas
My true love sent to me
Twelve drummers drumming
Eleven pipers piping
Ten lords a-leaping

Nine ladies dancing
Eight maids a-milking
Seven swans a-swimming
Six geese a-laying

Decorating directions start on page 190

Five golden rings
Four colly birds
Three French hens
Two turtle doves

And a Partridge

in a Pear Tree

Make it merry,
bake it bright,
Charm a child on
Christmas night

Santa-In-The-Box Directions page 191

Santa Star Cake Directions page 189

Decorating directions on page 189

Up on the roof top,
gay and quick,
Here's our hero,
old Saint Nick

Decorating directions on page 189

Christmas elves, a sight to see,
Dance around a flowery tree

185

Decorating directions on page 189

ENGLISH WALNUT TOFFEE

The inspiration is English, the flavor is delicious, in this English Walnut Toffee from **Phyllis Brown** of Hennepin, Illinois.

   1 pound butter or margarine
   2 tablespoons water
   2 cups sugar
   ½ teaspoon salt
   2 cups finely chopped walnuts
   10 ounces milk chocolate

1. Butter a 14x10-inch pan.
2. Melt butter with water in a heavy 12-inch skillet over medium-high heat. Add sugar and salt, stirring constantly with a wooden spoon. Bring to boiling; if using a candy thermometer, set in place. Cook until the boiling mixture begins to lose its yellow color and takes a whitish look. Mix in 1 cup chopped walnuts. Continue cooking and stirring until toffee is a caramel color (298° to 300°F). Turn mixture into buttered pan and cool slightly. Mark into squares with a sharp knife. Cool.
3. Melt chocolate in a double boiler over hot, not steaming, water.
4. Spread chocolate over cooled toffee. Sprinkle with remaining walnuts. Let stand until chocolate is set. Break toffee into pieces. About 3 pounds.

DARLENE'S CHRISTMAS CANDY

Two popular products of the South, pecans and bourbon, highlight this tempting treat from **Darlene Cumba** of Seymour, Texas.

   2 pounds confectioners' sugar
   ½ cup margarine
   ½ cup bourbon
   Pecan halves
   Semisweet chocolate pieces or chocolate coating (about 12 ounces)

1. Mix confectioners' sugar and margarine in a large bowl. Add bourbon gradually, mixing until a putty-like dough is formed.
2. Work with a small portion of dough at a time. Roll dough into balls about the size of small pecans. Press each ball between two pecan halves. Set upright on a cookie sheet covered with waxed paper or aluminum foil.
3. Melt chocolate in top of a double boiler over hot, not steaming, water.
4. Dip each pecan candy ball in chocolate to coat one half. Set on the cookie sheet and let stand until chocolate is set.
5. Store in an airtight container such as coffee cans or plastic ware with tight lids. Keep cool and away from moisture. 5 to 6 dozen.

TRIPLE LAYER DELIGHTS

Bonnie Kovatch of Denver, Colorado contributed her favorite candy recipe. Stored in the refrigerator, it will keep up to a month—if it isn't devoured!

First Layer:
   ½ cup butter
   ¼ cup sugar
   ¼ cup cocoa
   1 teaspoon vanilla extract
   1 egg, slightly beaten
   2 cups graham cracker crumbs
   1 cup flaked coconut

Second Layer:
   ½ cup butter
   3 tablespoons milk
   1 package (3¾ ounces) instant vanilla pudding
   2 cups sifted confectioners' sugar

Third Layer:
   1 package (6 ounces) semisweet chocolate pieces
   2 tablespoons butter

1. For first layer, combine butter, sugar, cocoa, and vanilla extract in the top of a double boiler. Cook over simmering water, stirring occasionally, until butter is melted. Stir in egg. Continue cooking and stirring until mixture is thick, about 3 minutes. Stir in crumbs and coconut. Press into a buttered 9-inch square pan.
2. For second layer, beat butter thoroughly. Blend in milk, pudding mix, and confectioners' sugar. Beat until light and fluffy. Spread evenly over first layer. Chill until firm.
3. For third layer, melt chocolate and butter together over simmering water. Cool. Spread over chilled second layer. Chill. Cut into bars, about 2x¾ inch. About 4 dozen.

CARAMEL DIVINITY ROLL

Mrs. Clara Burchfield of Terre Haute, Indiana sent along this recipe for an old-fashioned delight, divinity covered with caramel and pecans.

   2 cups granulated sugar
   ½ cup white corn syrup
   ½ cup water
   2 egg whites
   ¼ teaspoon salt
   ½ cup red and green candied cherries (optional)
   1 14-ounce package caramels
   1 tablespoon water
   1 7-ounce package pecans, chopped

1. Combine sugar, syrup and water, and heat until boiling, stirring constantly. Reduce heat and cook to 260 degrees.
2. When syrup reaches 250 degrees, beat egg whites with salt until they peak. Beating constantly, pour syrup **very slowly** over egg whites. Beat until stiff, about 7 minutes. Stir in cherries by hand.
3. Pour candy onto a buttered cookie sheet. With buttered hands, divide it into 2 rolls. Allow to stand 1 hour.
4. Place caramels and water in top of double boiler and melt, then spread onto divinity. Roll in chopped pecans. Wrap in foil and store at room temperature. Keeps 3 or 4 days. Two 12-inch rolls.

HOLLY WREATH CLUSTERS

Here's an old family favorite from **Mrs. Dean McGrew** of Randolph, Nebraska.

   ½ cup butter or margarine
   30 large marshmallows
   ¼ teaspoon green food coloring
   4½ cups cornflakes
   Approx. ⅓ cup red cinnamon candies

1. Heat butter in saucepan; when it starts to melt, add marshmallows. Stir until marshmallows are completely melted.
2. Add coloring and stir to blend.
3. Pour in cornflakes and stir until they are coated with color.
4. Immediately drop by spoonfuls onto waxed paper.
5. Sprinkle each cluster with red cinnamon candies before coating dries. About 60 clusters.

PEANUT BRITTLE

Mae Logue of Hartville, Missouri gave us a recipe for all-time favorite Peanut Brittle.

   2 cups sugar
   1 cup light corn syrup
   ½ cup water
   2 cups raw peanuts
   1 tablespoon butter
   1 teaspoon vanilla extract
   2 teaspoons baking soda

1. Butter a large shallow pan.
2. Combine sugar, corn syrup, and water in a heavy 3-quart saucepan. Bring to boiling, stirring until sugar is dissolved. If using a candy thermometer, set in place. Cook until mixture begins to thicken (242°F), washing down crystals from sides of pan.
3. Mix in peanuts and butter. Cook until light golden brown (about 300°F).
4. Add vanilla extract and baking soda; stir quickly. Pour over bottom of buttered pan.
5. Break cooled brittle into pieces. Store in a dry container with tight lid, such as a coffee can with plastic lid. 2 pounds.

Above all, Christmas is cookie baking time, and many homemakers continue the old tradition of baking dozens of holiday cookies. Some of the best are included in our Holiday Treat contest winners.

CHOCOLATE DIAMONDS

Mrs. Shirley Lorenz of Aurora, Illinois submitted one of her family's most loved recipes, Chocolate Diamonds. They'll freeze, but hers never last long enough!

   2 squares (2 ounces) unsweetened chocolate
   ½ cup butter or margarine
   1 cup sugar
   2 eggs
   ½ cup sifted all-purpose flour
   ¼ teaspoon salt
   ½ teaspoon vanilla extract
   ⅔ cup finely chopped walnuts

1. Melt chocolate and butter together in a saucepan. Remove from heat and stir in sugar, eggs, flour, salt, and vanilla extract.
2. Spread in a Wilton 9x13-inch sheet cake pan. Sprinkle with walnuts.
3. Bake at 400°F about 15 minutes. Cool and cut into diamonds. About 4 dozen.

ITALIAN CHRISTMAS BOWS

Here's a unique Christmas cookie with an Italian heritage. Not baked, but fried, so they're crisp and light, "Nocchi" came to us from **Mrs. Dorothy Yodice** of Yonkers, N.Y.

2 eggs
10 egg yolks
2 tablespoons brandy
3 tablespoons dairy sour cream
4 cups all-purpose flour
Pinch salt
Confectioners' sugar

Fat or oil for deep frying, heated to 375°F
1. Mix eggs, egg yolks, brandy, and sour cream gently until blended. Stir flour and salt together; add egg mixture gradually, stirring constantly until blended. Cover bowl and set aside 1 hour. Work dough until holes show.
2. On a lightly floured surface, roll out a small amount of the dough at a time and cut in 3-inch strips. Make bow ties or rose buds.
3. Fry one layer at a time in deep fat until lightly browned, 2 to 3 minutes.
4. As they are fried, put into a large bowl lined with paper toweling. When cool, sprinkle generously with confectioners' sugar. Keep for weeks wrapped in foil.

TAFFY APPLE COOKIES

Linda K. Coad of Champaign, Illinois invites you to try an unusual cookie recipe that has the look and the caramel nut coating of old-fashioned Taffy apples.

1 cup plus 2 tablespoons margarine
½ cup confectioners' sugar
2 egg yolks
1 teaspoon vanilla extract
3 cups all-purpose flour
½ teaspoon salt
1½ pounds caramels
½ cup water
Finely chopped pecans (about 4 cups)

1. Beat margarine, confectioners' sugar, egg yolks, and vanilla extract. Mix flour and salt; add to creamed mixture and mix well.
2. Roll dough into little balls about ½ inch in diameter. Set on ungreased cookie sheets.
3. Bake at 350°F about 12 minutes. Remove from oven and immediately place a round toothpick in each and cool.
4. Combine caramels and water in the top of a double boiler. Heat over simmering water until caramels are melted. Stir until smooth. Dip cookie balls in caramel and allow excess to drip off. Coat with pecans and place each in a candy wrapper. About 12 dozen.

MERRY CHRISTMAS COOKIES

Chock-full of fruits and nuts, these colorful cookies make attractive gifts at holiday time. **Mrs. Glenna R. Thomas** of Fort Bragg, California got this recipe from another Navy wife 18 years ago, bakes them every year.

1 cup butter, softened
1 cup firmly packed dark brown sugar
3 eggs
3 cups sifted all-purpose flour

1 teaspoon baking soda
1 teaspoon ground cinnamon
½ cup milk
2 tablespoons sherry
7 cups chopped walnuts
1 cup chopped candied pineapple
2 cups candied cherries (1 cup red and 1 cup green), chopped
2 cups chopped dates
¾ pound golden raisins
Candied cherries for decoration

1. Cream butter and brown sugar. Add eggs, one at a time, beating well after each.
2. Sift flour, baking soda, and cinnamon together; alternately add with milk to cream mixture, beating until blended after each addition. Mix in sherry, walnuts, fruits.
3. Drop by teaspoonfuls onto greased cookie sheets. Trim with candied cherries.
4. Bake at 300°F about 20 minutes. Cool cookies on racks. About 14 dozen cookies.

DREAM CHEESE CAKES

Your smallest muffin tins help turn out tiny cream cheese tarts that **Mabel Crown** of Rockville, Maryland submitted. You'll like their delicate cheesecake flavor.

Filling:
3 8-oz. packages cream cheese
1½ teaspoons vanilla extract
1 cup sugar
5 eggs

Topping:
1 pint dairy sour cream
¼ cup sugar
1 teaspoon vanilla extract
Red and green candied cherries

1. Line 1½-inch muffin pan wells with fluted paper cups.
2. For filling, cream the cheese with vanilla extract. Add sugar and eggs; beat well.

Spoon about 1 tablespoon mixture into each paper cup.
3. Bake at 350°F about 20 minutes, or until top cracks slightly.
4. Meanwhile, for topping, combine sour cream, sugar, and vanilla extract; mix well.
5. Spoon a small amount of topping onto each cake. Bake 5 minutes. Cool on racks.
6. Decorate with cherries. Refrigerate until ready to serve. 6½ to 7 dozen cakes.

CARROT CAKE

From **Mrs. James Swanson** of Royal Oak, Michigan comes a moist, flavorful Carrot Cake studded with nuts and dates or raisins. Bake several loaves for gifts or freezing.

2 cups sifted all-purpose flour
2 cups sugar
1 teaspoon salt
2 teaspoons baking soda
2 teaspoons ground cinnamon
1½ cups cooking oil
4 eggs
3 cups shredded carrots (easiest to shred in an electric blender)
1 cup chopped pecans
1 cup raisins or cut dates

1. Sift flour, sugar, salt, baking soda, and cinnamon into a large mixer bowl. Add oil and eggs. Blend on low speed, then beat at medium speed 2 minutes. Stir in carrots, pecans, and raisins.
2. Divide equally in 2 greased and floured 9x5x3-inch loaf pans.
3. Bake at 350°F about 1 hour.

Continued on page 188

Top left, Chocolate Diamonds and Merry Christmas Cookies; top right, Italian Christmas Bows and Taffy Apple Cookies; bottom, Dream Cheese Cakes.

FRESH APPLE CAKE

As a change from the usual fruit cake, **Mrs. Roland J. Latimer** of Waterbury, Connecticut, bakes a spicy Fresh Apple Cake.

1¼ cups oil
2 cups sugar
3 eggs
1 teaspoon vanilla extract
3 cups all-purpose flour
1 teaspoon baking soda
1 teaspoon ground cinnamon
1 teaspoon ground nutmeg
4½ cups chopped pared apples (5 medium)
1 cup chopped walnuts or pecans
1 cup raisins

1. Combine oil, sugar, eggs, and vanilla extract in a large mixer bowl. Beat at medium speed 3 minutes.
2. Blend flour, baking soda, cinnamon, and nutmeg. Add to oil mixture and mix well. Add apples, walnuts, and raisins.
3. Spoon into a lightly greased Wilton 11-inch ring-shaped mold.
4. Bake at 350°F 1 hour and 5 minutes, or until cake tester comes out clean. Cool slightly. Remove cake from pan and cool completely on rack.

PRUNE TART

Mrs. Carole MacKinnon of Fairview Park, Ohio, passed along this traditional German recipe she received from her mother.

Filling (see recipe)
3 cups all-purpose flour
1 cup sugar
1 teaspoon baking powder
¼ teaspoon salt
1 cup unsalted butter
1 egg
3 egg yolks
Juice and grated peel of ½ lemon
1 cup finely chopped walnuts

1. Prepare filling.
2. Mix flour, sugar, baking powder, and salt in a bowl. Cut in butter with pastry blender or two knives as for pastry. Add egg, egg yolks, and lemon juice and peel. Mix with a fork until a dough is formed.
3. Divide dough so one portion is enough to cover just the bottom of a 13 x 9-inch pan. Press dough into pan. On a lightly floured surface, use hands to roll remaining dough into round strips.
4. Spoon filling into pan over dough. Sprinkle with walnuts. Make a crisscross effect with the strips on top of filling.
5. Bake at 350°F until golden brown.
6. Cool. To serve, cut into triangular pieces.

FILLING

2 pounds dried prunes, rinsed
Juice and grated peel of ½ lemon
1 cup strawberry or raspberry jam

Cook prunes until soft in water in a covered saucepan. Cool prunes, remove and discard pits, cut into halves, and force through a food mill. Mix in lemon juice, peel, and jam.

A FAIRYTALE CHRISTMAS CENTERPIECE
Shown on page 173

The enchanting Gingerbread House on our cover was created especially for this holiday issue of CELEBRATE! by Larry Olkiewicz, CELEBRATE'S pastry consultant.

Making a candy-bedecked Gingerbread House is one of the most delightful Christmas customs throughout Germany, Austria and much of Switzerland. Origins of this tradition go back to the early 1800's, when the fairy tales of the brothers Grimm first popularized Hansel and Gretel and the Gingerbread House in the forest. Many authors and composers used the theme in plays, songs, even operas, and the charming edible cottage became a vital part of the holiday celebration in most German homes. Even now, many families feel that Christmas wouldn't be Christmas without it!

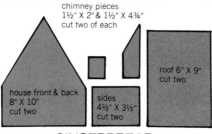

GINGERBREAD

Make two recipes of this dough, one for the house pieces and the other for the 14" circle that forms the base.

8 ounces sugar
pinch of salt
1½ pounds honey
3½ ounces lard
2¼ pounds flour
½ pound coarsely chopped almonds
½ teaspoon gingerbread spice
3 teaspoons cinnamon
2 eggs
3 teaspoons water
1 ounce baking soda

Mix sugar, salt, honey and lard in a saucepan and heat until blended (about 110-115 degrees); do not allow it to boil. Remove from heat and cool in the refrigerator. Place flour, almonds and spices in large mixing bowl. Make a well in center of flour and pour in honey mixture, eggs, and baking soda dissolved in water. Mix together well, working flour from outside into center. Knead dough lightly, then let it rest in refrigerator at least 2 hours.

Make paper patterns for the house pieces, enlarging the diagram shown here. Cut a 14" circle for the base pattern. Use Gingerbread Cutters, 5" high, for the boy and girl, or sketch your own figures to that height.

Roll out dough on lightly floured board and cut out pieces with a sharp knife. For shingles, cut rectangles about 1¼" by ¾"; for fence, you need two long strips, about 6" by ½", and at least 15 slender strips about 2" long for pickets. Make extras as they are apt to break. Logs are also about 2" long, and

slightly thicker. The basic dough recipe will make enough for the house, boy and girl, and the fence. Use second batch for the circular base, and for extra fencing, small heart and star cookies to use in decorating, and extra boy and girl figures. You will need a 14" cardboard circle to support the completed house. To transfer the walls and roof to buttered jelly-roll pans dusted with flour, take a cardboard circle larger than the piece of dough and dust it with a little flour. Lift edge of dough with spatula, slide cardboard under it, then slide it gently into the pan. Leave space between pieces, as gingerbread will spread during baking. Bake the circular base on a large, upside-down tier cake pan, buttered and floured. Bake in a 375-400 degree oven for about 25-30 minutes, or until firm and lightly browned. After 20 minutes of baking, check to make sure it is not too brown, and remove if done.

Assemble the house using royal icing to hold the parts together securely. Place gingerbread circle base on cardboard circle, attaching with dots of icing. To support walls while you work, set one or two clean, empty, #2 cans on the base. First, pipe royal icing around the sides and back wall, and put these together, allowing time for each piece to set firmly. Make the door and windows before putting up the front wall. Cut the openings with a very sharp knife. Place a cellophane square behind each window, attaching with dots of royal icing. Remove the cans from inside, then attach the front wall with royal icing. Let it dry well. To prepare roof, place both sections upside-down on work table, and pipe royal icing around all sides. Join top seams together, then pick up the complete roof, using both hands, and invert it over the wall opening. Hold it in place for about 5 minutes until you feel that it has set enough not to slide off. Have two coffee cups or small cans close by, so you can slide these under the ends of the roof when you let go; they should support it for at least 30 minutes. When the roof is firmly set, put on the chimney.

Now to decorate! Spread the roof with icing, letting some hang down like "icicles." Trim the eaves with shingles, each centered with an almond and frosted with "snow". Candy decorations, all attached with royal icing, can be as varied as you like; make your own marzipan fruits, buy them, or buy colorful fruit candies. Pebble candies for the "yard" may be bought or made from marzipan. Frost hearts and stars with royal icing and sprinkle with colored sugar and nonpareils. Hansel and Gretel are piped with royal icing. Don't forget a cap of snow on each fence picket! Finish with bulbs of icing piped all around the base with tube 7.

This charming Gingerbread House centerpiece will keep its beauty for years if you can restrain the family from nibbling at it. Do not freeze or refrigerate, as moisture will loosen trim. Simply cover in airtight plastic wrap or a plastic bag and store in a cool dry place for many happy Christmases ahead.

HOW TO DECORATE THE CHRISTMAS ELF CENTERPIECE
Shown on page 185

Make Christmas merry with a treat of a tree and six elfin sweets. They're so much fun to make! Use the Christmas Tree Kit which includes a 3-d pan for baking a stand-up cake and a lacy plastic tree-cake base. First "paint" the cake with softened green icing. Then, pipe plenty of bright drop flowers with tube 193. Dot flower centers with tube 1. When dry, attach to tree cake with icing. Trim all these flowers and cover the rest of the cake with icing leaves using tubes 67 and 69. To complete, attach a few more drop flowers to the cake base with icing and again decorate with tube 67 leaves. Now light up the tree top by propping a thin wax taper candle with tube 67 leaves.

To make the merry band of elves, bake cakes in the Small Wonder Mold Pan and ice in assorted colors. Add "fur" borders with tube 7, "feet" with tube 9. Figure pipe the arms with tube 12. Use standard size marshmallows "painted" with softened icing for the heads and attach to cakes with icing. Next, pipe the fluffy "beards" with star tube 13 by pulling icing out into peaks. Add the eyes, noses and mouths with tube 1; then figure pipe caps with tube 4B and decorate with tassels and "fur" trim using tube 7. For the sweet touch, attach candy canes with icing and pipe the elves' hands with tube 7 for additional candy cane supports. When you finish all these treats have a jolly holiday party and serve your sweet elves to six lucky children, while you slice the cake for other guests. Tree cake serves 12.

HOW TO MAKE THE HOLIDAY CAKE HOUSE
Shown on page 184

What a spectacular for Christmas morning—guaranteed to thrill all the little Santa-watchers at your house. And you don't need to be a master builder to put it together. It takes just five 5″ square cakes and very simple decorating techniques to complete.

Do as much as you can ahead. For windows and doors, draw patterns yourself. Do a ¾″ diameter circle and a 1½″ high heart for the smaller windows, a 2½″ square for larger windows (allowing ½″ shutter at either side) and a 1¾″ high, 1¼″ wide rectangle for door. Cover patterns with wax paper, outline with tube 2 and fill in with softened Color Flow icing. Make drop flowers for Christmas wreath at same time, using tube 225 and gay tints of royal icing. Pipe trees and bushes with tube 74, piping trees on a Tree-Former cone, bushes on standard marshmallows. Reserve all until day before party.

To "build" house, bake five cakes in 5″ square cake pans. After baking, chill and cut as shown on diagram given on this page. For base of house, fill and frost two cakes

together, one atop the other. Push in 3 dowel rods to support "roof". For roof, cut two cakes in half diagonally, line up 3 of the resulting cake triangles side-by-side, ice together and push a dowel rod through sides to add extra support. Set on a cardboard cut to fit and ice blue on top, red at each end.

Next, prepare front door section by cutting one cake into four even squares. Ice one square to match base of house, then secure to front of house with icing. Push a couple of dowel rods in to support its roof. For roof, cut another square in half diagonally and place one of the resulting cake triangles on a cardboard cut to fit. Ice top blue, front red and place atop door square. For chimney, take the third square and cut a wedge into one end to fit on roof of house. Ice it gold, place in position and mark in bricks with a toothpick.

Now assemble house on a styrofoam base, 12″ square and 1″ high. Swirl white boiled icing on base and roof tops for snow effect. Attach windows and doors with dots of icing and add tube 2 lines and dots to windows and doors, scrolls, drapes and dots to house and roof. Pipe balls on roof with tube 6 and add sprig of holly over front door with tube 66. (Pull out tiny points on leaves with toothpick while icing is still wet.) Draw a 1½″ diameter circle with toothpick and attach drop flowers with dots of icing to make the wreath. Add tiny leaves with tube 65s.

With house complete, you're ready to pop Santa into the chimney! Figure-pipe him with boiled icing as follows. Use tube 12 and maximum pressure to squeeze out his jolly pear-shaped body directly on chimney top. Start at base and work up, gradually easing pressure as you reach top. Add head with same tube, piping a ball shape and pausing momentarily to puff out cheeks. Pipe Santa's stocking cap with tube 12 again, using reverse shell motion to pull it to one side. Add features, hair, beard and fur trim with tube 1, using swirly motion for beard. Push toothpick into body at right shoulder to support waving arm. Push opening of tube 12 into pick and squeeze out arm with even pressure. Repeat for other arm but do not use toothpick. Just poke tube into body and pull out. Add mittens with tube 6, doing thumbs with separate motion. Do leg with tube 12, tucking it into base of body and pulling it out over chimney. Finish with an outward twist for foot. Add flat belt with tube 46. Wind polka dot ribbon around base and your masterpiece is ready to display!

HOW TO MAKE TOY-BOX ORNAMENTS
Shown on page 183

Jolly icing ornaments that look as if they popped right out of Santa's pack onto the Christmas tree! Child's play to make with ordinary royal icing and the Ornament patterns from CELEBRATE! II Pattern Book. Just tape wax paper or clear plastic wrap

smoothly over each pattern and fill in design as described. (Pipe everything very close together, so design will not "fall apart" after drying.)

First pipe face areas by forming a ball with tube 10. Add ears to elves with tube 2. Do the ribbon on the seated elf's gift package with tube 2 and smooth with a damp brush. Let faces and ribbon dry before completing ornaments.

Use tube 14 to pipe all stars, Santa beards, muff and fur trim and the rocking horse's mane and tail. With tube 101s, pipe ruffles on clown's costume. With tube 1, pipe eyes, noses, smiles and rosy cheeks. And use tube 2 to add locks of hair to elves and Santa. Use same tube for soldier's hat plume, trim and epaulets and horse's blanket trim and halter. Pipe Christmas tree held by larger Santa with tube 74, pulling out each "branch" separately.

Let all designs dry completely, then turn over. Place wire hanging loop at top of each and overpipe back same as front. Let dry again, then string top loops with golden cord and hang on the tree for the merriest, most talked-about ornaments ever! Ornaments are 4″ high (horse) to 6″ high (soldier).

HOW TO MAKE A SANTA STAR CAKE
Shown on page 182

Everybody's favorite Christmas visitor does a happy dance on this star-shaped cake while toys cavort around the sides. Perfect for Christmas parties and it couldn't be easier.

You'll need the Santa and Toy patterns from CELEBRATE! II Pattern Book. Cover patterns with wax paper, outline with tube 2 and fill in with softened Color Flow icing. Dry thoroughly and reserve while you prepare cake.

Bake a two layer cake in a pair of star pans, using a single mix. Fill and ice with snowy white buttercream, then place on a foil-covered star base, cut slightly larger. Edge with white stars at top and green stars at bottom, using tube 19 for both. Attach toys to sides, slanting this way and that, with dots of icing. Your Santa pattern comes in sections—legs, arms, body and head. Experiment with positions first, and mark where everything will go on cake top with a toothpick. Position legs first, then arms. Add body on a mound of icing to raise it off surface, then head on a slightly higher mound. This will give Santa a dimensional look and he'll really appear to be dancing! Serves 12 happy children.

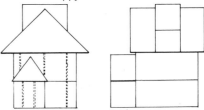

HOW TO DECORATE
THE 12 DAYS OF CHRISTMAS
Shown on pages 178-181

Now you can celebrate the twelve days of Christmas with cakes little to large in tune with the season. Each cake makes a very special family dessert or a thoughtful gift when holiday visiting with friends. All twelve cakes make a marvelous display on the dessert table for a really big party. Patterns for each are included in the CELEBRATE! II Pattern Book.

To reproduce each decorative Color Flow Christmas trim, tape wax paper over the pattern you wish to make, outline the areas with tube 1, then fill in with softened Color Flow icing. Let the trims dry overnight and when the cake is ready for decorating carefully peel the design off the wax paper backing and attach it to the cake top or sides with icing. Be sure to mound the icing slightly so attached Color Flow decorations are raised for a three dimensional effect. Now all you need to add are borders, (see decorating specifics for each cake below), and you're set to serve up a song of Christmas!

On the first day of Christmas, my true love sent to me a partridge in a pear tree. To decorate this 6″ x 3″ square cake, make all the Color Flow designs first—the pear tree, the partridge, the number ones and the sixteen half-hearts. Dry thoroughly. When the Color Flow pieces are dry, add the bird's features and all scrollwork and beading with tube 1. Pipe the tiny heart trims with tube 1 also, and attach a tube 16 drop flower to each Color Flow heart with icing. Position the Color Flow designs on the cake and add tube 1 beading to the cake corners where Color Flow hearts meet. Finish the cake with tube 6 bulb borders. Serves 8.

On the second day of Christmas, my true love sent to me, two turtle doves. To make the pretty designs that grace this 6″ round, 3″ high cake, outline and fill in Color Flow patterns for doves, cage top and bottom, and three numbers. To be sure numbers fit curved side of cake, tape pattern to side of cake pan, then outline, fill in and let dry in position. When Color Flow pieces are completely dry, add tiny hearts with tube 2, dots and scrolls with tube 1. So that bird-and-cage pieces will fit properly, mark an outline on cake top with toothpick, using original pattern as a guide. Then position top and bottom of cage on cake, securing with dots of icing. Pipe tube 2 string lines for cage "bars" and stringwork drapes above and below them. Then working carefully, so not to break strings, pipe two small mounds of icing within middle of cage and attach Color Flow birds. Position numbers on sides of cake with dots of icing, and add scrolls with tube 1, hearts with tube 2. Do star borders with tube 16. Use tube 2 again to drape a string beneath each number and tube 16 to pipe a star at ends of strings. Then, with tube 103, swing swag drapes about 2″ long all around cake

between numbers. Serves 8.

On the third day of Christmas, my true love sent to me, three French hens. To make the Color Flow hens and four numbers that decorate the 6″ x 3″ petal shaped cake, outline and fill in patterns as directed. Tape patterns for number on curved side of cake pan, then fill in and dry in position, so that numbers will fit curves of cake. When Color Flow pieces are dry, add dots, ring-and-dot eyes, comb and wattles to hens and dots to numbers with tube 1. Then, with tube 15, pipe cake borders, curving "C" scrolls at every petal of cake top and pressing out French fleur-de-lis between them. Edge bottom of cake with tiny shells, using same tube. Then position hens and numbers on cake and pipe tiny hearts next to numbers with tube 2. Serves 6.

On the fourth day of Christmas, my true love sent to me, four colly birds. The cake is baked in the diamond shape of the Grand Slam pans, or you can cut an 8″ wide diamond from a sheet cake layer. To make the fluttering Color Flow birds and number-decked hearts, outline and fill in patterns. When Color Flow pieces are dry, pipe dots on hearts and eyes and dots on birds with tube 1. At same time, pipe a number of tiny drop flowers, using tube 225 and pastel-tinted royal icing. Attach Color Flow hearts to top of cake first, then arrange birds in a circle around them. Pipe a neat shell border around base with tube 16 and use same tube to pipe a pair of free-hand scrolls on each side. Pipe small mounds of icing within scrolls and attach tiny drop flowers, adding leaves with tube 65s. Add a single flower and leaf to each heart at top. Serves 4.

On the fifth day of Christmas, my true love sent to me, five golden rings. First make the shining Color Flow ring design and the numbers that circle the 6″ round, 3″ high cake. Outline and fill in patterns, making sure to tape patterns for numbers to side of cake pan first, so resulting designs will fit curve of cake. When Color Flow pieces are dry, add dots with tube 1, tiny hearts to numbers with tube 2. Ice cake and position Color Flow ring design to top, numbers to cake sides. Complete cake with tube 9 bead borders. Serves 8.

On the sixth day of Christmas, my true love sent to me, six geese a-laying. As before, prepare the Color Flow designs first—the gaggle of geese on their nests and four numbers in heart plaques. Outline and fill in patterns, taping number plaques to sides first so they'll fit the sides of 6″ high, 2″ deep heart-shaped cake. (We used the heart shape from the Grand Slam pan set.) When Color Flow pieces are dry, add dot eyes to geese, tiny curves to nest, and dots to number plaques with tube 1. At the same time, pipe lots of tiny drop flowers with tube 16 and pastel tinted royal icing. Ice cake and secure Color Flow geese to top, hearts to

sides. Border bottom of cake with drop flowers and place more drop flowers on garland shaped mounds of icing at top. Add tiny leaves with tube 65s. Serves 5.

On the seventh day of Christmas, my true love sent to me, seven swans a-swimming. To decorate 8″ long, 4″ wide, 4″ deep cake (half of cake baked in Long Loaf Pan), first prepare Color Flow swans and heart-and-number plaques. Outline and fill in patterns. When all Color Flow pieces are dry, add scrolls and dots to number plaques, dots for eyes to swans with tube 1. When cake is iced, position swans on top and number plaques on sides and ends about 1½″ above base of cake. Pipe a border of tube 16 shells and with same tube, curve "C" scrolls—a pair at each corner, facing opposite ways, horizontal and vertical ones above these on sides, a long horizontal one at either end joined to base border with a single standing shell. Serves 8.

On the eighth day of Christmas, my true love sent to me, eight maids a-milking. The cake is baked in 8″ round pans, 2 layers, then a curve is cut off to create a crescent shape. To decorate, first make Color Flow designs—the eight little maids, milk pails and all, and one number-and-heart plaque. Outline and fill in, making sure to tape number pattern to side of cake pan first so that completed design will fit curve of cake. When Color Flow designs are dry, add dot eyes and tiny curved mouths to maids, and dots to number with tube 1. Pipe tiny red hearts on number plaque with tube 2. Then simply position Color Flow design on top and side complete cake with regular shells at base, reverse shells at top, both piped with tube 16. Serves 8.

On the ninth day of Christmas, my true love sent to me, nine ladies dancing. To decorate the 10″ round, 4″ high cake, first make Color Flow designs—three groups of dancing ladies and the heart they dance around and six number "9" plaques for sides of cake. Outline and fill in, making sure to tape number plaque patterns to sides of cake pan first, so finished designs will fit curve of cake. When Color Flow designs are dry, add features to faces, beads and dots to dresses of ladies and dots to center heart with tube 1. Add dots to side number plaques with tube 1 again and tiny hearts with tube 2. Next, ice cake and secure designs to top and sides. Pipe rosette borders—using tube 21 at bottom, and tube 18 at top. Finish with tube 18 fleur-de-lis between side plaques. Serves 14.

On the tenth day of Christmas my true love sent to me ten lords a-leaping—and what a merry troop on a 9″ oval cake! After you made all the Color Flow lords and numbered hearts; add all the eyes, noses, mouths, buttons, beading and scrollwork with tube 1. Position the Color Flow decorations on the cake top and sides; then pipe the shell borders using tube 16 for the base and tube 14 for the top. Serves 12.

On the eleventh day of Christmas my true love sent to me eleven pipers piping. And here they all are—a parade of pipers on an 8" x 4" cake square! Make all the Color Flow designs and when dry, pipe the faces, uniform trim, instrument details and tiny hearts with tube 1. Position the piper parade on the cake top, then add the ribbed stripes to the cake sides with tube 47. Complete the cake with bulb borders using tube 9 for the base and tube 7 for the top. Serves 12.

On the twelfth day of Christmas my true love sent to me twelve drummers drumming. The grand finale to the twelve days of Christmas rings the top of a 10"x4" cake. After making the twelve Color Flow drummers and number trim, pipe all the beading, stringwork, tiny hearts and faces with tube 1. Now position the number first, then attach the drummers one by one with toes and legs overlapping as shown. When drummers are in place, pipe their drumsticks with tube 2; then decorate the sides of the cake in a drumlike style by piping zigzag stripes with tube 17. Use this same tube to pipe the cake's top rosette border and tube 21 to pipe the bottom rosette border. Set out this cake to serve 14 and the happy recipients will want to sing out the Twelve Days of Christmas in praise of your decorative talents!

HOW TO MAKE A SANTA-IN-THE-BOX
Shown on page 182

All gingerbread and icing and fabulous fun! A happy surprise for Christmas eve or morning and not difficult at all for you to make. You'll need patterns for the cookie Santa and the Color Flow Box from the CELEBRATE! II Pattern Book. To make the box itself, just draw a 4" square pattern of your own. Mix your favorite gingerbread dough or use the gingerbread recipe on page 188. Just be sure dough will produce a good, stiff gingerbread. Roll it out to ¼" thickness and cut out one Santa pattern and 6 squares. Bake, cool and reserve. (Gingerbread pieces will spread out while baking to become slightly larger, but they will remain in proportion to one another.) For side trims, cover patterns with wax paper, outline with tube 2 and fill in with softened Color Flow icing. Dry thoroughly and reserve.

With cookie Santa, box sections and side trim ready, begin your masterpiece. First put box together with melted sugar. Keep it heating as you work, as melted sugar hardens the minute it cools. So work next to the stove and be careful—melted sugar is hot! Place one cup of sugar in a heavy skillet over low heat. Stir occasionally until it starts to melt. When it is a clear liquid, begin "gluing" box together. (Liquid will begin to carmelize and turn golden after awhile, but this won't make any difference.)

Place a gingerbread square on a 7" square foil-covered board for bottom of box. Dip edge of one side square in melted sugar and set against bottom square. Hold upright 30 seconds until sugar hardens. Repeat with second side, placing it opposite first. Then dip three sides of the back square and set it in place, pressing just the inside edges together to leave a space for side borders later. Repeat with the front square. Dip bottom of box top and attach at a slight slant to back side of box. When sugar has hardened, add additional support for box top by piping a mound of icing at base of it and pushing in three popsicle sticks. Let sticks stand against back of box on foil-covered base.

Now you are ready to decorate Santa and box. Paint on the jolly old saint's hat, suit, gloves, eyebrows and whites of eyes with softened Color Flow icing and let dry. Then pipe his rosy cheeks and cherry nose with tube 7, his mouth and pupils with tube 3, his mustache and beard with tube 16 and a reverse shell motion. Set him aside while you trim box. First attach Color Flow trees and stars with dabs of icing and add string lines, dots and garlands with tube 3. Print Merry Christmas on lid with same tube. Then edge box and lid with tube 21 shells.

Now pop Santa in the box! Stand him upright and stuff standard marshmallows in box all around him to keep him in place. Surround him with peppermint candy and candy canes. Then sit back and enjoy the excitement when the children see him.

INDIAN SUMMER
continued from page 169

Push in toothpicked nose and feathery headdress and treat a tribe of cake lovers!

A COLOR FLOW CHIEF is a topper for Indian Summer! To make, tape wax paper over Chief pattern from CELEBRATE! II Pattern Book, outline each section with tube 2 and fill in with Color Flow icings. When Color Flow chief is dry, carefully peel off wax paper and place on an iced 8" x 8" x 3" square cake. Decorate with rosette borders using tubes 17 for the base, 16 for the top and sides. All complete, serve your chief cake and celebrate!

Here's a festive snack that can be prepared in a jiffy—and pleases everyone!

Party Rounds

2/3 cup grated Parmesan cheese
1½ cups mayonnaise
3 tablespoons finely chopped onion
2 pinches oregano
Dash of Worcestershire sauce, garlic salt, pepper and seasoned salt to taste.

Mix all the ingredients and spread on thin slices of cocktail rye bread. Place on cookie sheet, broil until golden brown. Serve hot

---

A Classic Dessert

FRESH PUMPKIN PIE

Anyone who has ever eaten a pie made with fresh pumpkin will never be content with one made with the canned variety. Sure to draw applause at this year's Thanksgiving table!

Pie Crust

2 cups sifted flour
1 teaspoon salt
¼ cup ice water
1 cup vegetable shortening

Mix the flour with the salt and sift into a large bowl. Cut two thirds of the shortening into the flour with a pastry blender till it is the consistency of corn meal. Cut the remaining third of the shortening until the particles are the size of large peas. Sprinkle with water and blend lightly with a fork until it just holds together in a ball. Wrap in wax paper and chill for half an hour or more. (It will keep nicely for days in the refrigerator.)

Roll the chilled dough between sheets of waxed paper, lifting the rolling pin at the end of each stroke. Trim it in a circle one inch larger than the pan. Fold in half and lay the fold across the center of the pan. Then unfold. Fit it loosely into the pan, and make a crimped edge with your thumb and forefinger for a one-crust pie. This will make two 9" one-crust pies or one 9" two-crust pie.

Pumpkin Filling

¾ cup brown sugar
½ teaspoon salt
¾ teaspoon cinnamon
¼ teaspoon ginger
¼ teaspoon cloves
¼ teaspoon nutmeg
1½ cups prepared fresh pumpkin
1½ cups rich milk
2 beaten eggs
1 tablespoon dark molasses
2 tablespoons rum

Prepare the pie crust in a 9" pie tin, building up a fluted rim. Chill, do not bake. Combine the brown sugar, salt and spices, add remaining ingredients and mix well. Pour into the chilled pie shell. Bake at 450° for 15 minutes, then lower heat to 325° for an additional 30 minutes, or until a knife inserted in the center comes out clean. Serve with whipped cream or vanilla ice cream.

Preparing the Pumpkin

Wash a medium-size pumpkin and cut in half. Scrape out seeds and strings and place skin-side up in a large baking pan. Bake at 325° for an hour or more until it is tender. Scrape out pulp and put through a sieve or potato ricer.

From the American Heritage Chapter of the Wilton Book of Classic Desserts.

INDEX